Studded with inspirational stories from a range of schools, *Ha*
should spark some fundamental and much-needed changes ir
have been led to believe in practices that only make it hard
teachers to teach. This book provides a clear, accessible guide t
by cognitive science that can enable both teachers and students to reacn

Natalie Wexler
Author of *The Knowledge Gap* and co-author of *The Writing Revolution*

Teachers will treasure the guidance offered in this volume. Nathaniel's book is an accessible and entertaining combination of scientific research and anecdote. It's an invitation to all who work in education—teachers, school leaders, policymakers, or academics—to learn from examples of schools that have experienced success applying evidence-based practices.

This book offers a diagnosis—there is a disconnect between what we know about how learning happens and the practices that are used in our classrooms—along with a cure. In doing so, Nathaniel somehow avoids the trap of being prescriptive. You will find content in this book that is motivating, wise, never patronising, and grounded in pragmatism and evidence.

This book brings together the compelling case for the science of learning with the realities of classrooms. Nathaniel Swain applies his experience as teacher, school leader, and academic to offer an evidence-based, credible path to improvement. Combining science, real-life experience, and common sense, the authors deliver a recipe for school improvement that is evidence-driven and proven to succeed. This is the book we have been waiting for.

Dr Jenny Donovan
CEO, Australian Educational Research Organisation (AERO)

Published research has created a new science of learning based on new theories and voluminous data sets. That knowledge is now beginning to transform the teaching profession. The transformation has been slow because while there are innumerable research papers, there are far fewer resources aimed at the teaching profession. I believe *Harnessing the Science of Learning* has the potential to rectify this resource gap. The book is exceptionally clearly written. It contains critical information that every teacher and every teacher trainee requires. I can recommend it in the strongest terms.

John Sweller
Emeritus Professor of Educational Psychology,
Father of Cognitive Load Theory

I often warn students not to write in the way that they speak, since speaking and writing are such different beasts. But Nathaniel Swain does that very thing, and I'm glad. There is no time, in my experience, when Nathaniel hasn't spoken eloquently, intelligently, and with great empathy, and so his writing reflects that in this superb book. Bringing together a balance of expertise, research, and teaching with heart, this accessible book puts complex points across as a tool for teachers and education leaders alike.

Lyn Stone
Linguist, Literacy Specialist and Author, *Reading for Life*,
Spelling for Life, and *Language for Life*

This gem of a book is a highly readable introduction to a huge body of scientific research on effective teaching and learning. More importantly, it is intensely practical. Reading this book, I was infused with an overwhelming sense of optimism that we might yet deliver on our promise of providing an excellent education to all young people—a life-changing gift for many.

Dr Jordana Hunter

Program Director for Education, Grattan Institute

Dr Swain's *Harnessing the Science of Learning* is an essential read for educators looking to revolutionize teaching methods. The acclaimed authors in each chapter masterfully combine scientific research with practical classroom applications, offering a comprehensive guide to enhancing educational outcomes. The book's engaging narrative and real-world success stories provide a compelling argument for the integration of the science of learning into everyday teaching practices. A must-read for those committed to educational excellence in their context.

Bruno Reddy

Mathematics Educator, Disruptor, and Pedagogy Specialist.
CEO, Maths Circle Australia Pty Ltd

The last twenty years has seen a welcome increase in the number of books for teachers about the science of how we learn. Over the same period, there have also been many books on different approaches to school improvement. What we haven't seen, at least to my knowledge, is anything that integrates the science of learning with how schools might use this knowledge to effect radical improvements in their educational efforts, and that's why *Harnessing the Science of Learning* is so welcome. In it, the authors skilfully weave together what cognitive scientists have discovered about how to maximize learning with stories of how schools have used this emerging body of knowledge to improve student learning—often to an extraordinary degree. Highly recommended.

Dylan Wiliam

Emeritus Professor of Educational Assessment,
UCL Institute of Education

In the last decade, there's been a global revolution in the way teachers think about classroom practice. Techniques and resources based on cognitive science are becoming more popular than ever. In *Harnessing the Science of Learning* Nathaniel Swain has done a great service for teachers everywhere in explaining what this new science of learning is, why it matters, and how it can help you and your students.

Daisy Christodoulou

Award winning educator and author,
Seven myths about education

HARNESSING THE SCIENCE OF LEARNING

Drawing together the worlds of classroom practice, school leadership and scientific research, this is an essential how-to guide for initiating and maintaining a school improvement journey based on the science of learning.

What we now know about learning and teaching is vast; yet often, wading through the thousands of articles and books on this subject can leave even the most seasoned educator overwhelmed. This guide instead offers a distillation of key understandings—for teaching, literacy, mathematics, curriculum and implementation—to launch your school improvement work.

Harnessing the Science of Learning also features contributions from thought leaders across the fields of learning sciences and educational practice: Pamela Snow, Tanya Serry, Zach Groshell, Reid Smith, Toni Hatten-Roberts, Simon Breakspear, Katie Roberts-Hull, David Morkunas, Steven Capp, Shane Pearson and Eamon Charles.

This book illustrates practical ways to harness this knowledge, using a series of exemplary school case studies. These insightful narratives of transformation are interwoven with summaries of powerful teaching practices, forming a roadmap to drive improvement.

In this volume, you will learn how even discrete changes in a school can have marked impacts. It is suitable for those already versed in such principles, as well as anyone curious to plunge into what the science of learning has to offer.

Nathaniel Swain, PhD, is a teacher, instructional coach and teacher educator. He is a Senior Lecturer in Learning Sciences at La Trobe University School of Education, Australia. Dr Swain has taught a range of learners in schools and founded a community of teachers committed to educational excellence and equity: Think Forward Educators.

HARNESSING THE SCIENCE OF LEARNING

Success Stories to Help Kickstart Your School Improvement

Nathaniel Swain

LONDON AND NEW YORK

Designed cover image: Getty Images

First published 2025
by Routledge
4 Park Square, Milton Park, Abingdon, Oxon OX14 4RN

and by Routledge
605 Third Avenue, New York, NY 10158

Routledge is an imprint of the Taylor & Francis Group, an informa business

British Library Cataloguing-in-Publication Data
A catalogue record for this book is available from the British Library

ISBN: 978-1-032-52030-8 (hbk)
ISBN: 978-1-032-52029-2 (pbk)
ISBN: 978-1-003-40496-5 (ebk)

DOI: 10.4324/9781003404965

Typeset in Interstate
by Apex CoVantage, LLC

CONTENTS

LIST OF TABLES AND FIGURES

Tables

Figures

FOREWORD

Lorraine Hammond

Sir Isaac Newton famously said, "If I have seen further, it is by standing on the shoulders of giants." This statement has come to symbolise scientific progress. That is, you cannot have a very tall tree without deep roots. For example, Newton was born in the same year that Galileo died, and Newton would eventually pick up his predecessor's idea of a mathematical science of motion and bring this work to fruition. Despite his unquestionable intellect, Newton drew on the ideas of those who came before him. Education also has a long history of drawing on existing ideas, particularly about how best to teach.

When Dr Nathaniel Swain asked me to write a foreword to *Harnessing the Science of Learning*, I readily accepted, knowing that everyone who has contributed to and reads this book owes a debt of gratitude to the work of inspirational thinkers and educators who have come before them.

Like the teachers, principals and researchers who share their stories in *Harnessing the Science of Learning*, when I stood at the fork in the road in my career, I found knowledgeable and generous educators who showed me the way forward. One such example is my friend, colleague and international authority on explicit instruction, Dr Anita Archer, who first came to Australia in July 1991. Dr Archer spoke at Edith Cowan University in Perth, the university where I work, in a lecture theatre very close to my office, but it would be 20 years on from that visit before I'd eventually meet her. Dr Archer's influence on me and my teaching has been significant.

I have experienced many such Damascus moments during my search for effective instructional methods: From attending a serendipitous guest lecture on reading from Direct Instruction expert, Dr Trish Formentin, who first invited Dr Archer to Australia and would go on to be my PhD supervisor and mentor; to sitting in an un-airconditioned classroom on a blisteringly hot Perth day listening to academic Dr Kerry Hempenstall while frantically taking notes beamed on a wall from an overhead projector; to a lengthy email exchange with Professor John Sweller, who graciously took the time to answer my questions about cognitive load—I slowly built my knowledge about the most efficient and effective ways to teach. As my lived experience and my confidence implementing explicit instruction grew, I felt qualified to give back and began offering the kind of advice that is encapsulated in this book.

Perth is considered the most isolated city in the world, so it is significant that experts like Dr Archer made the long journey in 1991 at all. However, it is the tenacity of the WA Branch of the Association for Direct Instruction that warrants recognition. In the 1990s,

Direct Instruction (the scripted version and second cousin to explicit instruction) was distinctly unpopular, despite the well-established efficacy of the approach. Instead, the role of the teacher as the facilitator of student learning was celebrated. Reading results plummeted thanks to whole language and its more recent iteration, balanced literacy. But anyone advocating for research-informed instruction was seen as an anathema to the profession, as I soon realised.

However, by the late 2000s, I had some company in the naughty corner, when a visiting Victorian Principal John Fleming advocated for more explicit and direct teaching as opposed to the dominant, inquiry-based teaching methods of the day. His school change story and data were compelling, yet of the 300 educators in the room, only a small handful of principals followed his lead including Dr Ray Boyd, a determined principal who is today one of the most respected educational sherpas I know, guiding systems and schools across Australia. In 2010, I met Brooke Wardana, an awarded and exceptional early childhood educator, whose innovative, fast-paced and thoroughly engaging delivery of Daily Review is now common practice in many classrooms and has changed the literacy trajectory of many children.

As the School Board Chair of Dawson Park Primary School, and Deputy Board Chair of Challis Community Primary School, I have been privileged to work closely with highly effective administrators with an unwavering moral compass for over 10 years, including Pauline Johnson, Dennis Bussell, Jordan O'Sullivan, Jared Bussell and Lee Musumeci. These collaborations have shown me first-hand what it takes to transform and maintain improved student outcomes. Many of the contributors in this book have visited Challis and Dawson Park and spent time observing the classrooms of generous teachers. Visitors leave such schools inspired, usually loaded with resources, ready to replicate and finesse what they learned.

None of this should surprise us. Teaching is an altruistic profession, and student success is the greatest motivator for teachers to change their practice. When educators see evidence of improved student results, typically in someone else's classroom, ideas and materials are shared widely. This raises teachers' collective knowledge and is the reason why many teachers have burgeoning bookshelves and hard drives. Teachers want the best for their students, but they don't always have the right tools.

The question I am most often asked about explicit instruction is, "How do you get them to do it?" Depending on who is asking, the 'them' is students, teachers, schools or systems. *Harnessing the Science of Learning* answers this question and will build the knowledge and practical advice that has underscored the remarkable take up of explicit instruction in Australian schools to date.

As you read this book, please doff your hat to Dr Nathaniel Swain, to the contributors to *Harnessing the Science of Learning*, and to the many forthright educators who have gone before us, and whose collective wisdom is now in your hands.

Dr Lorraine Hammond AM
Associate Professor Edith Cowan University

ABOUT THE AUTHOR

Dr Nathaniel Swain, a teacher and teacher educator, has seen what educational failure looks like, having spent more than five years teaching and researching how to support disengaged learners sucked into the infamous *school-to-prison pipeline*. Family troubles and delinquent peers notwithstanding, Nathaniel's students taught him that school was not working for everybody. How else could one explain the one in five Australian Year 9 students at or below the minimum standard for literacy, the two-thirds of American children reading at or below a basic level, and the 70–90% of young offenders around the English-speaking world struggling with basic reading and writing?

Having repeated far too many conversations with teacher colleagues about just how at odds mainstream classroom practice was with the science of effective instruction, Dr Swain founded the charity Think Forward Educators, a community of teachers and educational professionals committed to achieving educational excellence and equity, using the science of learning. It was whilst facilitating the Think Forward Principals' Forum that Nathaniel realised the striking similarities of the schools showcasing their journeys and the power of sharing the step-by-step processes by which they changed their school from the ground up.

Upon leaving youth justice education, Dr Swain put these instructional approaches into practice at one of the few science of learning aligned schools in Melbourne, Australia. Here, he saw the benefits of schools utilising insights from the cognitive science to improve educational outcomes for all, as well as the power of such practices in his own classroom. Dr Swain is passionate about illuminating the complex issues within school leadership and change journeys, as well as working directly with school leaders focusing on how the science of learning can transform their schools. Now a Senior Lecturer in the School of Education at La Trobe University, Nathaniel is working with colleagues seeking to revolutionise how teachers teach and how schools work.

PREFACE

I wonder if you've ever had a nagging feeling that the way we teach our children could be better. I've felt it ever since I met Jai*, a 15-year-old student serving time for breaking and entering, who couldn't figure out the difference between a country and a continent. Unable to read more than a basic pamphlet or one-page diagram, Jai was nevertheless a passionate conversationalist who above everything else wished someone had taught him to read and do mathematics.

I have worked with hundreds of young people like Jai, both in and out of mainstream education, and I have always felt daunted by the work that would be required to right this educational injustice. How could we prevent so many students leaving high school without the skills and knowledge that a decent education should provide? What could be going so wrong in so many different places that educational casualties, like Jai, are all but expected across social strata?

You may have worked with students who have not benefited from their education, whether early on when red flags were being raised, or at the tail-end of their education when all the challenges seemed insurmountable. When I reflect on my own time as a high school student, I naively assumed that students like Jai just didn't want to try. It was only when I began to understand the history of education and the disconnect between the classroom and insights from scientific educational research, that I had any glimmer of hope that things could be different for such students.

What we now know about learning and the conditions that promote academic success is vast; hundreds of articles and books would need to be consumed to even scratch the surface. Many teachers and school leaders have plunged down this rabbit hole and have found it both inspiring and overwhelming. I hope in this book you'll discover that harnessing this research does not mean throwing out everything; but that the science of learning provides a compass which can point educators towards the helpful, and away from the wasteful.

In these pages, I provide example success stories from a collection of exemplary schools and one school system, representing proofs of concept and illustrations. I do not claim that these examples are empirical, and as with all anecdotal evidence, they provide merely a springboard for further investigation, and should be taken with a grain of salt. Nonetheless, I do hope they can exemplify some ways to apply the robust findings from the scientific research.

A word of warning: Much of what we will discuss in this book may come across as common sense. Indeed, these findings would not be so compelling for teachers if the educational status quo was not so firmly at odds with many of these insights. It is a cruel turn of history that certain philosophical ideas that have won out in the 20th century have turned out to be in stark disconnect with what we now know about the mechanisms of effective and equitable teaching. There is much to learn and much to implement if we are to collectively rectify this chasm between research and practice. I hope this book is the first of many guides towards greater learning for you and your students.

*Not his real name

Nathaniel Swain, PhD

ACKNOWLEDGEMENTS

To my wife and best friend, thank you for tolerating all the time and mental energy I have spent to write this. Please forgive my auto-pilot behaviour when deep in thought about this book, including *occasionally* locking you out of the house.

I dedicate this work to my darling wife and two children, and thank whole-heartedly my parents, parents-in-law, and extended family. I also especially thank Lyn Stone, the author and my friend who provided the kind introduction to make this book possible when I merely had an idea on a piece of scrap paper.

To my contributing authors and the school leaders who generously shared their stories, it is a great privilege to work with you and to share these insights and successes in this medium. I thank my colleagues at La Trobe University including Professor Pamela Snow, Professor Tanya Serry, and Professor Joanna Barbousas for sharing with me your passion and commitment to excellence and equity for all.

I also thank the Think Forward Educators membership, including all the principals, teachers, and educators who have contributed to this vibrant community and have continued to enlighten and inspire change. I also thank the hard-working system leaders and policymakers who are driving improvement for their schools, especially Catholic Education Tasmania and Catholic Education Canberra Goulburn. A special thanks for the time and expertise lent to this body of work by instructional expert and co-author of *Explicit Instruction*, Dr Anita Archer, who provided valuable feedback on early manuscript drafts and gave me the professional encouragement regarding the potential of this book for the work of teachers.

A final thanks to the family, friends, and colleagues who reviewed early drafts of these chapters and provided meaningful and substantive suggestions for improvement: Pauline Swain, Gabriella Gianni Swain, Peter Swain, Leah Myers, Helen Hughes, Jacqui Magee, Melissa Barnes, Brendan Lee, Jeanette Breen, Amanda Barrett, Karina Stocker, Russ Fox, Siobhan Merlo, Ollie Lovell, Tessa Weadman, and Alana Semerjian.

LIST OF CONTRIBUTORS

Simon Breakspear is an Adjunct Senior Lecturer at the University of New South Wales and an advisor to the NSW Department of Education on leadership development and curriculum reform. Simon began his work in education as a high school teacher and now focuses on the practical application of implementation science in schools. Simon is the co-author of the book *Teaching sprints: How overloaded educators can keep getting better* and serves on the Australia Institute for Teaching and School Leadership (AITSL) Expert Standing Committee.

Steven Capp is the former Principal of Bentleigh West Primary School and current Principal of Chelsea Heights Primary School in Melbourne. He has worked across the primary and secondary school sectors as an educational leader for the past 15 years, and has worked with schools and across Australia in bridging the gap from research to practice. He served on the expert advisory panel to the Federal Government for Year 1 Literacy and Numeracy Checks in 2017.

Eamon Charles, the Academic Intern in the Science of Language and Reading (SOLAR) Lab at La Trobe University School of Education, works on major research projects across the SOLAR Lab's key research priorities, maintaining a teaching focus in the areas of language development, emergent literacy, and reading instruction. He completed a Bachelor of Speech Pathology (Honours) at Australian Catholic University and has clinical experience as a senior speech pathologist in the education sector.

Zach Groshell is a secondary instructional coach in Seattle, USA, and an experienced elementary school teacher. Zach holds a PhD in Education and is a highly distinguished speaker and proponent of the science of learning. Zach hosts the popular teacher podcast, Progressively Incorrect, and is active on Twitter/X (@mrzachg) and his blog, educationrickshaw.com.

Toni Hatten-Roberts is an award-winning educator, the director of COGlearn, and Executive Director of Education at Mastery Schools Australia. She is also the author of the Centre for Independent Studies publication "The need for speed: Why fluency counts for maths learning."

David Morkunas is a primary school teacher and instructional coach, specialising in enhancing the impact of mathematics teaching across schools. David has presented his work on mathematics and 'daily review' for organisations, including Learning Difficulties Australia, Sharing Best Practice, and ResearchED. David worked as classroom teacher and as team leader at Bentleigh West Primary School from 2016 to 2022, at which time he joined Brandon Park Primary School as learning specialist in mathematics and explicit instruction.

Shane Pearson, a speech-language pathologist from Melbourne's south-east specialising in literacy education, leads Brandon Park Primary School's whole-school literacy teaching and intervention. Shane has developed a set of open-access curriculum materials for spelling, word reading, phonemic awareness, handwriting, and vocabulary known as PhOrMeS (Phonology, Orthography, Morphology, Etymology, and Semantics), and is now working with other schools to implement this with fidelity.

Katie Roberts-Hull began her career as a primary school teacher in the US, and for the last decade has led international research on teacher development as well as advising Australian school system leaders in education policy. Katie is currently the CEO of Think Forward Educators, a grassroots community committed to implementing practices that align with the science of learning. Katie holds an MBA from the Wharton School and a Master of Public Administration from the Harvard Kennedy School.

Tanya Serry is a Professor of Literacy in the School of Education at La Trobe University. Together with Professor Pamela Snow, she co-founded the Science of Language and Reading (SOLAR) Lab as a platform for research, teaching, advocacy, and community engagement. Tanya is currently leading large-scale funded research projects exploring the impact of in-school coaching for early years teachers and the processes that lead to successful embedding of structured literacy instruction in schools.

Reid Smith, a teacher and former Head of Curriculum, Assessment, and Instruction at Victorian school Ballarat Clarendon College, is founder and co-CEO of Ochre Education. Reid is experienced in developing coherent curriculum across a range of year levels and contexts, and bridging the gap between educational research and practice.

Pamela Snow is a Professor of Cognitive Psychology in the School of Education at La Trobe University, Australia, and Co-Director of the Science of Language and Reading (SOLAR) Lab. Pamela is a registered psychologist and a speech-language pathologist. Her research concerns the role of language and literacy skills as academic and mental health protective factors in childhood and adolescence and advancing evidence in the language-to-literacy transition in the early years of school.

PART ONE

The Orientation

1 Do we need to improve our schools?

Nathaniel Swain

One of the greatest drivers for me to write this book was the chance to share the stories of schools transforming the lives of teachers and students alike using the science of learning. I have seen for myself how insights from the science of learning can revolutionise *my own* teaching as well as the learning of my students, but the wider potential of this body of knowledge for teachers is arguably untapped.

Indeed, the gap between what we know about how children learn best and what actually takes place in classrooms has widened over recent decades. Despite this, *some* schools have been fortunate enough to stumble across these powerful insights that are proving revolutionary to their school and community. Such success stories need not be accidental.

The audience of *Harnessing the Science of Learning* includes those who are already keen on the science of learning and want to learn more, as well as school leaders and teachers who are sitting on the fence. It is also written for those who are perhaps in the dark on this topic, or are in need of some convincing. I hope the book can help.

To begin, let's hear from our first school, with quite the story of change.

Story Example 1.1 – Churchill Primary School

Churchill Primary is a 200-student public school, situated two hours south-west of Melbourne, Australia, in the La Trobe Valley, the former home of the State of Victoria's coal-fired power stations. The school has typically served a strongly working-class student group with up to two-thirds in the bottom quartile for socio-educational advantage. When current Principal Jacquie Burrows worked as Churchill's Head of Student Wellbeing in 2016, she expected to use much of her day facilitating five or six restorative conversations with students who would spend more time in the corridor outside her office than in class.

Not through a lack of trying . . . Churchill had spent considerable energy implementing Positive Behaviour Support (PBS) and was considered a leading school in 'tiered intervention' for behaviour. Despite this, teachers needed to steel themselves daily for the seemingly inevitable kicking, punching, or swearing from the 5–12-year-old students.

On the academic front, Churchill had core groups of students in every grade without functional literacy skills, with 2016–17 National Testing results revealing up to

DOI: 10.4324/9781003404965-2

two-thirds lacking basic reading skills in Grade 5, and 40% below minimum standards for spelling.

One particular boy, Jason*, would voluntarily escort himself to Jacquie's office every day to avoid reading time. He explained that sitting in class would be so frustrating that spending 50 minutes at the top of a basketball ring or waiting in the administration building was much better for everyone. After all, he could not read. He asked legitimately, what was the point? Jason's teachers, like all at Churchill, had nothing but passion for and belief in their students, and were committed to helping them as best they could.

Previous practice

Churchill teachers had diligently implemented the Readers' and Writers' Workshop Approach, 'benchmarking' assessments using levelled readers, and guided reading groups—common practice in Australian schools and other English-speaking countries under **balanced literacy**. Despite this, the staff were not seeing the gains in their reading outcomes that they had hoped for, and were even placed on the local network's list of schools at risk.

The term for a collection of approaches to teaching reading and writing. These share in common the idea of using a range of methods to teach students; includes elements of phonics and whole language

Churchill's troubles were in both students' behaviour and learning, and the students who had the most concerning behaviours were also nearly always the most affected by literacy and numeracy difficulties. Despite back then being considered a local leader in Positive Behaviour Support (PBS), wellbeing and engagement were significant concerns for the school.

Jacquie recalls a morning that was emblematic of the challenge that Churchill had at the time. She and a visiting psychologist were supporting a second-year teacher to organise her class of students for the second session of the day. Whilst the teacher repeatedly tried to refocus her group to the front of the room, one student began marching the full length of the classroom on his knees, thrilled with stealing every other students' attention. With four adults in the room, each were attempting to coax the children out from under tables, back onto the mat, and the crawling boy from his knees back to a seated position with the group. A thought struck the new principal, Jacquie, at that moment: This is a bloody circus.

The impetus for change

Beginning in 2015-16, a series of chance events set Churchill into a completely different direction—one where the behavioural, academic, and attentional challenges plaguing the school would be systematically addressed and turned around.

Some Churchill staff had begun searching for anything that would help their school's literacy challenges. They stumbled upon some 'Jolly Phonics' books and started giving some explicit phonics teaching a go. Even with what Jacquie now sees as a meagre attempt to teach decoding, the Early Years teachers observed some interesting improvements.

Still guided mainly by a balanced literacy paradigm, principal Jacquie attended a Learning Difficulties Australia event at the Collingwood Town Hall in Melbourne with renowned reading neuroscientist Maryanne Wolf and many other experts in the science of reading. The day was filled with ideas and recommendations quite foreign to Jacquie. She found it interesting but over-whelming.

During an afternoon presentation, Alison Clarke OAM, Melbourne speech-language pathologist and literacy expert, asked the audience to raise their hand if anyone used running records or levelled readers. Jacquie confidently raised her hand along with hundreds of others in the auditorium. Alison's next comment hit Jacquie like a brick: "Well you shouldn't be. They don't align well with reading science. There is a much better way."

Jacquie was sceptical. How could it be that none of her colleagues had heard of a different way to teach reading? The leadership team caught wind of a school in Melbourne's south-east that were innovating their practice. Jacquie would have loved to see it for herself but because of the behavioural incidents, only her colleagues Halie and Gail could attend a full day at Bentleigh West Primary in her stead. They excitedly rang Jacquie on the two-hour drive back to Churchill. *It was incredible. You should have seen how engaged the students were. They don't do running records and they don't even do guided reading.* Jacquie was puzzled. What do they do then?

The makings of a transformation

These events kicked off a steady but rapid transformation for Churchill Primary—which over six years has become one of the best examples around the country of instructional excellence aligning with the science of how we learn.

In a process of discovery and experimentation, Churchill developed an overarching vision and plan for what their school could be:

- They overhauled their literacy teaching, trained their school in **systematic synthetic phonics** and undertook many other changes to explicit reading and writing teaching across the school years;
- They engaged instructional experts like Associate Professor Lorraine Hammond AM to cement the shared definition of great teaching;
- They refined the connection points between supports for student behaviour and wellbeing including **trauma-informed practice**;
- They developed consistent routines, clear expectations, and structures so that teachers could effectively model, guide, and then facilitate student practice.

A structured and well-sequenced approach to teaching phonics which involves breaking words down into the individual phonemes and graphemes, and blending them together

An approach to practice underpinned by understanding of impact of trauma on student behaviour and learning, whilst creating a supportive environment

A short, daily session of practice of previously taught material, including concepts and skills that ensure students consolidate their learning and avoid forgetting

Notably, their dogged focus on implementing the **daily review** (a fast-paced 20–30 minute warmup aimed at retrieving and practising prior learning) ensured all students could master the foundations of reading, spelling, and mathematics. This has seen massive gains in student understanding and retention, and meant students felt more successful, then more engaged, and then progressively learnt much more, in a delightfully virtuous cycle.

And this list of changes only scratches the surface.

The new Churchill

Jacquie says people cannot recognise the school it has become today. Government required surveys into student perceptions of Churchill show they are stimulated, engaged in their learning, and feel successful, challenged, and supported. Despite still serving a highly disadvantaged community, the high level of school engagement is evident in the students' calm, respectful, and focussed behaviour. Following these changes, many Churchill staff would be happy to, and indeed do, enrol their own children in the school.

From a school at risk before this work, Churchill now leads the area, exceeding the expected performance of literacy and numeracy in Grade 3 and Grade 5, and outperforming similarly disadvantaged schools in several domains of the standardised national tests. Several other schools in the local Gippsland area have been curious about Churchill's success and have begun adopting similar practices themselves.

Before their change journey, Churchill did not see the link between behaviour and learning. But now it is as clear as day. The change to excellent teaching at Churchill improved not just the learning of students, but their very concept of success at school, addressing the link between school motivation, behaviour, and academic achievement: The students felt more confident as they experienced more success, and with the longstanding behaviour systems in place, were less likely to experience distress and behavioural issues.

Previously 'tied' to the day-to-day crises that would eventuate, the leadership team can now attend whole-day meetings and conferences without a second thought. Jacquie's previous role as wellbeing coordinator, managing the students' challenging behaviours, no longer exists. Churchill Primary even takes *all 200 students* to *whole-school excursions* to the city aquariums and zoos. Jacquie could not have dreamed of what would have been an occupational health and safety nightmare only six years earlier.

Much of the school's journey has not been easy. Challenges have involved the risk of overloading staff with too many changes too soon, and how to close the learning gaps in older students who had missed effective instruction in literacy and maths until recently. Nonetheless, the thrill of Churchill teachers seeing their students' learning and wellbeing transform before their eyes could not be more motivating. Churchill has been driven by the aphorism of Psychologist Anna Gillingham (1878-1963): "Go as fast as you can, and as slow as you must."

And as for the wayward boy who used to skip reading sessions, Jason became one of the school champions for daily practice and review, and he could not have been more excited to finally learn to read and write. Having since moved to high school, Jason and Jacquie keep in contact when they can.

Even only having benefited from Grade 5 onwards, Churchill's science of learning transformation meant Jason has stayed in school and stayed out of trouble. But deep-down Jacquie knows that if he attended the *new* Churchill from beginning to end, this school could have changed his life for good.

**Student names have been changed for privacy.*

Teaching is a profession under fire

This book comes at a time when a spotlight has been fixed onto the teaching profession for several years. In Australia, the US, and UK, for example, initial teacher education and teacher preparation have been subject to almost annual government reviews and inquiries.

Unfortunately, many teachers in English-speaking countries are considering leaving the profession or are already moving on (e.g., Räsänen et al., 2020), in the wake of ballooning administrative duties, increasingly tense behavioural challenges, as well as the pedagogical acrobatics required to differentiate for a myriad of individual learning trajectories with eye-watering gaps in student learning.

Is this a way forward?

From my perspective as a teacher, instructional coach, and now teacher educator, if there are better ways of engaging, teaching, and supporting learners to find success in their education, I would ask how we can ignore that opportunity?

We are not just addressing simple or one-dimensional issues. Indeed, Churchill's reasons for change were not about a singular problem with reading, spelling, mathematics, or how much students did not know about a topic, nor were they only about behaviour or attention. Churchill's journey demonstrates how profound the improvement of teaching practices can be on student outcomes, with knock-on benefits for school climate, teacher efficacy, and wellbeing.

I argue that such success stories demonstrate a wider opportunity for improvement here—changes that can make genuine improvement in the lives of students and teachers. As we look at another school's improvement journey, keep in mind the contrasts *and* parallels to Churchill.

Story Example 1.2 – Bentleigh West Primary School from 'okay' to exemplary

The context for Bentleigh West Primary's transformation could not *appear* more contrasting to Churchill. But I must note that the differences we are about to explore are only surface-deep. The story of Bentleigh West is of a middle-class suburban Melbourne school that changed from okay to exemplary in just a few short years.

Bentleigh West is a school of around 720 students in an affluent area of Melbourne. When Sarah Asome, a specialist literacy teacher who had worked in the Singapore education system, joined as a casual relief teacher ten years ago, the school had a fairly typical collection of instructional practices.

Large composite classes in open-plan learning spaces were the norm across the school, and **inquiry-based learning** was a dominant approach to teaching. There were also at least a quarter of students in the early years who were significantly behind in literacy particularly word reading and spelling. For intervention, the school had the Reading Recovery program in Grade 1, though it did not appear to be closing many gaps. Sarah described the school climate at this time as "all over the place." Disruptive and off-task behaviour was constant, and there was a sense that many students were not consistently engaged in learning.

A broad set of pedagogies involving students designing, implementing, and reflecting on student-led inquiry projects

The term for a collection of approaches to teaching reading and writing. These share in common the idea of using a range of methods to teach students; includes elements of phonics and whole language

The teaching of sound-letter correspondences

Bentleigh West's reading approach back then was firmly aligned with a **balanced literacy** philosophy. **Phonics** was not a dirty word, per se, but it did not feature strongly in the daily literacy program. As Sarah saw it, the school's mathematics approach was also failing to build up the foundations, and many students had flat-lined in numeracy progress.

Did the school really need to change?

On some fronts, the school did not have a strong impetus for a transformation. It was achieving the average results expected for the area. It was an 'okay' school to send your child. It had already rolled out various additional programs—including a personalised learning approach and five-star sustainability rating—and the staff culture reflected change fatigue, uncertainty, and a reluctance to part with well-used (and perhaps worn-out) teaching practices. *If it ain't broke, don't fix it, right?*

But the children *least* served at Bentleigh West at this time were the ones potentially at risk of learning or behavioural challenges. There was no cohesive approach for identifying and supporting such students. When Sarah joined permanently as an intervention teacher, she began trying her best to address the deluge of students with significant reading difficulties across the school.

Sarah was concerned at the scarcity of explicit teaching and guided practice. She also noticed the teachers had insufficient attention to the building blocks of Mathematics and English, including mathematical facts, computational skills, handwriting, phonics, morphology, spelling conventions, and sentence structure.

There was little focus on building background knowledge for students to use for inquiry projects, which often resulted in lovely dioramas, but as Sarah saw it, very little learning—mainly because the students did not know enough about what they were supposed to be investigating.

But how was an intervention teacher to address problems that were evident in the *core classroom instruction*?

A new leader

When Steven Capp joined as the new principal of Bentleigh West in 2015, he was told to go sort out "that crazy lady" who was supposedly "trying to diagnose everyone with dyslexia." Preferring to find things out for himself, Steve met with Sarah and understood that far from looking to diagnose anyone, Sarah was trialling new approaches that taught reading in line with the science, and wanted to help all students to learn best. Steve, a man who always did his research, found her message compelling.

As Steve saw it, the school had lost its identity:

- The school had changed leaders three times in four years;
- There were stark inconsistencies in teaching across grade levels and between classes, for example, in one grade-level alone they were running five different spelling programs;
- The number of students needing 'extra support' was ballooning;
- Parents of students with difficulties felt unsupported, and there were escalating complaints;
- The results from standardised testing (NAPLAN) were stagnant at best; and
- Enrolments were dropping.

Sarah's description of a drastically different approach to teaching reading initially, and teaching in general eventually, captivated Steve's interest. He began reading up on everything to do with explicit teaching, synthetic phonics, and later, went deep into the science of learning.

Planning for successful change

With Sarah moving up into high leadership roles as their work progressed, Sarah and Steve formed a strong partnership, with a crystalised focus and vision for change. This allowed for clear discussion and action alongside their staff, and a systematic implementation approach that ensured long-term success.

Starting slowly, with the present cohort of first year school students, Steve, with Sarah's strong support, began rolling out professional learning, training, modelling, and coaching, which continued to develop as that initial cohort worked its way through the school.

Over the next four years, they relentlessly focussed on the evidence base around learning and teaching resulting in:

- A calm orderly environment through consistent norms and high expectations outlined in school-wide **Positive Behaviour Support (PBS)**;
- A consistent, explicit teaching model with rigorous and aligned professional learning to support the mastery of teachers–from inductees to experienced instructional coaches;
- A **Response to Intervention (RTI)** framework to inform literacy, numeracy, and wellbeing where every teacher has expertise to identify and respond to students with dyslexia, dyscalculia and other learning difficulties;
- A well sequenced **knowledge-rich curriculum**, broken down into specific key understandings with clear expected outcomes and shared **low variance** curriculum materials; and
- A revamped approach to assessment to monitor the progress of all learners reliably and make changes to teaching in real-time (through **daily review**, **checking for understanding**, and regular screening and assessment).

By the time that first cohort of students had reached Grade 5, they had emerged as a shining example of how to align practices with the best possible evidence of how we learn.

A whole-school framework for ensuring explicit teaching of behavioural expectations and boundaries as part of Multi-Tiered Systems of Support (MTSS)

A tiered framework used in education to provide early, systematic, and targeted support to students who need it, with the goal of preventing long-term difficulties

An approach to curriculum design in which knowledge, well-structured and specified in detail, provides an underpinning philosophy for learning

A school in which teachers collaborate and have a shared understanding of what and how to teach the curriculum

A short, daily session of practice of previously taught material, including concepts and skills that ensure students consolidate their learning and avoid forgetting

The teacher checking if students are learning while the lesson is unfolding using short, specific checks of understanding and proficiency

Now an exemplary school for all

The outcomes at Bentleigh West have been transformational, not just for those who had languished with unmet educational needs, but for all its students.

The standards attained by its students now rival the top elementary schools in the country; and this is despite a huge proportion of Bentleigh West's families having relocated to the south-eastern suburb to enrol their child with learning difficulties. The school has developed strong supports for all students, including a learning enhancement team for those above or below grade expectations, tasked with complementing each teacher's whole class instruction. Twenty-seven percent of its students now qualify as having learning disabilities, and by Grade 3, all students with such disabilities achieve grade-level expectations or above.

Through 2015–2023 the school had secured:

- The highest standardised testing (NAPLAN) results in the school's history;
- A move from performing below like school groups, to well above, particularly in mathematics and spelling;
- Enrolment at maximum levels, with parents relocation (even from interstate) to the now tightly controlled school zone;
- A parent opinion survey with over 90% positive endorsement, up from 65%;
- A staff opinion survey with 89% positive approval, compared to like schools at 58%;
- Recognition as a flagship school for teaching excellence, particularly evidence informed literacy and numeracy teaching, culminating in the 2023 Outstanding Inclusive Education Team award for the State of Victoria;
- Success in extra-curricular programs, including becoming highly competitive in athletics, swimming, cross country, and inter school sport; and
- Developing an Art Walk and Biannual Performing Arts events.

Not just the basics; inquiry that means something

When Sarah and Steve look back at what even the brightest Grade 5s and 6s could do before the school's transformation, it was fairly run-of-the-mill: a big focus on the product at the end, but little on the substance or the rigour of learning.

By ensuring students gain sophisticated literacy and numeracy skills, build rich content knowledge from the humanities and sciences, and appreciate challenging literature, the school has enabled all learners to investigate and inquire from a knowledgeable start-point, and work to present their findings in a creative way.

Propelling system-wide change

Bentleigh West became well-known for its exemplary practice. By 2019, they had catalysed changes at scores of schools across Australia and internationally, including Churchill Primary's own journey, which was our first example in this chapter.

With Steven Capp seeking to create a similar change journey at his next school, Sarah Asome took over as principal 2023, and now continually works to support the system-wide changes in which they both so passionately believe. Sarah now runs a regular designated day to accommodate the teachers and leaders flocking to see their school in action. Steve and Sarah want as many students and teachers as possible to benefit from such journeys to better align teaching practices, and it is for this reason that they share their story for this book.

Do we need to improve our schools?

The stories in this book will highlight how much work there is to be done in school improvement. The phenomena of relatively shallow excellence and wide inequity is characteristic of Australian schools (and mirrored in many anglophone nations).

International educational decline and rising inequity

Wealthy English-speaking countries often exhibit great inequities in educational outcomes. In Australia, there has also been a decline or stagnation in educational standards in recent decades, as well as a chasm of inequity between advantaged and disadvantaged students, particularly affecting historically marginalised groups (see PISA data 2000–2023; OECD, 2024). Australia has one of the widest educational outcome gaps between its least and most disadvantaged groups (OECD, 2019). It also has wide-spread under-achievement that increases in the proportion of students across the school years (ACARA, 2023).

Looking at reading proficiency in the US, the National Assessment of Education Progress has shown consistently that 66% of American fourth graders are not proficient readers (NAEP; Irwin et al., 2023), with over 50% of Black and Hispanic 4th graders unable to meet basic levels of reading.

England has seen significant reform in the preparation of teachers and the teaching of reading and mathematics in recent years. Not all of these changes have been without controversy. However, England's focus on early reading, moves towards knowledge rich curriculum, and changing what we mean by 'great teaching' appear to be impacting outcomes on the international stage (e.g., PIRLS; Lindorff et al., 2023), with only minimal losses in ground following the pandemic period (OECD, 2024). We must remain cautious at this early stage, but these are hopeful indications.

In general, like the United States and England, Australia performs reasonably by international standards, but the stagnation of academic standards over the past 20 years has coincided with an unprecedented investment into educational reform and resourcing in the sector (Productivity Commission, 2023). Clearly, something is not working.

What can we learn from the schools in this book?

There are exceptions to this disheartening picture. Australia, the US, and the UK can all highlight examples of their schools and students that are doing remarkably well. Many students and schools do buck the trend.

Problems that only appear different on the surface

In nearly every classroom in English-speaking countries, there are handfuls of students dramatically below the expected standard. In leafy suburbs around wealthy urban centres, there are whole schools that are underperforming, but for the privileges and resources of their students' parents. For switched on and wealthy families, there is a flurry of activity to improve their child's progress with private tutors and specialists, at significant expense–*in spite of* the instruction within the school. In some at-risk schools, with much less privileged families, children performing at the expected level is the *exception* not the rule. Parents without financial resources to spare can do little to help their child further; they depend on the school to improve this situation.

The pre-transformation Churchill Primary and Bentleigh West Primary Schools appeared to have had different challenges regarding academic achievement and behavioural issues. The demographic differences of each school community made their problems appear as *mediocrity* at Bentleigh West, but as *crisis* at Churchill. Fundamentally, however, I would argue that the schools demonstrated the *same set of problems*, which were realised in differing ways due to the relative advantages of the school's families.

For example, both schools:

- were dominated by ineffective and inconsistent teaching practices;
- had generally poor behaviour and low engagement in meaningful learning; and
- had too wide a gap between the few high-flyers and the languishing middle and low achievers.

Despite these similarities, the post-transformation outcomes have not been identical. Bentleigh West is a middle-class school which has reached astronomical heights in terms of equity and excellence, with leaderboard-topping results in mathematics and literacy, and the entire quarter of their school with significant learning disabilities achieving 'at level' performance. Churchill remains a school serving a disadvantaged community, but now is punching *well* above its weight—improving the equitable outcomes of its students, and ensuring all can become successful, safe, and proud of their learning.

Obviously, even with the most effective methods available, student and family background can still have an impact on learning outcomes. But truly successful schools should strive for excellence, remedy inequities, and get all students on the path to learning, as is the case with these two examples.

Why should I consider change?

The most compelling evidence for why school improvement should be at the top of your list is the proof of concept from schools who have done it. Churchill and Bentleigh West are but two examples where the re-conceptualisation of the potential of our schools have led to profound improvements in the quality of students' and teachers' lives.

This book is also an invitation to consider what successes you could bring to your own school journey. I hope it will act as a wakeup call to spur educators into action.

Who can use this book?

If you are an *elementary/primary teacher*, you will find nearly all of the insights in this volume relevant to your practice. Many of the gaps between classroom practice and the science of learning affect foundational and core learning (e.g., reading, writing, mathematics, knowledge from sciences and humanities), which should ideally be laid in the Early Years of school.

If you are a *high school teacher*, you may search through this book for answers as to how your students have entered Grade 7 or 8 with such low skills or such noticeable gaps in their knowledge. You may also find answers to your questions about the importance of explanation and modelling, and when to reduce cognitive load.

If you are a *principal* or *school leader*, you will learn about the school applications of the science of learning as well as common misconceptions about teaching and how to resolve them. There are also numerous recommendations for effectively shifting practice in your school and for weathering the storms that such changes may bring.

If you are a *system or district leader*, you may be inspired to investigate what aspects from the research have supported the success of other schools and systems, and to take a critical lens to decision making around training, curriculum resourcing, and assessment requirements.

If you are a *parent* or *family member*, I hope you find useful explanations and illustrations of great teaching practice, and can use these understandings to better support your child's or family members' educational success.

Whatever your role or background, this book will not provide an exhaustive or complicated explanation of the science of learning. I hope you can close this volume with a passion to try it for yourself and to begin down the path of discovery to school improvement.

Starting the journey: The time is now

In the chapters that follow, you will hear five more success stories, captured from the school and system leaders themselves, provided to you as a roadmap to oversee your own school improvement journey. The schools in this book have made major advances in school climate, academic achievement, as well as staff satisfaction and wellbeing.

Having undergone these transformations, all schools in this book are now enacting both goals from the ambitious vision for Australian education, The Alice Springs (Mparntwe) Education Declaration (2019), to promote excellence and equity, and to empower their learners as confident, creative, successful, and informed members of the community. We cannot say the same for all schools, nor all students, in Australia or internationally. But every one of our children deserves an education system of such calibre. The conditions are ripe for change.

References

Australian Curriculum and Assessment and Reporting Authority [ACARA] (2023). *National assessment program*. ACARA.

Australian Government Productivity Commission (2023). *Report on government services: Child care, education and training (part B)*. Australian Government.

Department of Education Skills and Employment [DESE]. (2019). The Alice Springs (Mparntwe) Education Declaration.

Irwin, V., Wang, K., Tezil, T., Zhang, J., Filbey, A., Jung, J., . . . & Parker, S. (2023). Report on the Condition of Education 2023. NCES 2023-144. *National Center for Education Statistics*.

Lindorff, A., Stiff, J., & Kayton, H. (2023). PIRLS 2021: National report for England.

Räsänen, K., Pietarinen, J., Pyhältö, K., Soini, T., & Väisänen, P. (2020). Why leave the teaching profession? A longitudinal approach to the prevalence and persistence of teacher turnover intentions. *Social Psychology of Education*, *23*, 837–859.

Organisation for Economic Co-operation and Development [OECD] (2019). *What students know and can do (Volume I)*. OECD.

Organisation for Economic Co-operation and Development [OECD] (2024). *Reading performance (PISA) (indicator)*. doi: 10.1787/79913c69-en

2 Why the science of learning? Why not something else?

Nathaniel Swain

Generally, schools in the English-speaking world do a fine job of educating children who are basically ready to learn. Such children continue to do well (sometimes in spite of the instruction they receive). But are schools really serving the needs of children who need them the most? Wealthy countries like the US and Australia, which have invested millions in educational reform in recent years, still lag behind by international standards, and the gaps between children often fall along socio-economic lines.

Many school leaders are looking for new ways to support their students better, but the field is overrun with fads, opinions, and untested approaches which likely waste resources, effort, and precious time. For example, learning styles, a thoroughly debunked but equally pernicious example of pseudo-science, continues to crop up in mainstream professional learning for teachers.

As such, school leaders are torn in multiple directions. Schools and teachers are working hard but their efforts can be often wasted on ineffective practices. Teachers may not be teaching in ways that align with what we know about human learning. In this way, the science of learning is an unknown, neglected, or sometimes even shunned body of knowledge for educators.

What is the science of learning?

The 'science of learning' (as well as other terms like the science of learning and development and the learning sciences) "refer[s] to a multidisciplinary field of research that incorporates child neuroscience, psychology, sociology, behavioral development, and cognitive learning" (Chambers, 2020).

This field of scientific research comprises robust theories of learning and teaching, that are supported by **rigorous** and **relevant research evidence** (AERO, 2021). Such research evidence can be classified into a hierarchy from lowest quality (least confidence, such as small-scale case studies) to highest quality (highest confidence, such as systematic reviews of previous high-quality controlled studies). The most effective practices can be identified using this hierarchy.

> Evidence from research methods that isolate the impact of a specific educational approach
>
> Evidence from contexts similar to one's own or from a wide range of studies indicating that the findings are not dependent on context

DOI: 10.4324/9781003404965-3

This broad body of knowledge provides key insights into how learning happens, and how educators and school leaders can create the "optimal conditions for student learning" (Chambers, 2020). While it may include pivotal theories (such as **cognitive load theory**, see chapter 4), the science of learning is not limited or reducible to singular ideas or teaching practices.

A theory for understanding how learners interact with tasks, based on the evidence that working memory is limited and affected by the environment, the nature of the task, and student prior knowledge

Why the science of learning?

The science of learning points to certain instructional practices and whole school changes that are likely to be beneficial, based upon robust research evidence. Despite this, these particular practices (featured in this book) are largely under-utilised and even sound counterintuitive in the dominant educational paradigms.

What if you learnt there were more and more schools bucking the trend, and starting to use this knowledge to transform their classrooms and schools? I share this book with you not because there is a singular path that I think schools should take, but because there are insights and principles from the science of learning that are so compelling, yet so unnoticed in many English-speaking nations, that if left untapped they represent a significant wasted opportunity.

We can learn much from schools that have embraced the challenge of bringing the scientific research to life in their classrooms, making remarkable transformations. Let's meet two more.

Story Example 2.1 - Challis Community Primary School

Challis Community Primary School is a 900-student elementary school encompassing kindergarten and early learning centre to Grade 6, serving the community of Armadale, one of the most disadvantaged suburbs in Perth, Western Australia. Longstanding principal, Lee Musumeci has overseen phenomenal change. Ms Musumeci and her colleagues have been driven by a moral imperative to deliver education that enables social equity, powered by principles and findings from the science of learning.

Throughout Ms Musumeci's nearly 20-year principalship, significant proportions of Challis' students have come from homes experiencing high levels of socio-educational disadvantage, with half from the lowest quartile for disadvantage and another 25% in the second lowest. It is typical for many Challis students, even now, to have family members in (or just out of) prison, to have involvement from child protection, to arrive to school without clean clothes or food in their stomachs, and to have associations with older peers ready to get up to *no good* on late nights or school holidays. The school is diverse, with at least a quarter from language backgrounds other than English, and a fifth first nations children.

Before Ms Musumeci began the school's journey of transformation, Challis had such problems with behaviour, engagement, and school culture, that the principal had to do a check on any short-staffed morning to ensure all leaders were wearing *flat shoes*, in preparation for the inevitable chase of dysregulated students running down the road or onto the school roof. Classrooms were inconsistently engaged, with teachers trying their best, but many students lacking the reading, writing, and mathematics skills to function effectively, especially in the middle and upper grades. There was a consistent group of students who, as they progressed through the school, were increasingly at risk of ending up in youth detention. Ms Musumeci was literally seeing the **school-to-prison pipeline** in action, and before this journey had felt somewhat powerless to stop it. How do you counteract deep-seated generational poverty and unstable home lives? It was this picture of a 'school in crisis' that spurred Ms Musumeci to strive for a greater education for her students, knowing that successful experiences at school was the best she could offer to turn the tide. Teaching and learning was high-stakes work.

A phenomenon where marginalised and excluded young people are at an increased risk of juvenile and, eventually, adult incarceration

Bringing the science of learning into Challis

Ms Musumeci credits much of her early changes to the Principals as Literacy Leaders (PALL) program through Australian Primary Principals Association, with support from leadership and literacy experts from Griffith University (see Townsend & Bayetto, 2021). This program spelled out the core actions that a transformational leader needed to take including: family and community support, professional learning, curriculum, and conditions for learning. Embedded within this program were the fundamentals of reading science, including the big five of phonemic awareness, phonics, fluency, vocabulary, and comprehension.

Ms Musumeci knew she needed to rework the school's entire ecosystem to embed these practices, and she knew she needed to start at the beginning of the pipeline. This started a five-year process of change to embed the fundamentals of early reading into the day-to-day work of the elementary classrooms, as well as oral language and emergent literacy experiences like phonemic awareness and shared book reading into the preschool rooms: The beginnings of a science of reading and learning journey.

The evolution of Challis' behaviour and wrap-around responses

Before initiating these changes, there was a core group of students experiencing extreme disadvantage who exhibited significant behaviours of concern. This group had often been the focus of all of the leaders' attention as they tried to keep the students, themselves, and the rest of the school safe. One of the only ways for the school to function was to provide a separate program for these students where everything was stripped back, and in many ways they just tried to keep everyone calm.

Today, the school's behaviour and engagement approach is comprehensive and school-wide. The process for helping these students begins with school-based parenting and early childhood learning at the Challis Parenting and Early Learning Centre, and involves multi-disciplinary responses from co-located professionals, including psychology, occupational therapy, and speech-language pathology.

In addition to these wraparound services that seek to address the underlying challenges around learning, there is a laserfocus on supporting ALL students to learn how to behave appropriately for the benefit of their learning, self-regulation, and the safety of all. Using Positive Behaviour Support (PBS) systems, the school has a behaviour curriculum which is explicitly explained, modelled, practiced, and reinforced school-wide. All teachers are trained in **explicit and direct instructional** practices that have clear routines and expectations for learning. The benefits of the clarity and consistency of these approaches is that students are never assumed to just *know* what 'respect' or 'appropriate' means. They are provided countless opportunities to learn these concepts explicitly in multiple contexts, and fair and responsive consequences when rules are broken. These responses include questions to prompt students to consider their actions, what they were feeling at the time, their impact on others, and what replacement actions could be taken next time.

An approach to explicit instruction from Data-Works involving a set of prescriptive, but clear practices and techniques for teachers to implement

The results have been nothing but extraordinary. Previously unreachable children—who would prefer to be chased out of the school than sit through a lesson—have begun to find their groove, develop their identity as a learner, and make gains in their learning at an increasingly rapid rate.

But Ms Musumeci notes that you cannot "love these children out of this postcode," and that effort to provide responsive and effective teaching is required to have even a remote chance of making a difference.

Reading as the fundamental goal for students

The leadership team saw early on in their journey that it was incumbent upon the school to ensure all students successfully learned how to read at the very minimum, so as to maximise their chances for health, happiness, and contribution to society. Ms Musumeci also reminds whoever will listen that nothing is more crushing for students from poverty than low expectations.

As such, Ms Musumeci adopted the teaching of reading for every child as a goal of paramount importance, given the protective factor provided by this life skill. With support from reading and instructional expert, A/Prof Lorraine Hammond AM (now a Challis school board member), the school underwent wholesale changes in reading and writing instruction, aligning practice with the best available scientific research.

With relationships and behaviour curriculum intact, and teachers who were supported to be the best educators of literacy (and later all learning areas), Challis began to deliver on its promise of an excellent and empowering education for all students. Where previously Challis parents and families did not necessarily assume that their children would become readers, there was a growing family expectation that all children could and would learn to read and write in the early years, and would make progress in their learning year on year.

Focussing on success in learning, Challis' story demonstrates that students need to feel they can do the work, to reinforce the notion that effort is worthwhile, and that school is a good and safe place to be. The expectations and engagement of the school community can also lift alongside this when they see that the excellence and equity of outcomes are possible. Only then can the culture of a school begin the shift to one of safety and high expectations for learning and behaviour—as these go hand in hand.

A platform for school-wide changes

The science of reading was really just a starting point for the pedagogical changes at Challis. With support of deputy principal, Mark McClements, the school has continued to take on continuous cycles of professional learning and coaching to bring more and more insights aligning with the science of *learning* in any subject into their school including:

- Explicit and direct instruction;
- Talk for writing;
- Teach like a champion; and
- **Instructional coaching** (including via Steplab).

A professional development process where a coach works with teachers to improve their instructional practices and enhance student learning

The school began developing an ambitious two-year coaching and induction program, increasing shared planning time, and investing in staff development and knowledge building, so that all teachers had regular goals which they worked towards to improve their practice.

The steady course of school improvement

Challis has achieved cumulative and solid improvements for students and teachers, with:

- A profound reduction in number of children leaving elementary school as low or non-readers;
- An increase in student proficiency in writing, spelling, reading, and mathematics; and
- A well-established induction and teacher development program.

Most of all, this virtuous cycle of relationships, clear expectations, and routines, and an educational offering that is achievable and promotes real success, has transformed the culture of the school. Challis Community Primary is now a calm and enriching learning environment, despite the still high proportions of students living in poverty, with incredibly disadvantaged socio-educational backgrounds.

The disruption of the school-to-prison pipeline has also been steadily improving, and despite the immense risk factors amongst their school population, Challis has created a school of which parents and families are proud to be a part. The school sees its work as a cumulative process of development and growth that occurs lesson by lesson, year by year, with each successful learning experience providing more protective factors towards positive life outcomes for its students.

This is what teaching can be

The school is quite unrecognisable in terms of the high expectations (and high support) for its teachers now too. As the school leaders were rounding out their sharing for this book, they recounted the story of a returning teacher who had previously worked at Challis years before the change, followed by three decades of teaching at other schools. Ms Musumeci found this teacher shaken up and teary after the first few weeks back at Challis and inquired what was wrong. It seemed that the experience of joining such a high performing and high expectations workplace was somewhat overwhelming. This teacher had their work cut out for them to take in all the learning and coaching to teach effectively and in line with the science of learning, but the teacher was also floored by the realisation that they had spent nearly 30 years doing something else that barely resembled the impactful and powerful teaching that they now knew existed. If only they had discovered these ideas earlier, the teacher told Ms Musumeci, their impact on the learning lives of their students could have been far greater.

Story Example 2.2 – Yates Avenue Public School

Yates Avenue Public School in Sydney's western suburbs has seen rapid and significant improvements in both student achievement and improved behaviour, following its adopting of science of learning informed approaches. This smaller school (180 students) in Dundas Valley about 40 minutes west of Sydney began its journey as a fairly typical school serving a somewhat disadvantaged cohort, but with children also from middle class backgrounds. Back in 2016, when principal David MacSporran began his leadership, behavioural issues were not out of control, but he does recall having to sometimes rush down to the local creek or skatepark once alerted that a student had run off, and would often lose a day following up on minor and major (sometimes violent) behavioural incidents.

It was acknowledged that teaching the older students at the school was difficult work, and when leadership began investigating how instruction was working, they realised there was no coherent or consistent model for teaching and learning at the school, and that some children were languishing with a lack of foundational skills, whilst disrupting the learning of others with anti-social and sometimes violent behaviour.

Six years down the track, the school credits much of its success to bringing in 15-minute daily reviews at the start of every lesson to consolidate prior learning, as well as changing their instruction so it was clearer, more explicit, and embedded with **checking for understanding (CFU)** opportunities throughout. These powerful practices originated from the science of how humans learn and could be seen as the driving forces that turned the school around. That being said, like many schools on such journeys, Yates Avenue used their own resources as well as the expertise from high-performing local schools. So how did they get here?

The teacher checking if students are learning while the lesson is unfolding using short, specific checks of understanding and proficiency

The data wake-up call

In 2017, David was looking at the school's standardised (NAPLAN) data and it was 'not great.' The school was underperforming for like schools in reading, writing, and mathematics. What's more, there were some grade levels where over two-thirds of students were accessing small group reading intervention—an unsustainable and worrisome proportion. Rather than blaming individuals or teams, David acknowledged this as an opportunity to challenge what the school had been doing for a long time.

Working hard, on the right things

There was no dispute that teachers were trying hard, but Yates Avenue was a school with a very low level of staff collaboration and shared planning. They also had fairly typical literacy and mathematics teaching practices, as per balanced literacy and inquiry/discovery methods for numeracy. After doing the phonics screening check, it was discovered many Grade 5 students were under-performing in decoding. The school sought out an effective, evidence-informed intervention program, and were fortunate to have found MultiLit® and MiniLit. While the intervention improvements were swift, they initially had not considered a literacy program for the whole class (InitiaLit). But the timing for such a change was serendipitously right. With such high numbers needing support, it was logical to overhaul their teaching approaches wholesale, and luckily the dismal data had created an openness amongst teachers to trying new practices.

The training from these programs introduced the school to practices informed by the science of reading, and what followed was a stark improvement in their literacy results, as they implemented systematic explicit phonics and phonemic awareness teaching. In addition to this, the school's science of *learning* journey was spurred on by a series of visits to a school that had made big changes to their general *instruction* (Blue Haven Public School). This was instrumental in David's school's understanding where to go next. The leadership team wanted their teaching to become more direct and explicit. Nevertheless, as in most schools, a change in this direction did worry some of Yates Avenue staff: *Shouldn't we be focussing more on rich learning, and student-led inquiry? Wouldn't more guidance from the teacher limit our students' potential?*

Yes, the teachers had seen some interesting examples of explicit teaching on their visits, but it had not clicked for them as to *why* more explicit and guided approaches could be the solution they needed.

Lockdowns that created time for teacher knowledge

In many ways, the COVID-19 lockdowns created space and time for additional professional learning and knowledge building, previously impossible with the day-to-day running of the school. Using mostly free webinars, podcasts, and readings from Think Forward Educators and Learning Difficulties Australia, as well as groups overseas including APM Reports journalist Emily Hanford, the school undertook significant whole-staff learning around many topics that aligned with the science of learning.

One such topic was the importance of daily review, an efficient and effective way to embed active retrieval of prior learning. Upon implementing these short, sharp revision sessions utilising whole class engagement and mini-whiteboard responses, the school observed that students were no longer forgetting things, and instead were consolidating skills and knowledge. Behaviour in classes became more under control as student time was filled with much more learning, and previously reluctant students exhibited greater confidence in the work they were undertaking.

Perhaps surprisingly, this influx of teacher knowledge building was not dependent on increased funding, and instead was driven by the staff's passion and dedication to find high quality, and freely available professional learning, of which there is now an abundance.

Raising the bar: Learning not a 'spectator sport' anymore

The expectations for students in terms of learning and behaviour were no doubt raised following this renewed focus on practices that aligned with the science of learning. Some older students who were used to a more 'free-range' learning experience did express that classes were harder now, and required more mental energy than they were used to. But once teachers and students slipped into their groove, they found that lessons would go quickly, the pace was fun and exciting, and students saw that their hard work was paying off in English, mathematics, and increasingly in other subjects. The school put a strong emphasis on maximising instructional time, removing unnecessary disruptions to core learning periods, and pushing special events and announcements to afternoons. As a result, the culture of the school shifted, and students had more mental space to become engrossed in learning. School pride became 'a thing.'

Expectations were raised for students, but so too was the support and the rigour of the teaching. Implementing **explicit instruction** practices meant that teachers made it

> A systematic and structured approach to teaching that provides clear, direct, and explicit guidance to learners. It involves breaking down complex skills or concepts into smaller, manageable steps, and providing explicit explanations, demonstrations, examples, feedback and practice to ensure understanding

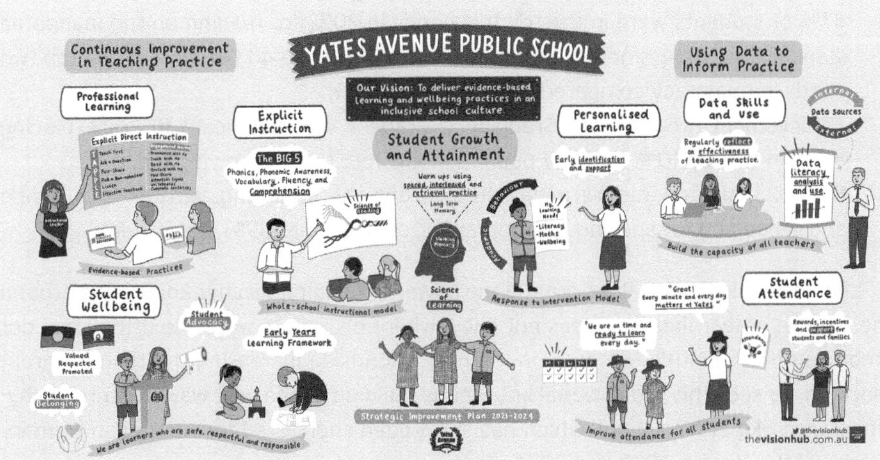

Figure 2.1 Yates Avenue School Strategic Plan.

Illustrated infographic by The Vision Hub at thevisionhub.com.au.

the norm for students to participate, but they would also pause lessons frequently to check for understanding and adjust as necessary. Alongside improvements in learning, the classrooms became calmer and more predictable. The school focussed on increasing teacher collaboration and consistency of teaching across all subjects, not just literacy and mathematics.

Teacher workload was carefully managed, and professional development was provided to support the changes. Teachers shared their experiences and strategies with each other, spreading good teaching practices throughout the school. They also embraced the messiness of the work, recognising that improvement takes time and patience.

Getting your profession back

Teachers at Yates Avenue have described the change in awareness of teaching and instruction as 'getting our profession back,' as they unfalteringly pursue best practice for every teacher for the benefit of every student. Teachers at this school can get really good at teaching (not just observing or facilitating learning); and students can learn how to focus, practice, and study effectively in all subjects, increasing their agency and self-efficacy. Looking at teacher turnover as an indicator of a strong school culture, the school has had very few teaching staff leave since the end of 2019, and have had the same leadership team for now five years.

In terms of student outcomes:

- In 2023, 100% of Grade 1 students met phonics check benchmark (meaning proficiency in decoding), compared to the average of only 59% for other public schools in the state;

- 47% of students were in the top two bands in 2022 for reading on the mandated standardised assessments, up from 26% in 2019, while 44.6% were in the top two bands in numeracy compared to just 27% in 2019;
- Achievement growth from Grade 5 to Grade 7 was significant in 2023, placing Yates in the top 10% for NSW public schools for student growth; and
- For 2023, all students were classed as proficient, in writing, with 84% in strong and exceeding for spelling and numeracy, compared to 69% state-wide.

Looking back, David values greatly the power of building teacher knowledge around the science of learning, and does not know where his school would be if they had not embraced the scientific research on learning. Alongside increasing the time for great teaching, he sees this professional knowledge building as the best way to improve anywhere, just like at his school, which has since been shortlisted for Australian Primary School of the Year in 2023 and 2024.

In this book, I aim to lift the hood on transformative schools such as Challis and Yates Avenue who are witnessing their school culture and outcomes improve beyond expectations, by aligning their teaching with the science of how we learn.

Does this book include *all* facets of the science of learning?

The focus of this volume is on the aspects of the science of learning that must be understood to have the biggest impact on practice in schools. While it is a contested space, the aim of the book is to highlight the potential effective instructional methods that are both empirically supported and reflected in the featured success stories. The complexity of translating findings from the science of learning into the classroom cannot be over-emphasised. However, what I aim to share here is that even when schools utilise a sample of key ideas from the science of learning, the impact can be enormous.

Explicit instruction as a set of coherent pedagogies

You may notice that this book features teaching practices that align with explicit instruction techniques (see chapters 5 and 11). This is not to be confused with the ten minutes of explicit teaching at the start of commonly-planned lessons, nor with a 'just-in-time' explanation after students return from independent exploration or inquiry.

Instead, in this book you will learn that explicit instruction is about (1) setting the scene for learning, (2) pitching your instruction right, (3) eliciting frequent opportunities for students to respond and participate, and (4) the teacher using verbal, non-verbal, and written information from students to adapt the lesson as it unfolds (see chapter 11 for a focus on checking for understanding). Explicit instruction techniques form part of a unified and coherent pedagogy that reflects the science of how humans learn and also the broad aims of education. You will learn more about the potential to use explicit instruction practices aligning with the science of learning as the book unfolds.

Is this just a pendulum swing?

There are many aspects that add together to create a comprehensive picture of learning and education. As has been prominent in the past 40 years, teachers today are used to hearing about affective, socio-cultural, and aesthetic aspects of learning as the *forgotten* pieces of the educational puzzle (e.g., Robinson & Aronica, 2016).

Ironically, such discussions have actually neglected the *cognitive* aspects of learning in recent decades, as learning in the brain has taken a backseat in discussions of 21st-century education. For this reason, it is the *cognitive* aspects of the science of learning that will feature strongly in this book, although the cross over into the emotional and behavioural aspects of teaching and learning will be frequently observable.

However, this is not an attempt at a pendulum swing towards purely cognitive views of education. If this was, it would mean these discussions are swinging back and forth between two poles (e.g., modern vs. traditional; or student-centred vs. teacher-centred). On the contrary, these discussions are not a swing back to the 'good old days' or 'back to basics.' The insights in this book reflect contemporary scientific understandings and real classroom/school applications that are truly innovative and often revolutionary. They can also be integrated with sociological and cultural understandings useful for learning and education.

Is the science of learning infallible? Is it the only source of knowledge to inform your teaching?

As with all science, insights from the science of learning are not beyond question or critique, nor do they represent the complete extent of everything teachers need to know. This evidence is an area of teacher professional knowledge which has been a blind-spot historically, often relegated to a few points in a once-off lecture. Other sources of knowledge should not be ignored, however, including socio-cultural accounts of education, and first nations knowledge-systems, for example.

Thus, I aim to ensure that insights from the science of learning makes it into the hands of teachers alongside the rich contextual understandings they already possess.

Concluding thoughts

I hope to provide a gentle awakening to the insights from the science of learning which should inform teaching practice. The stories and insights in this book indicate that schools currently in crisis *could* become places of safety, engagement, and success; and already average or fine schools *could* reach unforeseen heights—to the benefit of the communities they serve. There already exists a myriad of resources, books, videos, thought-leaders, and organisations that aim to inform and educate us about the science of learning and what it can do for education. I hope this book can be an accessible launchpad for any teacher or school leader.

References

Australian Education Research Organisation [AERO] (2021). *Standards of evidence*. https://www.edresearch.edu.au/. AERO.

Chambers, A. (2020). *Key terms to understand the learning sciences*. Education Domain Blog. Aurora Institute. https://aurora-institute.org/blog/key-terms-to-understand-the-learning-sciences/

Robinson, K., & Aronica, L. (2016). *Creative schools: The grassroots revolution that's transforming education*. Penguin Books.

Townsend, T., & Bayetto, A. (2021). Supporting school leaders to become more effective in leading reading improvements. *School Effectiveness and School Improvement, 32*(3), 363–386.

3 The science of learning lifts all learners

Nathaniel Swain

Our stories detail significant barriers to implementing approaches that align with the science of how we learn. Nevertheless, our schools report that such investments of time and resources are worth it for student outcomes and also indicate qualitative improvements in teacher satisfaction and sense of impact in their work.

At present the default or status quo approaches remain dominant. In some ways a *romantic* idea about teachers has become commonplace—one which has been advocated by social constructivists of old, explaining how individual students need to construct their own understandings, and which relegates the role of teacher to facilitator alone. Narrow interpretations of **constructivism** have left many teachers thinking they must not *interfere* with natural learning or risk stealing their students' chance to discover and construct for themselves.

> An influential theory of learning that emphasises learners actively constructing their own understandings

Quite the reverse, when teachers take a more in-depth and systematic approach to guide students' learning, it appears that many more students experience success, and those who would have been able to intuit the concepts or skills gain a more nuanced understanding of the learning. Teachers also report greater awareness of the content to be taught and of their students' growing mastery. In this way, the science of learning may hold the potential to *lift all learners*—student and teacher alike.

Let's hear from the final two school stories, and one from a school district/system.

Story Example 3.1 – Riverwood Public School

Before Anne Davis took on the principalship at Riverwood Public, this small south-western Sydney elementary school was considered a challenging place to work. A casual staff member at the school said, "Good luck!" to Anne on her first day on the job. Flanking the Riverwood public housing estate, 98% of Riverwood's students speak languages other than English at home, and the vast majority are from significantly disadvantaged backgrounds. The school serves a predominantly low socioeconomic community, with many highly vulnerable families with complex needs. It is a community with high markers of disadvantage, the impacts of which were evident in many children at the school. Riverwood's leadership have their work cut out for them.

DOI:10.4324/9781003404965-4

As you are about to read, the changes Anne and her colleagues put through for this little urban Sydney school would be monumental. What motivated (and continues to drive) this principal to do it? Anne Davis believes unapologetically that *no one's education should be defined by their postcode.*

Challenges and opportunities

As Anne remembers her first year at Riverwood, the teachers were well intentioned, but it was evident from classroom and playground observations, and negative staff-room discussion, that a great deal of work was needed to build their knowledge to better understand and respond to student behaviour. Inappropriate student behaviours were significantly disrupting the learning which was meant to be taking place.

Anne undertook significant work on re-building school culture, introducing workplace norms to set expectations for and to guide professional behaviour and practice, overseeing significant staff changeover, and introducing **positive behaviour support (PBS)**. Following significant changes to the timetable when behavioural issues reduced in frequency, and when the new school values and expectations were being demonstrated fairly consistently, the school leadership began to focus more squarely on learning.

Changing how reading was understood and taught

Previous instructional leadership had focussed on reading comprehension; but when Anne hired Sophie Roberts and Julie Mavlian to strengthen the instructional expertise of the leadership team, it was clear most students were struggling with decoding. The students had experienced years of **whole language** and **balanced literacy** teaching practices, including L3 (a government literacy program since retired) that neglected the foundations of reading. Using more fine-grained assessment tools, like a phonics screening check, a massive 69.5% of students in Grades 2–6 were identified as not having basic word recognition skills. This meant that the main problem was not in comprehension, but in lifting the words from the page. Considering the standardised national testing data (NAPLAN), the new leadership team was able to see overall low performance in literacy, but particularly low scores in reading for the most vulnerable children.

This made the school's priority for professional learning laser-focused. They needed to completely revamp the approach to teaching reading, and it was fortunate that the core team had achieved small-scale success with approaches aligning with the science of reading. The school set out to learn about and implement a range of initiatives including:

A whole-school framework for ensuring explicit teaching of behavioural expectations and boundaries as part of Multi-Tiered Systems of Support (MTSS)

A pedagogical philosophy which advocates for immersing children in rich, authentic texts as the main instructional tool. It pushes for the encouragement of students to 'sample' words in texts and to use multiple cues to predict written words

The term for a collection of approaches to teaching reading and writing. These share in common the idea of using a range of methods to teach students; includes elements of phonics and whole language

- systematic teaching of **phonics** and **phonemic awareness** across the entire school;
- explicit vocabulary teaching and use of rich texts to increase knowledge building and language comprehension;
- building knowledge and understanding of sentences and how to teach the building blocks of writing; and
- introducing a clear **Response to Intervention (RTI)** framework to guide targeted support for learning.

The teaching of sound-letter correspondences

The ability to hear, identify, and manipulate individual sounds (phonemes) in spoken words

A tiered framework used in education to provide early, systematic, and targeted support to students who need it, with the goal of preventing long-term difficulties

Building momentum

Within a year of big changes to the teaching of reading (and soon after, writing), Riverwood began to work on general instructional practices aligning with the science of learning, including a revamp using **Explicit Direct Instruction (EDI)**, as well as:

- increasing understanding of **cognitive load theory** and its impact on instruction;
- school-wide retrieval practices to reduce forgetting and increase mastery;
- engagement norms implemented to ensure students' attention was maintained, using in-house professional learning, demonstrations, and coaching;
- **checking for understanding (CFU)** practices to ensure teachers were monitoring student understanding, addressing misconceptions, and reteaching when required; and
- the introduction of the school's new Wellbeing Framework which provided a school-wide system and routines for developing successful learners (including **trauma informed practice**, PBS, student voice).

An approach to explicit instruction from DataWorks involving a set of prescriptive, but clear practices and techniques for teachers to implement

A theory for understanding how learners interact with tasks, based on the evidence that working memory is limited and affected by the environment, the nature of the task, and student prior knowledge

The teacher checking if students are learning while the lesson is unfolding using short, specific checks of understanding and proficiency

An approach to practice underpinned by understanding of impact of trauma on student behaviour and learning, whilst creating a supportive environment

The school today

Riverwood Public School is somewhat unrecognisable since these changes. Academic performance is improving, with successful readers becoming the new normal. In addition, other key results have included:

- wellbeing data indicating students believe they receive quality instruction, and they are learning;
- high levels of consistency across the school for learning and instruction;

- engagement of wider community—bringing them into classrooms, sharing and celebrating student growth;
- quality universal instruction ensuring all students are successful;
- teachers are valued and supported through high levels of professional learning and wellbeing practices, such as self-care plans; and
- high level of inclusion, high expectations culture, high levels of student and staff sense of belonging.

Resources for new staff include an instructional handbook featuring the non-negotiables from the science of learning. Because of the rigour of this school's practices, a new involved staff induction process has been required to ensure new teachers have the professional knowledge they need to thrive at Riverwood.

Previously, Riverwood was a hard-to staff-school. Today staff now seek out the school to secure a position there. It is indeed good fortune that Anne Davis and the school leadership came together at Riverwood, a school where now no child's education is determined by their postcode.

Figure 3.1 Riverwood School Strategic Plan

Illustrated infographic by The Vision Hub at thevisionhub.com.au.

Story Example 3.2 - Brandon Park Primary School

I have great pride in sharing this school's success, which I was fortunate enough to join halfway through their journey in 2021 as instructional coach. I miss the joy of teaching and leading change in this hub for excellent practice, but I trust their success can inspire many others. Brandon Park's story should be of use for school leaders who may have heard of this science of reading and learning 'stuff,' but may not know what to make of it.

Brandon Park's monumental shift from an average suburban Melbourne school to a leading school operationalising principles from the science of learning has been swift. Previously, like many government schools in Australia, the United States, or the United Kingdom, Brandon Park was a bastion of **balanced literacy**.

The term for a collection of approaches to teaching reading and writing. These share in common the idea of using a range of methods to teach students; includes elements of phonics and whole language

Hired by 20-year tenure principal Sheryl Chard, a new assistant principal Janice Corbett would open up a window of opportunity for her school to become exceptional. Janice and Sheryl were puzzled by their stagnating academic results, particularly in spelling. The school served a highly culturally and linguistically diverse community, with over 85% of families speaking a language other than English in the home; but their literacy program had always used what they saw as the supposedly *latest* pedagogical practices—'guided reading,' 'daily five,' and 'café reading,' and writing programs like 'seven steps to writing success.'

They had recently bought the spelling and morphology program Words Their Way, and wondered why they had not seen the gains they expected. Kate Buck, who had recently returned from maternity leave to a role as Assistant Principal, saw this spelling 'fix' as students learning to cut out lists of words, rather than learning to spell them.

Looking for solutions, Janice had worked previously with an educational speech-language pathologist named Shane Pearson and suggested to her fellow leaders, Kate and Sheryl, that someone with expertise in English spelling might be able to help them out. But what would a speech-language pathologist who worked mainly with students one-on-one know about teaching literacy?

What Shane Pearson brought was an intimate knowledge of the English spelling system, and an entrée into the science of learning to read and write, previously unheard of among Brandon Park's 30 teachers. Starting with part-time support for spelling, Shane's work blossomed into more in-depth conversations with staff about what else the school could consider updating, in line with the research.

Broadening the scope: Dabbling in explicit instruction

By the time I joined the school in early 2021, the school had made significant changes. It was one of the leading settings in Melbourne for adopting and utilising approaches that aligned with the science of reading and learning. My own contributions to the school sent it on the improvement of writing instruction, the implementation of **knowledge-rich curriculum**, and the tightening of explicit instruction techniques,

An approach to curriculum design in which knowledge, well-structured and specified in detail, provides an underpinning philosophy for learning including **checking for understanding** and **engagement norms.**

While the current school leadership, including now Principal Kate Buck, head of literacy Shane Pearson, and learning specialist David Morkunas, admit they still have significant work to do to improve the instructional expertise of their teachers, the success of the school demonstrates that even implementing aspects of an explicit and responsive pedagogical model can have marked improvements on student engagement and academic outcomes.

The teacher checking if students are learning while the lesson is unfolding using short, specific checks of understanding and proficiency

Taught, practiced, and expected routines for student responses and participation (e.g., attention signal, choral or tracked reading, pair shares, mini whiteboards)

Managing and responding to staff uncertainty

Would we describe Brandon Park's transformation as smooth sailing? Let's just say there were BIG discussions, and many concerned conversations in principal Sheryl's office, as devotees to balanced literacy, three cueing, and explicit teaching sceptics warned against changes that some felt were foreign and more rigid than they preferred. There was some significant resistance from certain staff members at the extent and nature of the changes. Much of what Brandon Park decided to do directly conflicted with what was popular and valued in many Australian classrooms.

To the credit of the leadership team, such concerns were handled with care, and some concessions were made. In the end, though, the force of the school executive, the guidance of the literacy expert, and the groundswell of teachers seeing massive success and benefit in their classroom, allowed the school to continue their work to align practice with the science of learning.

Brandon Park's example shows clear methods for managing particular voices, and ensuring that people in positions of leadership are aligned to the schools' vision and plan of action.

Outcomes

Like many of the stories in this book, Brandon Park has been on an upward trajectory ever since it began its science of learning work:

- The long tail of underachievement, especially in spelling, mathematics, and grammar and punctuation on national testing has disappeared, with all but a few students achieving strong or exceeding by Grade 5;
- The school's national testing results now sit above or well above like schools in all five domains tested in Grades 3 and 5;
- The school was one of the top three performing schools across the country for writing in recent assessment projects via No More Marking; and
- There is a consistent upward growth trajectory in the key indicators via national testing, and standardised assessment (e.g., DIBELS®).

What's more, there is no longer a group of students who work their way through Grades 3 to 7 unable to read or spell proficiently. Those who would have previously continued to the end of elementary school without functional reading and writing skills, now have their needs identified, supported, and continually monitored for progress. As per Brandon Park's outstanding **Response to Intervention (RTI)** framework, all students receive excellent Tier 1 classroom instruction, and there is additional, responsive Tier 2 and 3 intervention programs for those who need more support.

A tiered framework used in education to provide early, systematic, and targeted support to students who need it, with the goal of preventing long-term difficulties

The impact has meant that in a school of 600 students, only a handful with profound learning challenges are sitting below the expected standards in national testing (NAPLAN), but even these students have continued to make progress each year.

Endnotes

When long-standing principal Sheryl Chard left Brandon Park, it was a school transformed, both through the science of learning work, and the leadership's innovation and good management. Succeeded by Kate Buck, and Assistant Principals Rebecca Pal and Todd Bates, the school continues their science of learning journey taking the lead from instructional and curriculum experts Shane Pearson and David Morkunas (both contributors to this volume).

It has become a school that is able to support and challenge its students in all aspects of learning, as well as develop its teachers into instructional experts and future leaders. By ensuring educational equity, with no more **instructional casualties**, and excellence by continually raising expectations across the learning areas, Brandon Park acts as a beacon for other schools to learn from their successes, impacting the wider education context in Victoria and Australia.

Students struggling with reading who would not necessarily qualify for a learning disability, but whose outcomes have been affected by a lack of effective reading instruction

Is it all about science and no art?

The science of learning is a collection of insights we can use to inform how to best teach to maximise learning. But is there still an *art* of teaching? Of course! Teachers can be creative and unique in their enacting of effective teaching. And a pull between effective practices and personal preferences will always exist.

You can be *artful* and enact your own *finesse*, whilst also making good decisions about:

a) what should be most efficacious (best bets), and
b) what traps or fads should be avoided.

Let's look at the story of Catalyst, an ambitious school system-wide program for teachers and school leaders, harnessing the science of learning to optimise teaching and get effective and responsive practices into all schools.

Story Example 3.3 - Catalyst: Catholic Education Canberra Goulburn

Catholic Education Canberra Goulburn is the governing body for 56 catholic schools and nine Early Learning Centres (preschools) in Canberra and surrounding regional and rural areas of New South Wales which encircle Australia's capital city and territory. The office supports a wide variety of school sizes, regionality, and levels of socio-economic disadvantage, but in general serves fairly well-off communities, and should logically lead the country for outcomes, though some years ago this was not the case.

Originally from a business and policy background, Ross Fox joined the Catholic Education Canberra Goulburn office as Director in late 2016, and had always been inspired by the fundamental role of teachers in society, especially for the promotion of academic excellence and equity.

It was not until Ross began researching how reading develops and is best taught, considering the education of his own son, that he stumbled upon the plethora of scientific research sometimes referred to as the 'science of reading.' Another key driver behind the program of work which was to come was a sticking point in discussions about where explicit teaching should feature in the system's instructional models. In many ways, even asking that question was taboo, as the 56 schools had operated with a predominantly **inquiry-based learning** model, and the system did not at that stage have an account of the role of explicit teaching. This puzzled Ross, given the stark disconnect with the implications of the science of learning.

> A broad set of pedagogies involving students designing, implementing, and reflecting on student-led inquiry projects

Investment and knowledge building of system leadership

The system leaders began a deep dive into the nuances of the implications for practice provided by the cognitive science research particularly: *Where does the role of the teacher fit? How do we rectify the needs for agency and self-efficacy of the student with the necessity of guided and* ***explicit instruction*** *by the teacher?* Not all in the archdiocese's teaching and learning team stayed on following these discussions and decisions about the future direction of the system.

> A systematic and structured approach to teaching that provides clear, direct, and explicit guidance to learners. It involves breaking down complex skills or concepts into smaller, manageable steps, and providing explicit explanations, demonstrations, examples, feedback and practice to ensure understanding

Working with implementation partners, Knowledge Society, including CEO Elena Douglas, Ross Fox and the teaching and learning leadership began mapping out its large-scale, long-term plan for learning and change with school leaders and teachers. Indeed, the time spent understanding models of practice and implementation strategies was significant, and it took a few years before they were ready to bring this work to schools.

From here, the grand plan for 'Catalyst' was born: Catalyst being the system's teaching and learning approach and implementation strategy launched in 2021. Informed by the science of learning and reading, Catalyst would deliver excellent learning experiences for teachers focussed on science-aligned teaching practice and high-quality resources.

Investment in professional knowledge building of school leaders

The initial building of understanding around the research and implications for change were not always straightforward. Many principals and teachers did not think they needed to change. However, spending time reading about the sciences of reading and learning opened up opportunities for dialogue:

- Now that we know about **cognitive load theory**, what does that mean for my practice?
- What does our understanding about novice versus expert learners mean for my leadership, the structures, processes, and frameworks?
- How are these concepts enabling and supporting the teacher to evolve and change their practice?

A theory for understanding how learners interact with tasks, based on the evidence that working memory is limited and affected by the environment, the nature of the task, and student prior knowledge

For the new leader of teaching and learning in the Catalyst team, former principal Patrick Ellis, this process included significant reflection on prior beliefs and practices, and how these insights were shifting his views on what great teaching looked like.

Drawing upon subject matter experts to provide tailored professional learning was instrumental to the precision of this process, including Professor Pamela Snow (co-author in the volume), Associate Professor Lorraine Hammond AM., Dr Jennifer Buckingham and Ingrid Sealy.

Steady, people-focussed planning and implementation

One caution to learn from Catalyst, was that there was significant time and effort spent working with principals and school coaches to 'socialise' the principles and possible actions to be taken that aligned with implications of the scientific research. Considerable time was invested to unpack ideas, give nudges towards change, build knowledge through professional reading and discussion forums. The system leadership agenda was always clear, and the plan for what ideas were important were always held close. However, implementation was steady in the early days as trust and 'positive envy' of the success at early adopter schools could be generated.

Refocussing the work of the system

One of the biggest enablers for all this work was a reduction on professional development that did not align with the work of Catalyst. Indeed, Ross Fox firmly believed there was no point developing teachers to lead, when they are still to master the fundamentals of how students learn. In this way, the saying "the teacher is the most important learner in the system" became a focus, not to diminish the students, but to point out that system transformation happens with changing the teacher: their knowledge, beliefs, practice, and efficacy.

Fox also lessened the focus on school data for the teacher in the early days of Catalyst implementation, and instead promoted the concept that the 'mini-whiteboard' (a tool for checking student understanding in real time) was more important than the data 'dashboard.'

Setting up, then scaling up coaching and professional learning

Core work involved reframing professional development to encompass four main stages for each area of learning, comprising: Theory, Demonstrations, Practice, and Coaching. This allowed a clear discipline to be followed relating to the design of learning for teachers and leaders. There was also a reshaping of support structures, including observation and curriculum sharing, to increase accountability and expectations for teachers and their development.

Getting the most knowledgeable and experienced instructional coaches to lead initial implementation in schools helped communicate a strong message to leaders and teacher in schools that Catalyst was a worthwhile initiative.

In its first iteration, Catalyst was framed an opportunity for schools, with different leaders deciding to go faster or slower in some ways, though as time passed, all schools were supported to be part of the system-wide changes.

Once leaders and teachers had a taste of excellent instructional practice, they wanted to know how best to develop the curriculum (what to teach), so they could focus more effectively and efficiently on how to teach and how to respond to student learning.

Successes and next steps

Catholic Education Canberra Goulburn has already received positive signs of system-level improvement following the launch and staged roll-out of Catalyst. Whilst the work of system-wide change is ongoing, early indications are promising, including a distinct lift in outcomes at Grade 3 national testing (NAPLAN).

Table 3.1 Percentage of Canberra Goulburn *underperforming* schools, compared to students in similar schools nationally.

	2019	*2022*
Reading	42%	4%
Writing	71%	13%
Spelling	71%	21%

There is ongoing work to coordinate the innovation of instruction, curriculum and assessment in the system, including:

- reading, writing, and mathematics teaching practice and programs;
- effective instructional practices aligning with the science of learning in all subjects (see chapter 11);
- modelling and **instructional coaching**;
- bespoke professional learning modules to continue teacher knowledge building in the science of learning;
- curriculum scopes and sequence implementation for English to Grade 6 and Mathematics to Grade 6; and
- continued work focusing on developing expertise and materials for a **knowledge-rich curriculum** (see chapter 9).

A professional development process where a coach works with teachers to improve their instructional practices and enhance student learning

An approach to curriculum design in which knowledge, well-structured and specified in detail, provides an underpinning philosophy for learning

Concluding thoughts

The team behind the trail-blazing Catalyst initiative, emphasise that system leaders must beware of the potential for **lethal mutations** (Jones & Wiliam, 2022) that likely await other system leaders as they begin their own change implementation. A protective factor noted by design partner Elena Douglas is that the executive leadership needs to be just as knowledgeable about the actual content of the science of learning and its implications for practice. This ensures that there is high-level leadership and oversight over what is implemented, what is de-implemented, and how the system's conception of practice excellence evolves.

In education, occurs when an evidence-informed practice is modified beyond recognition from the original practice, and loses its utility

Fundamentally, the outcomes from Catalyst are demonstrating that this initiative is supporting students who have traditionally languished under less explicit and less guided approaches. The work is also beginning to extend and develop *all* students to achieve greater academic excellence. This powerful system-lead (but school powered) approach allows all within the archdiocese to undergo a process of gradual but consistent transformation, driven mainly by the experimentation and refinement of practice in every classroom every day.

Lifting all learners

As demonstrated in the stories above, the schools exemplify the benefits to those students *below grade expectations* who would otherwise be languishing, as well as to those *above grade expectations*, whose engagement and achievement appears to also increase even further following such transformations.

Hopefully, now I have your attention. I expect you are wondering *what* we are really talking about . . . And how can you get started?

The structure of this book

Sections

You are about to leave PART ONE: THE ORIENTATION, where you have met the schools sharing their science-informed changes that have driven their success.

In PART TWO: THE FOUNDATIONS, you will be introduced to key insights and implications from the sciences of learning and reading; you will look at effective teaching for literacy, mathematics, and other curriculum areas; and the implementation piece for potential school improvements.

PART THREE: THE TAKEAWAYS provides advice about kickstarting your science of learning journey, becoming a leader in the space, as well as next steps. The aim is to provide practical step-by-step processes for teachers and leaders to follow to commence their own science of learning journey.

Chapter overviews and knowledge organisers

From here on, you will notice the inclusion of a chapter overview at the beginning, and a knowledge organiser at chapter's end, to provide a summary of each chapter's main points.

Success story snippets

You will hear more about the changes and practices that comprise these school improvement journeys throughout the book. These are real experiences of teachers, students, and school communities, and have been shared in this book in the hope that they can inspire and inform a new interest in the science of learning in your school.

Where to next?

At the end of each main chapter, some key further reading and resources will be provided to launch your understanding of how to apply the chapter ideas to your classroom or school.

On-track indicators and discussion questions

There isn't just one way to go about using the science of learning to change your school. But there are some non-negotiables and key drivers that will ensure you are on the right track. Look out for the *check your indicators* tools at the end of the subsequent chapters.

Discussion questions are also available to guide your reflection and unpacking of the content of each chapter, individually or with your colleagues. You are encouraged to make connections within your own school/workplace and the issues and stories explored.

Progressing through the book

The book does not aim to be exhaustive or definitive. Rather, along with my fellow contributors I hope to have woven a cohesive and insightful narrative, combining school transformation stories with the insights from the science. Readers are encouraged to move back-and-forth between sections as they need. For example, you may wish to go straight to specific content chapters and then return to takeaway chapters in Part Three.

How do I begin?

What is stopping you from making changes like the schools in this book? Nothing. The evidence and knowledge are out there. Depending on your work context, you may be able to begin implementing changes tomorrow! And if not, this could be the book to give to leaders that are yet to join the discussion. I hope you can start your science of learning journey right now with the turn of a page.

Reference

Jones, K., & Wiliam, D. (2022). Lethal mutations in education and how to prevent them. *Evidence-Based Education*. https://evidencebased.education/lethal-mutations-in-education-and-how-to-prevent-them/.

PART TWO

The Foundations

4 Key insights from the science of learning

Cognitive load theory and beyond

Nathaniel Swain and Zach Groshell

What we now know about how humans learn is remarkable. The scientific research illuminates that learning is complex and, quite often, challenging. Here, you will read about key insights from the science of learning, including fundamental ideas like Cognitive Load Theory. In this chapter, we will begin our exploration of how learning and teaching happen, and what teachers can do to optimise these processes to benefit all students. Such insights can be grouped into four themes.

Box 4.1 - Chapter 4 overview - Insights from the science of learning illuminate:

- Why learning is hard;
- How knowledge powers all learning;
- How great teaching facilitates student learning; and
- Why we forget most of what we learn, but do not have to.

Why learning is hard

What we can learn is limitless, but our attention and working memory are powerful buffers

A lesser-known fact is that there are no known limitations of our **long-term memory** (Sweller, 2016). This means that we never have to stop learning. Our long-term memory is the store of all our knowledge, skills, and personal experiences. Whenever we recognise a word, solve a problem, connect an idea, design something new—we draw upon facts, ideas, concepts, and procedures from our long-term memory, which is practically infinite.

The **environment**—including the physical, social, cultural, and intellectual stimuli that surround us—is also a limitless source of learning.

The storage of previous learning and experiences which can be drawn into working memory for mental work

A source of learning external to the learner, including what can be observed, heard, sensed, and/or experienced

DOI: 10.4324/9781003404965-6

Many definitions are possible. See Dehaene's *How We Learn* for an overview

The work of getting information from the environment into our long-term memory is the process of *almost all* **learning** in schools. Kirschner, Sweller, and Clarke (2006) define learning as a change in long-term memory. If something has not changed in long-term memory, then learning has not happened.

Unfortunately, other than evolved skills such as how to speak our first language, information cannot go straight from the environment to our memories (although that would be the epitome of information overload). Instead, learning from the environment is hampered by two important buffers: (1) attention and (2) working memory.

Attention

Our focus on specific information, and ignoring of other stimuli

Our **attention** system is constantly shielding us from all but a few things at a time (van Moorselaar & Slagter, 2020). As we focus on one sound, one image, or one sentence on a page, the attentional system can literally block out incoming stimuli.

The power of our attention to buffer us from irrelevant stimuli is demonstrated in numerous studies–for a great example see Simons and Chabris' (1999) selective attention video on YouTube™. In this clip of six basketball players, the viewer is asked to count the number of passes made by the white team. All the while, a person in a gorilla suit casually traipses through the frame, completely unnoticed by the focussed observer. The viewer concentrates so hard on counting the number of passes that their attentional system blocks out the interloper.

Working memory

Our mental workspace, which can hold a limited number of items at any time

The second buffer is our **working memory**, described as both a mental workspace–which is cleared constantly unless we maintain our focus–as well as the seat of our consciousness, including our internal monologue and our mind's eye (Baddeley, 2003). Working memory is where we do our active thinking, and while it is a powerful part of our cognitive architecture, it is also incredibly limited. The magic number of items that can be held in working memory is fiercely debated, but for some individuals it can be as low as two to three items, and others mostly between three and five (Cowan, 2010).

Try remembering a new bank account number you have just been shown (without writing down the digits), and you will realise just how short your working memory is.

A learning mechanism that is prone to distraction and overload

Working memory and attention make the prospect of successfully learning uncertain. These are, however, the realities within which teachers must work when teaching anyone. As Sweller et al. (1998) outlined:

> *Limited working memory is one of the defining aspects of human cognitive architecture and, accordingly, all instructional designs should be analyzed from [this] perspective.* (p. 262)

Take this example. Your students might be successfully using mental arithmetic as they solve a multi-step mathematics problem, but if their attention is taken, or if the number of items exceed their working memory capacity, then all that mental work will be lost. Distraction and cognitive overload are the occupational risks for learners everywhere.

So how can we hope to teach when learning is so hard?

Teachers harnessing the science of learning know that gaining and maintaining student attention is the first step to teaching. By creating powerful **engagement norms** and routines, teachers can make it easy for students to focus and preserve precious working memory capacity for the cognitive tasks at hand (Smith et al., 2016). Some example routines include:

> Taught, practiced, and expected routines for student responses and participation (e.g., attention signal, choral or tracked reading, pair shares, mini whiteboards)

- attention signals, to gain students' focus quickly and reliably;
- choral reading (read with me) and tracked reading (track with me) prompts; and
- routines for completing tasks, answering questions, or working with partners.

> Breaking learning tasks down into bite-size pieces, so that each component of a task can be taught, practised, and mastered before it is connected with another component or chunk

It is also important to break learning down into **manageable chunks** so as not to overwhelm students. This means taking complex tasks or multi-step problems and breaking them up into bite-sized pieces which you teach and master with students one at a time, before proceeding to the next.

Teachers can also use numerous opportunities for students to respond to promote active engagement in new material. This *does not* mean doing various activities centring on the same learning intention (e.g., writing words on whiteboards, coloured pencils, keyboards, and in sand). Rather, it is about increasing the number of opportunities to respond in real-time while you are teaching (see Archer & Hughes, 2010) using engagement norms, as well as interspersing moments for checking for understanding, as students grapple with new content (Twyman & Heward, 2018). This could include using techniques such as: **pair shares** or turn and talks, **mini-whiteboard** responses, multiple choice questions, and **cold call** answering.

> A brief learning routine where students share their responses or thinking, regarding a particular question or prompt about the learning
>
> A small dry erase board that can be used for individual responses to tasks
>
> Calling upon a 'non-volunteer' to answer a question, as opposed to taking hands up volunteers

Story Example 4.1 - Riverwood Public School - Engagement norms

At Riverwood, before their science of learning journey began, low student engagement and disruptive behaviours impacted learning and wellbeing on a daily basis. Starting

A systematic and structured approach to teaching that provides clear, direct, and explicit guidance to learners. It involves breaking down complex skills or concepts into smaller, manageable steps, and providing explicit explanations, demonstrations, examples, feedback and practice to ensure understanding

with general professional learning around **explicit instruction** (Rosenshine, 2012; Archer & Hughes, 2010), followed by a distinct roll out of engagement norms from Explicit Direct Instruction (EDI; Hollingsworth & Ybarra, 2017), this shift created a common language for the school, as well as a clear conception of what the new practices looked like.

Using techniques like attention signals and prompts like 'read with me' and 'track with me,' Riverwood teachers saw a significant turn-around in behaviour as students were engaged in their learning and the teachers' consistent use of these norms reduced the strain on students' working memory, supporting even higher levels of engagement. This was not a 'set and forget' initiative, and leaders have continually revisited and practised these techniques through professional learning and coaching and induction for new staff.

The many sources of cognitive load

Once we attend to something and it enters our conscious awareness, it uses up some of our working memory. *Cognitive load* refers to how much working memory capacity is used up when completing on a task, remembering that anything can take some of our working memory.

A theory for understanding how learners interact with tasks, based on the evidence that working memory is limited and affected by the environment, the nature of the task, and student prior knowledge

Cognitive load theory (see Sweller et al., 2019) is a way of conceptualising how a learner will interact with a task, how their working memory is likely to be under- or over-used, and what instructional designers can do to optimise this. We want our students to grapple with the learning tasks we give them. However:

- *Underloading* working memory leads to boredom, disengagement and self-distraction (and less learning);
- *Overloading* working memory leads to feeling overwhelmed or confused, and thus leads to disengagement and self-distraction (and less learning).

Like Goldilocks, we need our students to have the 'just right' experience when it comes to cognitive load: not too little and not too much. Scientists consider that there are two main types of cognitive load: intrinsic and extraneous (Sweller et al., 2019).

The kind of load associated with the task itself and the level of complexity within it. Intrinsic load will differ based on the background, knowledge and skills of the learner

Intrinsic load is the kind of load we want, as it is associated with the intended learning, and the students' relevant prior knowledge. Tasks will differ on their intrinsic load based upon the number, complexity, familiarity of the task items, and how these elements might interact.

Extraneous load is cognitive load to do with the manner and structure in which the information is presented. This refers to anything we use to provide the information (intentional or otherwise) which takes students' working memory away from the task at hand. It also comprises any other aspects in the learner's purview that could detract from learning (including *internal* distractors like other competing thoughts, or *external* distractors in the environment).

The kind of cognitive load that takes students' cognitive energy away from the task at hand. This is to do with the manner or structure of instruction

Table 4.1 Sources of main types of cognitive load.

Sources of Intrinsic Load

The number of elements or steps in a given task.
The density of information within the task (how difficult to read, or analyse the task).
The abstractness of the concepts (concrete items are easier than abstract ones).
The number and complexity of the connections between individual elements (**element interactivity**).
The novelty of the items, for each learner (new information adds more cognitive load than the familiar).
The restrictedness or open-endedness of task (tasks that are open-ended and unguided have higher intrinsic load).
Whether the task is static or dynamic: Are stimuli unchanging (e.g., paper-based task), or are they dynamic (live discussions, or driving a vehicle)?

The number and complexity of the connections between individual elements within a learning task. It reflects how much mental effort is required to process the information

Sources of Extraneous Load

Complex, unfamiliar, conflicting, or ambiguous language or visuals used to convey the information.
Additional information that is unneeded (**redundancy**) and causes students to look in more than one place.
Verbal instruction that is too fast, slow, loud, quiet, off-topic, or long-winded.
Distracting information (within task):

- Superfluous, redundant, irrelevant writing, spoken language, or visuals
- Teachers speaking too much or for too long when delivering content or instructions, or speaking about things that are not directly related
- Unnecessary animations, GIFs, or overcrowded slides/worksheets
- Unnecessary decision points (i.e., choices within task that do not contribute to learning outcomes, but occupy working memory)
- Lack of familiarity with format of task or technology used.

Unnecessary double up or repeated information

Distracting information (outside task):

- Irrelevant visual or physical stimuli within view or reach (e.g., unnecessary posters, displays, decorations, clutter, fidgets, or other physical items)
- Background noise of any kind within or outside class
- Novelty of a visual, auditory, or even olfactory (smelly) nature!
- Verbal or nonverbal off-task behaviours from peers (or teachers!).

Important information disappears from view or is inaccessible (**transiency**), when it is still relevant to the task.

An effect on cognitive load where important information is only heard or seen briefly, meaning learners have to simultaneously try to remember the information and use it for the task

For illustrative examples of resources that have low and high extraneous load, see Lovell's (2020) guide to cognitive load theory.

As our attention and working memory are limited, effective teachers make it their mission to protect their students' learning apparatus. Thus, Lovell (2020) has summarised that cognitive load theory can be operationalised to increase learning by doing the following:

> *[R]educe extraneous load and optimise intrinsic load.* (p. 17)

Teachers harnessing the science of learning work hard to minimise sources of extraneous load in the manner or format of information shared for learning; and to remove sources of distraction in the environment (*reduce extraneous load*). They also modulate the level of difficulty or complexity of a given task, so that no student is significantly overstretched or under-activated (*optimise intrinsic load*).

Story Example 4.2 - Riverwood Public School - Intrinsic and extraneous load

Riverwood Public School also undertook professional learning to understand cognitive load theory, and its impact on instruction. Initially, their teachers had limited awareness of this theory, so professional development was needed to upskill staff. Then as a first point of action, the school made a concerted effort to reduce extraneous load, through tightening up routines and expectations (see Bennett's Running the Room, 2021), along with consistent resource templates (including PowerPoint slides) that were clear and lacked clutter or redundancy.

The school then considered ways of optimising intrinsic load, including by: activating prior knowledge, breaking content down into small manageable chunks, providing modelled and guided practice of all variations in the lesson and constantly checking for understanding. The implementation was underpinned by professional learning and instructional coaching. Also, workplace and professional learning norms helped to build a positive and productive learning culture among staff.

In terms of benefit, teachers noted that learning time and quality was maximised, with a reduction in wasted time, a decrease in problematic behaviours, and increasing student growth data.

How knowledge powers all learning

Prior knowledge is the start of all learning

An inescapable fact about learning is that all learning is based upon facts. More accurately, learning to do any task requires the accumulation of increasingly sophisticated knowledge (Willingham, 2006). Despite the appeal of the idea that knowledge is *unnecessary* in our digital/information age, if we were to try outsourcing our long-term memory to a Google search result–or a ChatGPT-written response–we could never compete with what experts of a domain can do.

The reason we cannot circumvent expertise by 'Googling it' is that our working memory constraints make complex tasks impossible if we do not have the right background. Yes, experts in a field will consult external information sources to cross-check and complement their long-term memory, but they are critical consumers of this information *because of what's in their long-term memory* (Hirsch, 2000). For instance, most surgeons would be terrible at diagnosis via cardiovascular imaging; and cardiologists would work like beginners when attempting complex plastic surgery. This highlights that domain-specific knowledge must be remembered, mastered, and applied for any learner to move from novice towards expert.

Knowledge isn't merely the accumulation of disconnected or meaningless facts. When experts begin to master any domain–from mechanical engineering to symphonic composition–they acquire and construct interconnected and organised schemata of knowledge about that discipline (Kirschner, 2009). This includes **declarative knowledge** of facts or truth propositions ('knowing that . . .'), and **procedural knowledge** of skills and tasks and the ability to apply these flexibly ('knowing how . . .'), see Table 4.2. Experts will also have personal experiential knowledge that connect the cognitive with the emotional.

Knowledge of facts, terminology and key ideas and the connections between them; 'knowing that'

Knowledge of how to complete a task or demonstrate a skill; 'knowing how'

Biologically primary vs. secondary

The cognitive science also teaches us that there are two kinds of knowledge, which are acquired very differently: biologically primary and secondary knowledge. Geary (2008) proposed a kind of everyday knowledge that is easily acquired through social

Table 4.2 Declarative versus procedural knowledge.

Declarative knowledge ('knowing that . . .') Facts or truth propositions	**Procedural knowledge** ('knowing how . . .') Skills and tasks including the ability to apply these flexibly
PRIMARY/ELEMENTARY SCHOOL	
The human body has 206 bones.	Labelling bones in a skeletal system diagram.
The Earth is the third planet from the Sun.	Identifying the planets in order from Mercury to Neptune.
There are 60 minutes in every hour.	Telling the time to the minute.
Stories have a beginning, middle, and end.	Retelling a story including major components.
SECONDARY/HIGH SCHOOL	
Shakespeare's *Romeo and Juliet* is about love and hate.	Writing a paragraph arguing how *Romeo and Juliet* is more about love.
World War II ended in 1945.	Analysing primary sources from World War II.
Mitochondria are the powerhouse of the cell.	Drawing a model of cellular respiration.

interaction and has conferred an evolutionary advantage: **biologically primary knowledge**. This knowledge is passed on with minimal or no effort through immersion and exposure. It is easy to learn this kind of knowledge, as limits of cognitive load do not apply here.

Fundamental knowledge that is innate or develops early in life, such as language acquisition or recognising faces

Classic examples of this kind of knowledge include:

- mastering your first language;
- finding your way around your local environment; or
- recognising faces.

This is contrasted with **biologically secondary knowledge,** which is the understandings that have only been important for humans in our recent evolutionary past. Some examples include:

Knowledge that is acquired through explicit educational experiences, such as reading, writing, and specific academic skills or knowledge

- learning to read and write;
- mastering the human invention of mathematics; and
- any other disciplinary knowledge tied to specific academic areas (e.g., science, humanities, the arts).

Cognitive load theory is primarily concerned with the *acquisition of biologically secondary knowledge* (Paas & Sweller, 2012). Thus, if not properly managed, material from the subjects of school will most certainly overload the working memories of our students.

It is the *biologically secondary knowledge* that we want all students to master. So, how we teach most knowledge in school should be explicit, systematic, and not be left for students to 'pick up.'

Experts have more domain-specific knowledge

Interestingly, knowledge (and lots of it) is exactly what individuals need to acquire in order for them to gain expertise in a given domain. Classic experiments with chess masters, for example, have demonstrated that it is not innate problem solving or strategising abilities that separates novice from professional within a specific domain. In fact, what is more important is the magnitude of knowledge that experts have (Sweller et al., 2010).

Box 4.2 - How studying chess masters taught us that expertise is about accumulating knowledge

It is the intimate knowledge that chess masters possess about thousands of games, potential moves and stratagems that makes them an expert (e.g., De Groot, Gobet, & Jongman, 1996).

In a series of studies on expertise, master chess players were shown an image of a board from the middle of a game for just five seconds. They were able to recall the entire chessboards, piece for piece from memory, but were reduced to the recall of novices when pieces were placed around the board in random configurations.

In the experiments, when the chess player looked at the board taken from the middle of a real game, they did not see single chess pieces, but rather a constellation of bigger patterns and explanations of how the pieces got there and what the player should do next. With a board that was randomly configured, there were no larger meanings or patterns they could draw upon to create a complete picture in their heads.

What we know about the knowledge of chess masters is true of all experts: When you have sufficient knowledge about your area of expertise, you do not get overwhelmed by all of the individual components of a problem or situation. Instead, you use the knowledge you already have in long-term memory to see larger, meaningful chunks; you notice irregularities, and predict logical next steps (Sweller et al., 2010). This is because you can connect the items in front of you to wider understandings of how this domain works.

This same phenomenon occurs when a literate person glances at an excerpt of a Shakespearean play. They are undistracted by the squiggly lines that form together to make words, nor are they drawn to superficial features of the texts, such as stage directions and translations in the footnotes. Rather, they analyse the underlying meanings within the entire segment and connect it with their wider knowledge of the Bard's work. It would be laughable to compare this reading of content to the way a five-year-old would approach such a task, when they are figuring out how to decode a word like 'cat.'

In both the chess and Shakespeare examples, the difference between a novice and an expert is the amount of **domain-specific knowledge** they have accumulated about that area (Christodoulou, 2014), not their abilities to think critically or solve a problem.

Refers to information, concepts, and skills that are specific to a particular field or subject area, such as mathematics, history, or biology

We solve problems, create, and critique using knowledge in our long-term memory

As a part of wider educational trends to separate *deep* learning from (boring old) knowledge, you may have been swayed by arguments that students do not need much factual knowledge anymore as they can simply look things up. You may have agreed that it seems logical to spend more time teaching students broader concepts or durable skills like problem solving, critical thinking, or creativity (see 21st-century skills; Rotherham & Willingham, 2010) rather than requiring students to remember knowledge and facts.

On the contrary, for our students to become independent, inquiring, and critical learners, they must possess sufficient knowledge of whatever it is they are inquiring about or critiquing. Knowledge isn't all students need to access higher order learning and application, but it is a necessary first step. A novice, by definition, does not know much about the topic (e.g., the Silk Road), which limits the kinds of questions they can generate when searching the internet. You may have sent your students off on independent inquiry projects about which they have relatively little understanding with the hopes they can independently research and form their own connections through exploration. A risk of relying on such approaches is that students acquire information inefficiently (Kunar et al., 2016), and end up, as we put it, *inquiring up the wrong tree*!

Box 4.3 - An anecdote about the dangers of unguided, premature inquiry, from Nathaniel

A Swain family favourite that illustrates this phenomenon is the story of my wife's secondary Humanities classes where students were set an inquiry project on Ancient Rome. Having been discouraged to teach this vast body of knowledge explicitly or sequentially, my wife, Gabriella, first sent her Grade 8 students off to inquire, only to later find a group of them spending significant time creating a PowerPoint presentation on Roman cars.

The preposterousness of such an inquiry topic was lost on the group, however. They simply had not understood what 'ancient' meant, and how the very name of the topic should have eliminated automobile exploration as their focus.

Contrary to much of the push from the 21st-century skills movement, focussing on knowledge *does not* waste time that should be reallocated towards developing problem solving or critical thinking skills. Quite the opposite, building knowledge paves the way for students to gain sufficient understanding to learn successfully from later unguided learning tasks like problem solving or creative/critical thinking (Witherby & Carpenter, 2021).

Becoming a proficient reader, writer, mathematician, or thinker requires sufficient domain-specific knowledge

The inescapability of knowledge is also demonstrated when students learn to read, write, and do mathematics. As the subsequent chapters will detail, effective literacy and numeracy educators teach in a systematic and explicit manner to ensure their students master the **declarative** (knowing that) and **procedural** (knowing how) knowledge they need to become literate and numerate. It is through the interactive process of modelling the material, facilitating practice, and providing feedback on errors that students begin to master these domains (Stockard et al., 2018). Just like all biologically secondary knowledge, the process of becoming proficient readers, writers, and mathematicians is not a natural one (Geary, 2008).

Knowledge of facts, terminology and key ideas and the connections between them; 'knowing that'

Knowledge of how to complete a task or demonstrate a skill; 'knowing how'

How great teaching facilitates student learning

Highly effective teachers manage students' cognitive load

As we have learnt so far, the science of how we learn indicates the effectiveness of teachers who:

- manage and optimise their students' cognitive load;
- build students' knowledge solidly and in a sequential manner;
- maximise the time spent on explicitly teaching students, directed and guided by the teacher (the expert in the learning at hand); and
- ensure all learners are benefitting from the instruction as they progress along the path from **novice** to **experts** (see below).

A learner who lacks the expertise of a particular task or domain, and may get overwhelmed with the complexity of complex tasks in that given area

Someone who has a well-organised and elaborate mental schema (knowledge system) related to a particular domain

Given how such insights rub up against widely held beliefs in education, most teachers would need to rethink many aspects of their work to align their practice with the science of learning. This would include rethinking how they:

- structure their teaching;
- create a calm and predictable classroom;
- plan to build the foundational skills and knowledge of students; and
- embed questioning and tasks during teaching, to constantly check for student understanding and respond to those checks in real-time.

In this book, the stories from schools who have undergone this 'rethink' provide a roadmap for you, as you consider the utility and effectiveness of these principles in your practice. Rosenshine's (2012) ten principles of instruction is a useful framework for understanding how explicit teaching can be effective and responsive (see chapter 11).

Novices benefit from fully guided instruction, and experts from less guided

What works best for supporting students comes down to whether they are relative novices or relative experts at the task or domain at hand. We might have been led to believe that as long as we were 'engaging' our students, and that they were busy during each lesson, then learning would happen.

It is surprising for teachers to hear that students can successfully complete tasks whilst actually learning very little. Tasks requiring activity or behavioural engagement do not necessarily foster actual learning, that is a change in long-term memory (Mayer, 2004). Studies of problem-solving tasks (e.g., Sweller, 1988) show that novice learners without guidance can end up working very hard cognitively, as they struggle through the task with methods such as trial and error. As novice students use very inefficient strategies to solve the problem, often they will completely exhaust their working memory capacity on figuring out what to do next. This means that novice learners can be left with no working memory remaining with which to *learn from* the experience itself (Sweller, 2006).

Box 4.4 - Successfully solving a problem does not necessarily guarantee learning

Dr Greg Ashman, cognitive load theory researcher and deputy principal at Ballarat Clarendon College, has used the following example in several blogposts, podcast episodes, and in his book *A little guide for teachers: Cognitive load theory.*

In many inquiry-based approaches to teaching, investigations and exploration are said to be ideal. In science teaching, there is a focus on students experimenting in order to figure out for themselves if something is true. A classic chemistry experiment using marble chips and hydrochloric acid is designed so students learn about the importance of surface area for how quickly a substance will react. In Ashman's own teaching experience in high schools, he would work intently to set up the experiment so that in the process of exploration, students were meant to discover the learning intention: that smaller chips would react to the acid faster because smaller pieces had greater surface area than chunkier pieces.

Of course, Ashman's efforts were always thwarted by students becoming distracted by the complexity of the task and its many interacting components. Students would fail to come to this conclusion as they were instead thinking: 'Where are the test tubes kept?' and 'I have no acid left . . . Where can I get some more acid?'

Ashman found that with students wrapped up in the task, they may have successfully dissolved a lot of marble chips, but usually failed to figure out the core learning about how fast the differently sized pieces would dissolve. He should have just taught them that first.

Worked example effect: Relevant for novice learners

In cognitive load theory, the **worked example** effect shows that novices benefit from looking at well-structured and fully-solved example problems for them to study and understand. So, novice learners will learn much more from watching a step-by-step explanation, than struggling through the same task without guidance (Sweller, 2006).

A fully-worked problem which has already been solved for the student, showing each step explained clearly

Learners who are new to a task or topic benefit most from teachers breaking it down for them. Willingham (2002) reminds us that learners' first job is to *understand* a solution to a problem, *not to create* their own solution initially. As students systematically acquire more knowledge in their long-term memory, they have more fuel in the tank to power their solving of future tasks.

Expertise reversal effect: Relevant for expert learners

When students do move from novices to more expert-like in a given domain (e.g., easily identifying the effect of surface area in the marble chip reaction), a different cognitive load effect comes into play. Known as the **expertise reversal effect** (Kalyuga et al., 2003) this shows that explicit instruction can actually interfere with the *expert* learner's knowledge about the task.

A research finding that shows that novices need step-by-step instruction whereas experts can learn better from more independent problem solving

When students have become proficient in a certain domain, this is the time to actually pull back on the level of guidance, and let students independently apply their understandings.

Despite this effect, much of what we seek to teach students (i.e., new learning) will place students firmly back into the novice seat, at least initially. And thus, there is a strong rationale for initial explicit instruction and guidance to move students along the expertise continuum effectively (Kirschner et al., 2006). That is what great teaching seeks to do!

Fully guided instruction provides a pathway to higher order learning

Nowhere might we find a more polarising topic as the question of when and how to teach explicitly. Despite many popular theories and edu-thought leaders who say otherwise, there is immense power in teachers using instructional practices that ensure learners are not left to struggle alone. **Fully guided instruction** (as summarised by Kirschner, Sweller, and Clark, 2006) is often pitted against **minimally guided approaches** such as problem-based learning, inquiry, or discovery learning. What is forgotten in the critiques of explicit instruction (e.g., Groshell, 2022) is that *modelling is not the end point*; it should only be considered the entry instructional mode which is aimed at taking learners from absolute novices to intermediates, or perhaps quasi-experts in a given domain.

A collection of approaches to instruction that has high levels of teacher guidance at the beginning of the learning process, and only withdraws this guidance when students are ready to progress

A set of instructional approaches that gives students the prime responsibility of structuring and managing the learning; providing a task or project without ensuring students have the prior skills and knowledge may occur here

Fully guided instruction builds the learning foundations in a given domain

When teachers start to teach in a way that incrementally guides students through the learning process, they systematically add knowledge, skills, and tools to their students' mental toolboxes. When this change in instructional design occurs (as we will hear more about from our school stories), we begin to close the gaps between the most advanced students in the class and those needing the greatest support. For example, proficiency in the domain of reading begins with teaching the building blocks of language—that is the sound-letter patterns (graphemes)—and having students recall these automatically, then combine them together to blend sounds into words (Buckingham et al., 2019). These incremental milestones—that is the accumulation of increasingly sophisticated knowledge about sounds, words, and phrases—is what allows students to gain sufficient expertise to read their first book, and then their tenth, and hundredth.

Of course, some learners will build this knowledge and skill elsewhere. Teachers are not the sole sources of learning for our students. That being said, spending most of our time teaching in a way that neglects such building blocks can actually *increase* the gaps between our lowest and highest students. In contrast, the use of fully guided instructional approaches (at least initially) can ensure ALL your students can make progress towards *expertise* in their learning.

As discussed in chapter 2, teaching in line with the science of learning is a social justice imperative because such work can efficaciously address student inequities by closing gaps in all students' foundational knowledge and skills.

Why we forget most of what we learn, but do not have to

The final insight we wish to share is that learning is not a set-and-forget endeavour: The new knowledge and skills acquired by students as a result of our teaching must be actively maintained, or else these will likely be forgotten. The last inconvenient truth of our chapter on cognitive architecture is this: Most of what we focus on (attention), think about (working memory), and even learn, does not stay in our long-term memory. Students forget the vast majority of what we teach them (Bjork, 2011).

The forgetting curve means that teaching is always a moving target

The phenomenon in which learners tend to immediately forget most of what they have learnt the previous day, with sharp declines over time, unless content is reviewed

Hermann Ebbinghaus (1850–1909), a German psychologist, carried out a series of recall experiments on himself to produce one of the most helpful insights about our brain. Known as the **forgetting curve**, Ebbinghaus was the first to map the rapid decline of memory retention over time on any set of information, illustrating just how swiftly new learning is lost from our mind. On the forgetting curve in Figure 4.1, we can see that the majority of new learning is lost one day after first exposure. Nevertheless, teachers harnessing the science of learning understand this harsh reality and plan for it: If you review prior material with students by engaging in frequent practice and testing, you can counteract this effect. For example, also in Figure 4.1, you should see that one re-teaching (review) of the content can reduce the speed of loss significantly.

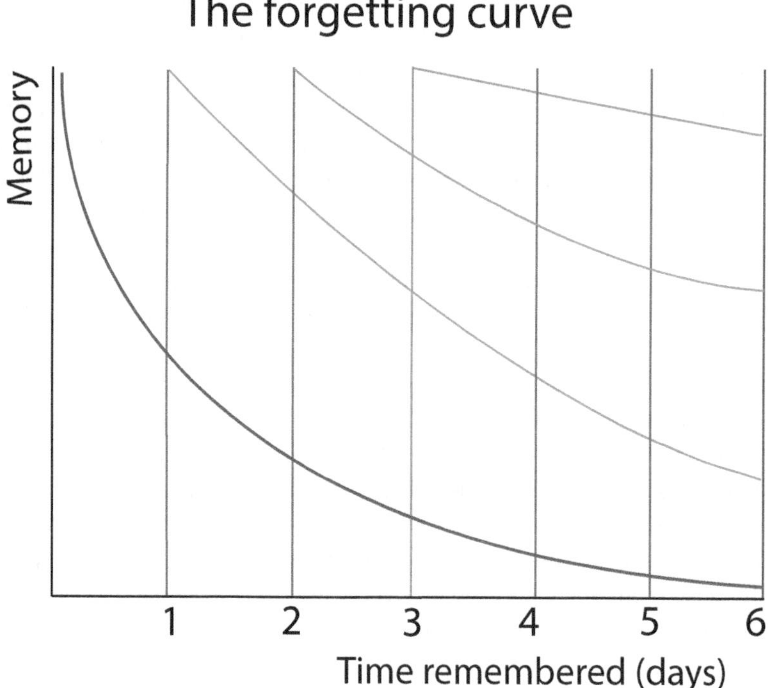

Figure 4.1 A typical representation of the forgetting curve with spaced repetition.

Icez at English Wikipedia.

Retrieval practice reduces forgetting: It's 'use it or lose it'

How can we counteract Ebbinghaus' troublesome discovery? The rate and magnitude of students' forgetting can be minimised when we facilitate frequent student **retrieval practice** (i.e., self-testing; Karpicke, 2012). Though it can feel effective when we read over or revisit our notes from previous learning, what really prevents our memory from being whittled down to nothing is actually putting our memory to the test.

Opportunities for students to attempt to remember how to complete previous learning tasks or recall previously learnt concepts, facts, or skills

One way to facilitate frequent retrieval practice is to make **daily review** part of your everyday non-negotiables as a teacher. Daily review involves fast-paced practice to see if students can remember prior learning, including:

A short, daily session of practice of previously taught material, including concepts and skills that ensure students consolidate their learning and avoid forgetting

- **concept review** for previously learnt concepts, vocabulary, and facts (e.g., 'What is the word for this shape?,' 'Which is an example of a simile?'); and
- **skill review** for procedures and applications of concepts (e.g., 'Complete this sentence using the conjunction *even though,*' 'Solve this perimeter problem on your whiteboard').

The review of key concepts and vocabulary from prior learning

The review of skills or tasks that have been previously taught

Other retrieval practice opportunities can include:

- frequent student quizzes on prior topics and skills; and
- warm-up tasks including previous topics before each lesson begins, for example 'Do nows' (see Lemov, 2021).

Spacing and interleaving structures learning better

In addition to retrieval practice, research into the efficacy of **spaced practice** and **interleaved practice** (e.g., Dunlosky et al., 2013) has determined that the forgetting curve can also be reduced by:

Structuring learning, so that it is spaced out over time, meaning there are time gaps between the lessons that allow students to better consolidate their learning

The interspersing of different learning tasks and topics, overtime, as opposed to blocked practice

- breaking learning across several days and weeks (spacing); and
- mixing things up to move through a variety of topics and skills (interleaving).

See further reading at the end of the chapter. As opposed to **massed** and **blocked practice** (learning one topic all at once and not revisiting it), spacing and interleaving create a significant memory advantage for our learners.

The practising of the same set of learning tasks in an intense way for example, cramming; in contrast to spaced learning

Studying one topic or skill for a period of time without breaks or interspersing other topics; in contrast to interleaved practice

It may be tempting to demarcate student practice into different sessions, so we do not confuse or overwhelm them. This may be the case for initial learning. However, when students begin to show some fluency with the target learning, starting to interleave and space out practice is much more beneficial. For example, the left side of Figure 4.2 shows traditional massed/blocked practice where in one session there is:

- practice in a singular topic A (e.g., addition problems);
- followed by a separate session on topic B (e.g., subtraction); and
- another session on topic C (let's say worded problems with addition).

If teachers facilitate blocked practice like this continuously, they may see students forgetting each topic as they move from one to the next.

By contrast, with interleaved practice (see the right-hand version in Figure 4.2), students have a chance to practice many different kinds of problems from A, B, and C, therefore can harness the spacing and interleaving effect.

Intuitively, we know that cramming for an exam the night before may produce immediate benefits of passing the exam (with flying colours, perhaps). We also know that this learning is unlikely to be still in our brains, even after just a few weeks, let alone years. Spaced and interleaved practice, on the other hand, have such benefits for mastery of study that they have been dubbed 'powerful learning' tools (Agarwal & Bain, 2019).

One way to facilitate retrieval practice and spacing/interleaving: Daily review

With daily review, students are taken through a fast-paced daily experience where they recall and reconnect with (almost forgotten) learning from previous weeks. This daily practice and self-testing ensure that all the great knowledge from topics and the complex connections in between are not lost (Dunlosky & O'Brien, 2022). Instead, these are strengthened. In the

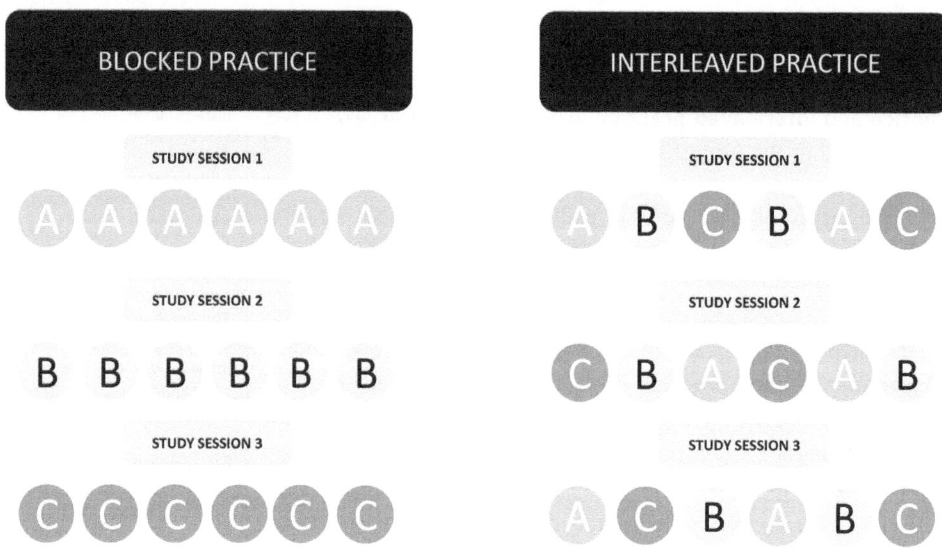

Figure 4.2 Blocked vs. interleaved learning, showing practice for topic A, B, and C.

following examples, you will hear how spacing and interleaving principles can transform the performance and confidence of students.

Story Example 4.3 - Churchill Primary & Catalyst - Benefits of daily review

Churchill Primary

Churchill Primary's practice of daily reviews started in the literacy space, with daily practice of phonics, spelling, morphology, grammar, and vocabulary. Here, the school also developed their Explicit Direct Instruction (EDI) teaching-learning model. Though not a school-wide implementation focus, these approaches organically transferred to numeracy, as teachers adopted explicit teaching for mathematics spontaneously and began reviewing these concepts in their own version of mathematics daily reviews. Teachers created a list of non-negotiable concepts that had to be in their reviews every day. These included concepts from all strands of numeracy.

Following the next round of standardised testing, principal Jacquie Burrows' supervisor requested that she give a talk on how the school had improved its numeracy results. This was much to Jacquie's surprise as Churchill Primary had not undertaken any school-wide work on improving mathematics. This just demonstrated the power of daily review and explicit teaching.

Catalyst: Catholic Education Canberra-Goulburn

A big focus in Catalyst schools has been professional learning into retrieval practice of previously taught material and how it helps students learn (via a change in long-term memory). Daily review has been a beneficial initiative, as it has supported teacher practice including pace, frequency of **checking for understanding (CFU)**, and other questioning techniques.

> The teacher checking if students are learning while the lesson is unfolding using short, specific checks of understanding and proficiency

Initially, daily reviews require a lot of work from teachers (they might be lacking a bank of instructional materials including PowerPoint presentations). However, the investment of time can very soon pay off as such resources are used and adapted each year. This has been the experience in Catalyst schools.

Results across the schools within the system have indicated a decrease in problem behaviours and increase in engagement, following the introduction of daily review. Leaders see this as a result of the structure, predictability of practice, pace, and consistent CFU throughout.

Teachers have fed back that content previously forgotten with the change of school year was now being retained, because students were consistently revisiting what was taught daily, weekly, and monthly.

Schools who have implemented retrieval practice as well as spacing/interleaving have seen these research-informed practices revolutionise the retention of their students (see Agarwal & Bain, 2019). You should not underestimate their potential for your teaching.

Summary

The scientific research indicates that learning, which can be defined as a change in long-term memory, is a complex process. It is fundamentally about a learner taking insights from the environment and moving these into long-term storage in their brain. However, all information must first pass through our working memory, our temporary mental workspace. Unfortunately, working memory is a somewhat temperamental feature of our cognition, extremely limited in capacity, and can hold only a few items in the mind at a time. Often hindered by distractions and cognitive overwhelm (as per cognitive load theory), learning is often hard.

Knowledge, the foundation for all learning, is crucial for expertise in any domain, and includes both declarative and procedural knowledge. **Biologically primary knowledge**, acquired with minimal effort through social interaction, differs from **biologically secondary knowledge**, which necessitates explicit teaching and often overloads working memory when first encountered.

> Fundamental knowledge that is innate or develops early in life, such as language acquisition or recognising faces
>
> Knowledge that is acquired through explicit educational experiences, such as reading, writing, and specific academic skills or knowledge

We have outlined how teachers must manage their learners' cognitive load and systematically build the domain-specific (and often biologically secondary) knowledge of their students, so they progress along the continuum from novice to expert, and thus lay the groundwork for later exploration, inquiry, creativity, and critique.

Table 4.3 Chapter 4 knowledge organiser.

1. Why learning is hard • There are no limits to *what* we can learn, but our attention and working memory are powerful buffers. • Anything can create cognitive load for a learner.	***2. How knowledge powers all learning*** • Prior knowledge is the start of all learning. • We solve problems, create, and critique using knowledge in our long-term memory. • Becoming a proficient reader, writer, mathematician, and thinker requires sufficient domain-specific knowledge.
3. How great teaching facilitates student learning • Highly effective teachers manage students' cognitive load. • Novices benefit from fully guided instruction; experts from less guided. • Fully guided instruction builds the learning foundations and provides a pathway to higher order learning in a given domain.	***4. Why we forget most of what we learn, but do not have to*** • The forgetting curve means that teaching is always a moving target. • Retrieval practice reduces forgetting: It's 'use it or lose it.' • Spacing and interleaving structures learning better. • Daily review is an efficient and effective mechanism to ensure retention.

Finally, we have demonstrated how easily students forget what we teach them, and that great teaching will build in retrieval practice, spacing and interleaved learning to ensure maximum retention. See the chapter knowledge organiser in Table 4.3.

As you continue your journey into how schools have used these insights in their work, remember that there is more than one way of harnessing the science of learning for school improvement. Nevertheless, there is a need to address some of the popular, yet problematic, ideas that–in light of the research evidence–are plaguing teachers and students from getting the most out of school-based education. Join us in the next chapter, as we unpack four misconceptions that can be resolved by the science.

Where to next?

Science of learning principles

- Australian Education Research Organisation [AERO] (2023). *How students learn best.*
- *Why don't students like school?: A cognitive scientist answers questions about how the mind works and what it means for the classroom.* Daniel T. Willingham.
- *Understanding how we learn: A visual guide.* Yana Weinstein, Megan Sumeracki, and Oliver Caviglioli.

Cognitive load theory

- *Cognitive load theory in action* by Ollie Lovell.
- *A little guide for teachers: Cognitive load* theory by Greg Ashman.

Retrieval practice, spacing, and interleaving

- *Powerful teaching: Unleash the science of learning* by Agarwal & Bain.

Check your indicators – Cognitive load theory and beyond

On-Track Indicators	*Off-Track Indicators*
• Familiarity with cognitive load, including optimising intrinsic load, and minimising extraneous load. • Awareness of the importance of student knowledge and planning for the building of knowledge-rich learning experiences. • Understanding of the uses of fully guided instruction and how novices benefit from this. • Use of less guided approaches as novices move closer to mastery. • Planning for student forgetting using retrieval practice, review, and interleaving.	• A focus on stimulating or appealing learning materials and environment. • Working to often throw students into the 'deep end' without prior instruction (i.e., 'productive struggle'). • Belief that knowledge of facts and details are less important than critical thinking and creativity. • A focus on inquiry-learning first and foremost and 'just-in-time' teaching. • Massed/blocked practice including focussing on one topic or skills for an extended series of lessons without returning to review this material till next term/semester.

Discussion questions

1. What are some ways that you currently optimise cognitive load in your teaching? How could you minimise extraneous load further?
2. Consider the idea that novices benefit from fully guided instruction, while experts benefit from less guided instruction. How are you currently catering for students at the novice stage? Do things shift when they gain expertise?
3. Why is it important to ensure that your students acquire and retain essential knowledge for long-term learning?
4. How do you currently effectively activate and leverage students' prior knowledge to enhance their understanding of new concepts?
5. Reflect on the statement "We forget most of what we learn, but we don't have to." What practices and approaches can you implement to enhance long-term retention and application of knowledge among your students?

References

Agarwal, P. K., & Bain, P. M. (2019). *Powerful teaching: Unleash the science of learning*. John Wiley & Sons.

Archer, A. L., & Hughes, C. A. (2010). *Explicit instruction: Effective and efficient teaching*. Guilford Publications.

Baddeley, A. (2003). Working memory: Looking back and looking forward. *Nature Reviews Neuroscience*, *4*(10), 829–839.

Bennett, T. (2021). *The Running the Room Companion: Issues in classroom management and strategies to deal with them*. John Catt.

Bjork, R. (2011). On the symbiosis of remembering, forgetting, and learning. In *Successful remembering and successful forgetting* (pp. 19–40). Psychology Press.

Buckingham, J., Wheldall, R., & Wheldall, K. (2019). Systematic and explicit phonics instruction: A scientific, evidence-based approach to teaching the alphabetic principle. In *The Alphabetic Principle and Beyond* (May, pp. 49–67).

Chi, M. T. H., Feltovich, P. J., & Glaser, R. (1981). Categorization and representation of physics problems by experts and novices. *Cognitive Science*, 5(2), 121–152.

Christodoulou, D. (2014). Minding the knowledge gap. *American Educator*.

Cowan, N. (2010). The magical mystery four: How is working memory capacity limited, and why? *Current Directions in Psychological Science*, *19*(1), 51–57.

De Bruyckere, P., Kirschner, P. A., & Hulshof, C. D. (2015). *Urban myths about learning and education*. Academic Press.

De Groot, A. D., Gobet, F., & Jongman, R. W. (1996). *Perception and memory in chess: Studies in the heuristics of the professional eye*. Van Gorcum & Co.

Dunlosky, J., & O'Brien, A. (2022). The power of successive relearning and how to implement it with fidelity using pencil and paper and web-based programs. *Scholarship of Teaching and Learning in Psychology*, 8(3), 225–235.

Dunlosky, J., Rawson, K. A., Marsh, E. J., Nathan, M. J., & Willingham, D. T. (2013). Improving students' learning with effective learning techniques: Promising directions from cognitive and educational psychology. *Psychological Science in the Public Interest, Supplement*, *14*(1), 4–58.

Finn, J. D., & Zimmer, K. S. (2012). Student engagement: What is it? Why does it matter? In S. L. Christenson, A. L. Reschly, & C. Wylie (Eds.), *Handbook of research on student engagement* (pp. 97-131). New York: Springer. http://doi.org/10.1007/978-1-4614-2018-7

Geary, D. C. (2008). An evolutionarily informed education science. *Educational Psychologist*, *43*(4), 179–195.

Groshell. (2022, September 17). Dead ends from the explicit teaching vs. inquiry-based learning debate. *Education Rickshaw*. https://educationrickshaw.com/2022/09/17/dead-ends-from-the-explicit-teaching-vs-inquiry-based-learning-debate/

Hirsch, E. D. (2000). You can always look it up . . . or can you? *American Educator*.

Hollingsworth, J. R., & Ybarra, S. E. (2017). *Explicit direct instruction (EDI): The power of the well-crafted, well-taught lesson*. Corwin Press.

Kalyuga, S., Ayres, P., Chandler, P., & Sweller, J. (2003). The expertise reversal effect. *Educational Psychologist, 38*(1), 23–31. https://doi.org/10.1207/S15326985EP3801

Karpicke, J. D. (2012). Retrieval-based learning: Active retrieval promotes meaningful learning. *Current Directions in Psychological Science, 21*(3), 157–163. https://doi.org/10.1177/0963721412443552

Kirschner, P. A. (2009). Epistemology or pedagogy, that is the question. *Constructivist Instruction: Success or Failure?, May*, 144–157.

Kirschner, P. A., Sweller, J., & Clark, R. E. (2006). Why minimal guidance during instruction does not work: An analysis of the failure of constructivist, discovery, problem-based, experiential, and inquiry-based teaching. *Educational Psychologist, 41*(2), 75–86.

Kunar, M. A., Ariyabandu, S., & Jami, Z. (2016). The downside of choice: Having a choice benefits enjoyment, but at a cost to efficiency and time in visual search. *Attention, Perception, and Psychophysics, 78*(3), 736–741.

Lemov, D. (2021). *Teach like a champion 3.0: 63 Techniques that put students on the path to college*. John Wiley & Sons.

Lovell, O. (2020). *Sweller's cognitive load theory in action*. John Catt.

Mayer, R. E. (2004). Should there be a three-strikes rule against pure discovery learning? *American Psychologist, 59*(1), 14–19.

Murawski, L. M. (2014). Critical thinking in the classroom . . . and beyond. *Journal of Learning in Higher Education, 10*(1), 25–30.

Paas, F., & Sweller, J. (2012). An evolutionary upgrade of cognitive load theory: Using the human motor system and collaboration to support the learning of complex cognitive tasks. *Educational Psychology Review, 24*(1), 27–45.

Robertson, D. A., & Padesky, C. J. (2020). Keeping students interested: Interest-based instruction as a tool to engage. *Reading Teacher, 73*(5), 575–586.

Rosenshine, B. (2012). Principles of instruction: Research-based strategies that all teachers should know. *American Educator*, 12–20.

Rotherham, A. J., & Willingham, D. T. (2010). "21st century" skills: Not new, but a worthy challenge. *American Educator, 34*(1), 17–20.

Sealy, C. (2019). Memorable experiences are the best way to help children remember things. In C. Bardon (Ed.). *The researchED guide to education myths*. (pp 31–39). John Catt.

Simons, D. J., & Chabris, C. F. (1999). Gorillas in our midst: Sustained inattentional blindness for dynamic events. *Perception, 28*(9), 1059–1074.

Smith, J. L. M., Sáez, L., & Doabler, C. T. (2016). Using explicit and systematic instruction to support working memory. *Teaching Exceptional Children, 48*(6), 275–281.

Squire, L. R. (1987). *Memory and brain*. Oxford University Press.

Stockard, J., Wood, T. W., Coughlin, C., & Rasplica Khoury, C. (2018). The effectiveness of direct instruction curricula: A meta-analysis of a half century of research. *Review of Educational Research, 88*(4).

Sweller, J. (1988). Cognitive load during problem solving: Effects on learning. *Cognitive Science, 12*(2), 257–285.

Sweller, J. (2006). The worked example effect and human cognition. *Learning and Instruction, 16*(2 SPEC. ISS.), 165–169.

Sweller, J. (2016). Working memory, long-term memory, and instructional design. *Journal of Applied Research in Memory and Cognition, 5*(4).

Sweller, J., Clark, R. E., & Kirschner, P. A. (2010). Teaching general problem-solving skills is not a substitute for, or a viable addition to, teaching mathematics. *Notices of the American Mathematical Society, 57*(10), 1303–1304.

Sweller, J., Van Merrienboer, J. J., & Paas, F. G. (1998). Cognitive architecture and instructional design. *Educational psychology review, 10*, 251–296.

Sweller, J., van Merriënboer, J. J., & Paas, F. (2019). Cognitive architecture and instructional design: 20 years later. *Educational Psychology Review, 31*, 261–292.

Twyman, J. S., & Heward, W. L. (2018). How to improve student learning in every classroom now. *International Journal of Educational Research*, *87*, 78–90.

van Moorselaar, D., & Slagter, H. A. (2020). Inhibition in selective attention. In *Annals of the New York Academy of Sciences, 1464*(1), pp. 204–221. Blackwell Publishing Inc.

Wiliam, D., & Leahy, S. (2016). *Embedding formative assessment*. Hawker Brownlow Education.

Willingham, D. T. (2002). Ask the cognitive scientist inflexible knowledge: The first step to expertise. *American Educator*, *26*(4), 31–33.

Willingham, D. T. (2006). How knowledge helps. *American Educator*, *Spring*, 1–5.

Willingham, D., & Daniel, D. (2012). Teaching to what students have in common. *Educational Leadership*, *69*, 16-21.

Witherby, A. E., & Carpenter, S. K. (2021). The rich-get-richer effect: Prior knowledge predicts new learning of domain-relevant information. *Journal of Experimental Psychology: Learning, Memory, and Cognition*, *48*(4), 483.

5 How can the science of learning change my teaching?

Four teaching misconceptions resolved by the science

Nathaniel Swain and Zach Groshell

The science of learning is a vast body of knowledge accumulated through countless studies of the human brain, learning and teaching, as synthesised into themes in the previous chapter. Unfortunately, many insights from the science of how we learn are largely absent from classrooms, schools, and graduate programs around the world. There are indeed longstanding tensions within education that have perhaps prevented these scientific findings from reaching the hands of teachers.

Here we disentangle four popular and pervasive ideas used in education. They are listed here as misconceptions given that principles from the cognitive science reveal these to be misaligned at best, misleading at worst. We hope they grab your attention, and we encourage you to explore this rabbit hole further using the suggested reading at the end of the chapter.

Box 5.1 - Chapter 5 Overview - Four misconceptions we plan to resolve

Misconception 1: Students will learn best when provided with a stimulating environment.
Misconception 2: Be a guide on the side, or risk interfering with learning.
Misconception 3: Knowledge and basic skills don't prepare students for the 21st century.
Misconception 4: Every child knows how they learn best, and every child learns differently, so we must teach in differentiated groups.

Misconception 1: Students will learn best when provided with a stimulating environment

Learning can be described as an interaction between the individual and their environment. However, a commonly held misconception in education is that a 'rich' environment is sufficient or superior for learning, compared to teaching the material explicitly (e.g., Parker & Thomsen, 2019). This misguided belief is often expressed by an approach in which teachers fill their classrooms with stimulating materials and activities and hope that their students will effortlessly absorb the knowledge and skills they are meant to master. Learning Centers, Choice Menus, The Daily 5, Genius Hour, or Investigation Time are familiar manifestations of this misconception (Groshell, 2021).

DOI: 10.4324/9781003404965-7

Not all knowledge is equal

The first problem with the 'environment = teacher' idea is that it ignores an important concept from evolutionary psychology: The distinction between biologically primary and biologically secondary knowledge (Paas & Sweller, 2012). As we discussed in the previous chapter, **biologically primary knowledge**, such as the ability to speak one's native language, or learn to recognise facial expressions, is acquired naturally through social immersion, as these abilities are essential for our survival.

Fundamental knowledge that is innate or develops early in life, such as language acquisition or recognising faces

However, **biologically secondary knowledge**, which makes up the majority of material taught in schools, cannot be learned so easily due to its recent emergence in our evolutionary history. The assumption that effective teaching mainly involves immersing students in a 'rich' environment is therefore deeply flawed since it presumes that human beings can acquire academic subjects as effortlessly, and through the same processes, as they do their native language (Sweller, 2021).

Knowledge that is acquired through explicit educational experiences, such as reading, writing, and specific academic skills or knowledge

The example of reading: Why a natural approach has failed

While the 'natural approach' is certainly appealing, the failures of Whole Language and its successor, Balanced Literacy, underscore why replacing explicit instruction with 'stimulating' materials and activities is unlikely to work. Both the Whole Language and Balanced Literacy approaches share a philosophy that emphasises immersion in a language-stimulating environment (see chapter 6). By increasing students' exposure to print and de-emphasising or forgoing explicit teaching of letter-sound relationships, it is assumed that students will naturally pick up the **phonic code**.

Sound - letter correspondence knowledge

After several decades of research into this theory, the National Reading Panel (2000) published a landmark report that concluded that systematic, explicit phonics programs significantly outperform programs that approach phonics unsystematically and incidentally. Whole Language and Balanced Literacy philosophies and practices persist to this day (*Sold a Story*, 2022) despite the overwhelming evidence for their ineffectiveness. This remains one of the greatest educational tragedies of our time.

Story Example 5.1 - Letting go of literacy rotations - Brandon Park

Before undertaking wider changes to their literacy program, Brandon Park Primary was a big advocate of the Daily Five and CAFE approaches, which saw students move through rotations of self- or peer-guided activities, as one group at a time would sit with the teacher for **guided reading.** This structure was manageable for the average or advanced students, though some teachers wondered how much they were being challenged. However, the school eventually saw that hours spent each week on self-directed activities and

A popular teaching practice involving small group, or individual conferencing with students, talking about a text, reading a text, or teaching a reading skill independent reading without accountability was a poor use of time, and that it had a huge opportunity cost for students performing below grade expectations. Reading *Where's Wally/Waldo* was rightly not counted as a quality literacy activity.

When these practices were questioned, some teachers were worried about losing this individualised time with students. However, once the alternative was trialled and teachers realised there was significantly more time available for whole class quality discussions about texts and literacy concepts, this concern about individualised interactions went away. Brandon Park now primarily runs literacy at the whole class level with follow-ups and small group instruction after initial whole class teaching. The level of engagement by students in the learning could not be more exciting, as teachers facilitate high-quality discussions and frequent checking for understanding.

The impact of achievement on *motivation is under-rated*

Too often we assume that students become demotivated because the learning does not interest them enough. A commonly touted solution (e.g., Robertson & Padesky, 2020) is for the teacher to choose something that will 'hook' them into it; or to make the work about student interests to get them engrossed in the learning: *If only we can get them to engage, then their learning will soar.*

At most schools today, educators can forget that the relationship between engagement and achievement is actually bi-directional (Finn & Zimmer, 2012). This means feeling bad about school or learning can obviously reduce academic achievement, but equally (if not more so) lacking skills or confidence for academic work can also create a sense of failure and de-motivation. Teachers should be more aware of the phenomenon of a lack of success or confidence in learning causing de-motivation in any learner.

So, do students at risk of disengagement need different curricula? Or different modes of learning? No, not usually. All students respond well to impactful, pacey, bite-sized, and responsive instruction. Such instruction uses **engagement norms** and **checking for understanding** to ensure that all students are given frequent opportunities to have a go and receive on-the-spot feedback (Kirschner et al., 2006). Thus, these bite-sized opportunities for feedback and success can increase the motivation to keep trying, and thus create a virtuous cycle from success to connection to school and back again.

Taught, practiced, and expected routines for student responses and participation (e.g., attention signal, choral or tracked reading, pair shares, mini whiteboards)

The teacher checking if students are learning while the lesson is unfolding using short, specific checks of understanding and proficiency

Story Example 5.2 - A focus on relationships and success in learning - Challis Community Primary

Alongside culturally responsive practice, Challis has constantly innovated to increase the wellbeing supports for all its students, especially those experiencing less than ideal home circumstances, and challenges like developmental delays and disorders.

When the school began to improve its behaviour support processes, they attempted to integrate these students into the rest of the school. The high needs students would meet most mornings with certain staff members, who tried to settle them down, before they went into both differentiated and mainstream learning programs. Even still, Principal Lee Musumeci reflects that at this point the school was doing little to support their connection to their own emotions, and teachers were not yet teaching replacement behaviours.

In contrast to its previous attempts, Challis now takes a proactive, explicit, and guided approach to developing their students' understanding and ability to follow the norms and routines and develop self-regulation. In the NURTURE program for students not yet ready to attend mainstream classes, students receive increased frequency and intensity of praise and support, whilst also learning the fundamentals of the school-wide behaviour curriculum. Learning experiences are set up so students are successful and then build more trust and a stronger relationship with Challis teachers.

High expectations for even their most vulnerable students have been raised sky-high, and the supports to achieve these goals have been elevated to match. Alongside its strong focus on relationships, wraparound service and the behaviour curriculum, fundamentally Challis has changed such students' trajectory. They are achieving this by helping students experience success in learning, by teaching effectively and in a supported way.

Great teaching is not just edu-tainment

It is tempting to conclude that we should make learning exciting and special so as to ensure our students *cannot resist* remembering what we teach. Unfortunately, it is likely we have all been hoodwinked by this misguided idea at some point. When we think back on our own schooling, we often recall the memorable moments, like school excursions, book weeks, and mind-boggling science demonstrations. So, why shouldn't we ensure students remember what we teach them, by making learning experiences 'unforgettable'? This approach would be ineffective, and it is very likely that students would remember the excitement of special activities, but not necessarily the learning behind them.

Instead, teachers harnessing the insights about **cognitive load theory** and novice vs. expert learners will utilise methods that increase the guidance for students when they are at the novice stage of their learning. This is so that students can sufficiently build their foundational knowledge and skills. Teachers using these insights would also work to adjust this level of guidance using checking for understanding as students progress. They would also manage the extraneous load so that the novelty (of an explosion in a science class, for example) does not detract from the new learning at hand. This is a very different way of thinking about teaching than expecting the environment to just stimulate learning.

A theory for understanding how learners interact with tasks, based on the evidence that working memory is limited and affected by the environment, the nature of the task, and student prior knowledge

An immersive approach neglects the science of how we learn

Here is a straightforward explanation for why it is a bad idea for students to spend extended periods engaging independently in activities as the mode of instruction: Attention is a limited resource and working memory can only hold onto a vanishingly small amount of information at a time (Cowan, 2001; Sweller et al., 2019). Thus, is it unrealistic to expect our students to be able to tune out the noise and disruptions of others and resist the temptation to multi-task, differentiate between relevant, irrelevant and alluring information, whilst also trying to organise their own spaced-out retrieval practice regime to solidify the material in long-term memory (Kirschner & van Merriënboer, 2013).

Yes, the learning environment should be conducive to learning, but should not be the *source* of all learning. That is why the teacher should be unafraid to assume the role of expert in the room, and just teach it directly and explicitly. It's a sure-fire way of getting all students to learn.

Box 5.2 - Misconception 1 Summary

Misconception 1: Students will learn best when provided with a stimulating environment.

Resolution: Your students should use our evolutionary advantage of learning from knowledgeable others. Making learning a self-directed endeavour gives the *illusion of agency* in your classroom, but the *reality of inequity* as your advantaged and disadvantaged learners progressively diverge. Control the learning environment so it does not distract from the learning at hand, but do not expect students to always work things out independently. Rather than seeing direct teaching as 'cold' or 'inauthentic,' embrace the interactivity and responsiveness of explicit instruction for the majority of your teaching.

Misconception 2: Be a guide on the side, or risk interfering with learning

One of the most well-known catchcries in education is *Don't be the sage on the stage, but a guide on the side*. What follows the previous misconception—that activities in the environment are a better catalyst of learning than teaching the material explicitly—is the corollary that students learn best when teachers are 'decentred' and students are given 'agency' to lead their own learning (e.g., Byrne et al., 2016). In these classrooms, students are supposedly 'empowered' to decide whatever they will learn and how they will learn it, whilst the teacher's role is reconceptualised as a curator of the environment and a *facilitator* of the learning (Kirschner & van Merriënboer, 2013).

Constructivism is a theory of learning, not teaching

Most teachers are prepared for the classroom with messages in favour of student-centred and student-directed learning, justified usually with the almost hallowed works of Jean Piaget, Lev Vygotsky, and Jerome Bruner (see Sweller et al., 2023).

One of the biggest misreadings of this socio-constructivist literature is that these works are theories of *teaching*, when in fact they fit better as theories of *learning* (Mayer, 2004). This does not in fact justify the teaching imperative that students must be left to 'construct' things on their own or discover the answers independently.

Fully guided instruction, not minimally guided please

In their influential 2006 paper, cognitive scientists Kirschner, Sweller, and Clarke made the compelling case *against* the teacher taking merely a supportive role in the learning process. Grouped under the umbrella term **minimally guided instruction**, the authors concluded that such approaches lacked evidence that they work well at all, especially for novice learners.

A set of instructional approaches that gives students the prime responsibility of structuring and managing the learning; providing a task or project without ensuring students have the prior skills and knowledge may occur here

Table 5.1 Minimally guided versus fully guided approaches.

Minimally guided approaches	*Fully guided approaches*
• Discovery learning (see critique in Mayer, 2004). • Problem-based learning (PBL; e.g., Schmidt et al., 2007). • Inquiry learning (e.g., Byrne et al., 2016). • Interest-based learning (e.g., Manurung & Mashuri, 2017). • Constructivist learning (e.g., Tobias & Duffy, 2009).	• Explicit instruction (Archer & Hughes, 2010). • Explicit direct instruction (EDI; Hollingsworth & Ybarra, 2017). • Responsive teaching (Wiliam & Leahy, 2016). • Direct instruction (DI; Kinder & Carnine, 1991). • Explicit teaching and direct instruction (Rosenshine, 2012). • Load reduction instruction (Martin & Evans, 2018).

Fully guided instruction, on the other hand, involves regulating the flow of information so that *relevant* information is presented in small steps, and *irrelevant* information is minimised, in accordance with the well-established limitations of cognitive architecture (see chapter 4). The common feature of all fully guided instructional systems is the gradual fading of guidance. As students demonstrate progress through exposure to models, feedback, and part-task practice, this instructional **scaffolding** is removed to allow students to complete whole tasks independently.

A collection of approaches to instruction that has high levels of teacher guidance at the beginning of the learning process, and only withdraws this guidance when students are ready to progress

Support provided to learners to enable them to complete learning tasks; intended to be faded out over time

In minimally guided situations, students could indeed still independently find the information they need to solve problems or complete a complex task. However, the problem is that searching the environment for answers, and/or trialling and erroring with minimal guidance is inherently inefficient for novices and may well embed misconceptions (Sweller, 2006).

You can get the right answer, but not learn anything

As teachers, we might assume if children get to the right answer without help from an adult, then they have learnt it more thoroughly. You may have also been convinced that in providing answers directly to students we are making learning too easy and stealing their chance of constructing their own understandings. Contrary to this, students engaging in activities (no matter how successfully) may still attain *no learning* if their underlying knowledge about the domain has not changed over time (Kirschner, Sweller, & Clark, 2006).

That's not to say that minimally guided approaches cannot facilitate compelling learning in some students. Our concern is that such approaches do little for those students who are already educationally disadvantaged. When students inquire from a place of relative ignorance, they are unlikely to end up *discovering* something of substance and value. On the other hand, *when teachers guide instruction for novices fully, it benefits all and harms no one.*

The goal of levelling the playing field can be realised when we teach in a way that benefits all students. Also, teaching in this way does not preclude other students learning for themselves and indeed going much further with their curiosity. By giving your students a shared body of knowledge, *all* can develop their mastery over that domain. Even for those who do not appear to *need* this explanation, having a more explicit understanding (of something the student perhaps had previously intuited and understood only tacitly) takes student awareness to higher echelons. This enables them to dig deeper and learn faster when they do begin to explore independently.

Will this stop them becoming independent, free thinkers? Quite the opposite. After explicit instruction, all students can begin to inquire, question, create, and critique—building upon the explicit knowledge they have developed.

> *In this way, fully guided instruction creates a low floor for all learners and no ceilings!*
>
> Inspired by comments from Tristan Lanarus, Principal of Westall Secondary College, Victoria, Australia.

To create 'low floors' means to always have an accessible starting point, and 'no ceilings' refers to never putting a limit on the end point of the learning. The above saying was adopted as a philosophy at Bentleigh West Primary School (see chapters 1 and 11).

Times when you can become the guide on the side

We are not arguing that teachers must sage it up all day. In fact, when students have sufficient knowledge and skill and are more like experts on a given task, this is the time to step away your role as whole class teacher and to instead meet with small groups and individuals as they apply their new understandings.

For example, when students can already fluently solve addition problems by themselves, providing additional unnecessary modelling can actually make the task harder, as the teacher might be suggesting conflicting or redundant strategies the learner does not need (see **expertise reversal effect** in chapter 4; Kalyuga, 2007).

> A research finding that shows that novices need step-by-step instruction whereas experts can learn better from more independent problem solving

Common concern: But the sage on the stage cannot differentiate!

There is a *myth* among some popular educational approaches, that if we are going to teach directly, we must do so in differentiated groups, as we cannot possibly cater for such differences in a whole group (Boushey & Moser, 2014).

Indeed, a recurring thought you may have as you work through this book is *how does this apply to my students with diverse learning needs?* Schools have been plagued with myths and fads that distract from great teaching: learning styles and multiple intelligences to name but two (De Bruyckere et al., 2015).

We can all agree that every student is unique and that students do differ in the amount of knowledge they bring to a given task. Fundamentally though, the science of learning has made great strides to describe how humans learn in common (Willingham & Daniel, 2012). This makes teaching less about different approaches for different learners, and more about excellent teaching that supports *all* learners.

So, how do I get whole class instruction to work for everyone?

To do this we must use responsive and adaptive teaching practices (see Rosenshine's principles, 2012):

- Review and maintain past learning;
- Understand and activate prior knowledge;
- Create explicit modelling and explanation;
- Check for understanding (CFU) constantly;
- Guide students towards independent practice;
- Respond by changing speed, reteaching, and adding support or extension to learners.

And when should small groups happen? (see misconception 4). Spoiler: Differentiation should mainly happen through differing levels of support provided to individuals within the whole group, when they need it, in real time.

Story Example 5.3 - Becoming a whole class teacher again - Catalyst: Catholic Education Canberra-Goulburn

Changing to more whole class instructional methods was a steep learning curve for some schools in the Catalyst project, as many leaders did not think that change was needed. However, looking at research from the sciences of reading and learning opened up opportunities for dialogue about effective teaching. The implementation of Catalyst involved Theory, Demonstrations, Practice, and Coaching.

- The *Theory* allowed teachers to understand the what and why, they learnt about the importance of ensuring students attend to their learning and **engagement norms** and how the teacher could facilitate whole class learning using checking for understanding (CFU);

Taught, practiced, and expected routines for student responses and participation (e.g., attention signal, choral or tracked reading, pair shares, mini whiteboards)

- *Demonstrations* allowed them to observe the 'how' and for them to reflect upon their own practice and see really precise exemplars of whole class teaching practice. They observed an expert coach demonstrate engagement norms and CFU techniques;
- Teachers were given opportunities to *Practice* and rehearse the new teaching techniques; and finally
- They received *Expert Coaching* including feedback to continually hone their craft.

This process allowed for a smoother uptake and a sense of success for teachers, seeing a decrease in off-task behaviour in students, less unnecessary variations between classes, and increased engagement of students (who remembered more than they would have in student-directed groups). This established the 'buy in' for further change.

Box 5.3 - Misconception 2 Summary

Misconception 2: Be a guide on the side, or risk interfering with learning.

Resolution: Don't just watch to see if learning happens. Make sure it does. Give your learners fully guided instruction which is gradually released to independent learning, to ensure they all flourish. Remember, students will nearly always be novices in the domain we seek to teach (otherwise, why are we teaching it?). You don't have to be a sage on the stage per se, but you need to take a front-and-centre responsibility for making learning happen.

Will this stop them becoming independent, free thinkers? Quite the opposite. By giving your students a shared body of declarative and procedural knowledge in the domain, you give them all a chance to be independent, mini-experts in that area. From here, they can begin to inquire, question, create, and critique using that very knowledge as the base.

Misconception 3: Knowledge and basic skills don't prepare students for the 21st century

Twenty-first-century competencies like creativity, collaboration, and critical thinking have been heralded as the solution in a world in which infinite knowledge is freely available at the click of a button. Ironically, these 21st-century skills are predicated on skills of 19th-century education: including oral language (although that is much more ancient), reading, spelling, writing, mathematics, science, history, geography, and literature.

The 21st-century competencies movement (e.g., Rotherham & Willingham, 2010) has contributed to the demise of the importance of *knowledge* in education. This is unfortunate as our cognitive architecture makes knowledge an unavoidable prerequisite to deeper understandings.

Knowledge is what we think with

Becoming a learner who can create, collaborate, and critique is inexorably tied to the knowledge one has about a particular domain. There are serious limitations with drilling domain general skills like reasoning or problem solving without fluency and master of foundational skills and knowledge (see more in chapter 9). Remember that the learning of biologically primary knowledge is naturally acquired and has no observable effects for cognitive load (Geary, 2002).

Fundamental knowledge that is innate or develops early in life, such as language acquisition or recognising faces

Knowledge that is acquired through explicit educational experiences, such as reading, writing, and specific academic skills or knowledge

A systematic and structured approach to teaching that provides clear, direct, and explicit guidance to learners. It involves breaking down complex skills or concepts into smaller, manageable steps, and providing explicit explanations, demonstrations, examples, feedback and practice to ensure understanding

Unfortunately, through the teaching decisions we make, it has been commonplace for educators to treat the academic knowledge taught at school as natural (**biologically primary**) when it is in fact the opposite. Largely, what we teach in schools is **biologically secondary** and from the academic disciplines (Tricot & Sweller, 2014). So, we are not setting up our students for success when expecting them to pick up the knowledge from science, humanities, mathematics, and reading for example by osmosis. This is because our brains have not evolved to naturally obtain this kind of knowledge without **explicit instruction** (Sweller, 2021). Novel biologically secondary knowledge creates significant cognitive load effects.

There are issues with focussing on creativity and critical thinking whilst neglecting knowledge. What's the alternative?

Recall from chapter 4 that experts have expertise because they have deep and sophisticated knowledge in the domain. Thus, if we want our novice students to acquire such knowledge, we must teach explicitly and responsively based on how well students are handling the cognitive load of the tasks.

We recommend the consistent use of fully guided approaches, including explicit instruction and a knowledge-rich approach given that:

- Explicit teaching helps regulate the flow of information and avoid cognitive overload;
- Explicit instruction leads to mastery of foundations, levelling the playing field, and increasing education equity in your classroom; and
- A **knowledge-rich curriculum** puts knowledge back into the fore, rather than focussing on the drilling of generic skills (see chapter 9).

An approach to curriculum design in which knowledge, well-structured and specified in detail, provides an underpinning philosophy for learning

Story Example 5.4 - Bentleigh West - Building the foundations of mathematics (not just teaching through problem solving)

When Bentleigh West pulled back on teaching numeracy through problem-solving, to focus more on mastering the foundational knowledge and skills in mathematics, there was scepticism from many teachers. Some believed that shifting to a more basic skills focus could compromise deeper understanding. Yet, the school leadership were able to demonstrate how successful mastery of foundational knowledge (e.g., initially every daily review had skip counting, arrays, and number lines) could then facilitate later applications of that knowledge. This started to show teachers that understanding was being built cumulatively and efficiently through careful presentation and demonstration of the material.

Before this change, students were not sufficiently practising mathematical facts and procedures to automaticity. When Bentleigh West teachers began expecting and supporting students to master these basics, they discovered that students, with a solid grasp of fundamentals, could then engage in more complex mathematical thinking.

This approach, aligning with the idea that knowledge is what you *think with*, not just *about*, led to improved performance on standardised tests, as well as **rich tasks.** Improved mathematics performance also increased the number of students accepted into the state-wide gifted and talented programs. Additionally, the gender gap in mathematics performance became non-existent.

Complex, open-ended problems, often with multiple entry points, that require students to apply multiple strategies to find a solution

Rather than starting inputs into the instructional process, competencies like critical and creative thinking are the *outcomes* of fully guided instruction. Remember that we should teach explicitly not because that is the goal, but because it is the *pathway* to higher order learning and teaching. Students will begin to work critically, creatively, and collaboratively because they have the foundational knowledge and skills to do so.

Box 5.4 - Misconception 3 Summary

Misconception 3: Knowledge and basic skills don't prepare students for the 21st century.

Resolution: Teaching knowledge of a particular domain systematically, cumulatively and explicitly is the best path to learning. Giving students sufficient opportunity for guided and independent practice allows students to master knowledge and automate skills to become quasi-experts in that domain. No matter how much we wish books, the internet, or now AI would outsource our long-term memory, nothing can replace the complex and interconnected schemata that experts acquire. Expertise is the accumulation of increasingly sophisticated bodies of declarative and procedural knowledge, so our teaching should seek to build it, step by step. Yes, we want to release students to undertake independent exploration, critique, and creation, but we cannot do that when their knowledge is insufficient to make such tasks fruitful.

Misconception 4: Every child knows how they learn best, and every child learns differently, so we must teach in differentiated groups

Common concern: Shouldn't we let students choose how they want to learn?

No. It is highly questionable whether young, inexperienced, and unknowledgeable learners are the best judges of teaching and learning effectiveness (Carpenter et al., 2020). In general, learners tend to be unaware of what they know and do not know (Kruger & Dunning, 1999) and are overconfident that they have mastered the material they are meant to learn. Studies indicate that students frequently choose learning strategies that lead to less learning, such as re-reading their notes instead of self-testing, and cramming before tests instead of spacing out their practice.

What about voice and agency?

There has been a push in recent times to invoke the voices and empowerment of students as a primary goal of education (Kohn, 1993). Unfortunately, however, attempts at obtaining student agency or voice are tokenistic if students are not experiencing an effective and responsive education. We would argue that authentic voice and agency comes from students learning how to optimise and maximise their own learning. By understanding their growing intellectual power, they can master the subjects of school and come to see the world and themselves differently as a result.

Please forget about learning styles and multiple intelligences. They don't exist

Students also tend to hold unproductive beliefs about learning, such as the notion that their learning is maximised when instruction matches their preference for a particular modality. While a student may think they learn best from either visual, auditory, or kinaesthetic materials, there is no credible research evidence that these learning styles exist, and, regardless, research would suggest that students typically pay little attention to their self-reported learning styles when attempting to learn something (Husmann & O'Loughlin, 2019).

Rather than learning styles, student preferences, or multiple intelligences, it is the *content* that should drive the use of modalities (De Bruyckere et al., 2015). Mathematics is enhanced when verbal (the teacher's words) and visual (the worked problems on the board) are combined, rather than taught with a single modality (Mesghina et al., 2023). Sometimes a physical object will help develop concepts and build connections so that students can later understand more abstract representations.

Some students need more instruction than others, which is an increase in time and support rather than a change in modality (Tran et al., 2011). We do not teach music visually or kinaesthetically alone; it will always involve listening to and/or performing music. We do not teach geometry just verbally; it will always involve lots of diagrams. It should be the learning at hand that dictates the combination of modes, not the preferences or perceived intelligences of the learner (Kirschner & Hendrick, 2020).

Common concern: Doesn't every child learn differently?

A popular argument against starting with whole class, teacher-led instruction is that individual children vary considerably in how they learn. Teachers are often encouraged to hand over the reins of instructional control to their students, in the belief that only the student knows how they learn best.

Remarkably, the cognitive science shows quite the opposite (Willingham & Daniel, 2012). Yes, students are unique, and each has relative strengths or weaknesses in different aspects of learning. However, we all basically learn via the same cognitive mechanisms, and benefit from instruction that is clear, well-structured, connected to prior learning, responsive, later applied and then reviewed frequently (Rosenshine, 2012).

Common concern: How can you argue that one-size-fits-all?

This is a common critique of more whole class teaching, and less individualised curricula—and this truism can be appealing. While the uniqueness of each of our students should be acknowledged and celebrated, it does not follow that the fundamental structures of their cognitive architecture vary to such a degree that we cannot identify any set of universal principles or high yield teaching techniques as a broad starting point for instruction. Just as we know that all human digestive systems share important commonalities, we can be confident that students' cognitive systems take in, process, and retrieve information in similar ways.

Story Example 5.5 - The problems with 'personalised' learning - Bentleigh West

Steven Capp, former principal of Bentleigh West Primary and current Principal at Chelsea Heights Primary in Victoria, could not have been a bigger advocate for personalised learning when working in previous schools. Moving away from subject based learning, helping teachers to collect performance and preference data on each student, he oversaw each school (primary and secondary) expecting teachers to design individualised curriculum programs and cater for students' unique interests and competencies. Despite such ideas aligning well with prominent advocates of personalised learning, Steve became sceptical about such approaches when results actually worsened under these conditions.

When Steve joined Bentleigh West in 2015, he was less confident about teachers' individualising their teaching for students as the default teaching strategy, yet still committed to the idea.

Over the course of Bentleigh West's journey to implement practices aligning with the science of learning (including a focus on mastering whole class teaching, with high expectations AND high support curriculum for all students), Steve's views on this shifted dramatically. Bentleigh West has obtained outstanding results academically and socially for their school when teachers began teaching at the whole class level 80% of the time, as part of a **multi-tiered system of support (MTSS)**. This is where students who need more support or extension receive this in addition to the mainstream classroom offering. Following the initial wins, and subsequent astronomical gains in results, today you could not find a bigger sceptic about personalised or individualised teaching than Steven Capp. It's all about teachers teaching fantastic lessons to the whole class.

A framework of multi-levelled systems to support students' learning and behaviour; intended to take a preventative approach

Steve now suggests that the problem with personalised learning is that the teacher cannot provide a high-quality learning experience for 26–30 individuals. There is a huge time and effort cost, and students inevitably spend much less of each lesson receiving instruction from the expert (the teacher). When Bentleigh West teachers use whole class pedagogies, and vigorously check for understanding, they can better teach the entire class and provide additional supports or even extension when needed.

Are we arguing that all students have to fit into one 'size'? Well, no. But we are saying that great teaching should begin with an initial delivery of excellent instruction at the whole class level, with additional support and **scaffolding** within class, usually individually or in small groups as needed. This should then be followed by further opportunities for second and third waves of that teaching and support at increasingly intensive levels and in smaller groups (see **Response to Intervention** and Multi-Tiered Systems of Support in chapter 6).

Support provided to learners to enable them to complete learning tasks; intended to be faded out over time

A tiered framework used in education to provide early, systematic, and targeted support to students who need it, with the goal of preventing long-term difficulties

All students will benefit from what Willingham and Daniel (2012) call the 'must haves' of the science of learning. Three of these are systematic practice, feedback from a knowledgeable other and a strong base of factual knowledge. Moreover, when we neglect to provide our students with an education program consisting of a steady diet of these essential ingredients, we are almost certain to penalise the students who need them the most (e.g., Agarwal et al., 2017; Knous et al., 2020).

At the other extreme, designing learning environments with the assumptions that (1) all students learn differently and (2) each student knows how they learn best, inevitably leads to serious logistical problems that serve to undermine learning. When a class of 30 students is put on a path to pursue 30 independent learning journeys, teachers are left fighting to keep up with the subject knowledge and planning requirements of providing 30 personalised lessons (Pozas et al., 2023).

So, less group rotations?

In 'over-differentiated' classrooms where we feel restricted from teaching with the whole class, teachers regularly need to turn their attention away from 30 students to *conference* with a single student or small group. While it may feel nice to provide such 'individualised' instruction, it often amounts to reduced supervision of the other students and extended periods of self-directed discovery learning (see Misconception 2). A comprehensive review of self-directed learning is not possible in this chapter, but it is clear on balance that students do not always make good choices when left on their own to determine the most effective route for their learning (Nugteren et al., 2018).

The other reason to reduce your small group instruction is that you can get the same benefit when you provide initial whole class instruction most of the time, and often with much less repetition and duplication by the teacher (Kime, 2018).

So, how DO you differentiate?

If we were to bring our class together and teach them as one group, how could we possibly cater for this range of differences? How can we ensure we are not just 'teaching to the middle' or ignoring the need to differentiate or extend?

Put simply, we must use **adaptive teaching** (Mould, 2021; Wiliam & Leahy, 2016). This term is more specific compared to the often-slippery concept of **differentiation**, and will be returned to frequently in this volume. The headline is: when teachers change their practice to provide an excellent learning experience for the whole class, they can then make changes based on the responses of their students to extend or provide additional support where needed.

> An alternative to differentiated lessons; in adaptive teaching, whole class teaching is planned, and teachers make real-time adjustments for learners based on checking for understanding tasks
>
> Embedding differing levels of challenge and support into the main, whole-class lesson, to allow students to experience success at various levels

While you might not believe it, whole class explicit teaching represents the 'sweet spot' of differentiation, allowing teachers to efficiently target a single learning objective with heavy doses of whole class modelling, practice, and feedback, which can then be followed by targeted small group support and additional practice for those who need it (e.g., Tran et al., 2011).

Fortunately, when teachers gain a sense of control over these whole class pedagogies, it can be much easier to teach this way, as our success story schools can attest.

Story Example 5.6 - Yates Avenue - Catering for difference with adaptive and responsive teaching

At Yates Avenue Public School, teachers used to facilitate much of the core learning through traditional differentiated groups. The staff had the commonly-held belief that the only way to cater for the diversity of learners in their classrooms was to have different activities or even different learning intentions for levelled groups of students.

As Yates Avenue teachers became familiar with the importance of foundational knowledge for *all* learners and that students all benefited from excellent teaching as a starting point, they started to dramatically change their planning and teaching.

Teachers began creating literacy, numeracy, and other lessons that had an accessible entry point (**low floor**), and provided different levels of challenge throughout the lesson using **built-in differentiation** (see EDI; Hollingsworth & Ybarra, 2017).

Providing an accessible entry point to the learning, so that all students can experience some success

Embedding differing levels of challenge and support into the main, whole-class lesson, to allow students to experience success at various levels

Enabling any student to continue to challenge themselves through to application and open ended creation or critique

For example, mathematical tasks during guided practice would have one accessible starting problem; and on the same task or slide there would be a medium or difficult (or even an open-ended) problem ready to be attempted (**no ceiling)**, without an expectation that all students would succeed at it. In this way, Yates Avenue teachers were able to keep their students as a whole group for the majority of the lesson, and provide additional prompts and supports where needed (responsive teaching).

Critically, this approach meant that even students needing extension could continue challenging themselves as there were built-in extension tasks within the examples in the main lesson, as well as extension tasks to take their learning further during independent practice (no ceiling).

Prepared with the key practice of constant **checking for understanding**, teachers could be responsive and adaptive in the moment to ensure that at least 80% of students were understanding at all times. This practice helped ensure that students grasped the fundamental concepts before progressing to more advanced material; if not, teachers would go back and reteach. Then, if some students needed further support after the main lesson, they would follow this with additional small group instruction, while others went to independent work.

The teacher checking if students are learning while the lesson is unfolding using short, specific checks of understanding and proficiency

In this new whole class teaching mode, Yates Avenue educators also used careful seating organisation, allowing children requiring more support to be placed strategically to enable teachers to provide in-the-moment assistance, as well as extending prompts to students seeking additional challenge.

As teachers worked through the teething issues of using whole class teaching for the majority of new learning experiences, one of the biggest pieces of feedback was their surprise at how well students accessed and kept up with the main lesson more often, even those who were placed into lower groups for literacy or numeracy previously. The resounding observation was that greater student success and self-challenge increased the motivation and rigour in their classrooms. Teachers also reflected that they felt there was more quality learning time. Rather than students losing focus whilst trying to manage their own learning in rotations or group work, they were engaged with responding to tasks, sharing with partners, and practising the skill of the lesson.

Hopefully we have begun to demonstrate that students do not actually need highly differentiated, small group instruction. This is because all students benefit from more time with the expert in the room—the teacher! For those who need it, more guided instruction and support can follow, usually when other students head off to independent practice for that lesson (Kirschner et al., 2006). When whole class teaching is working well, there is more time for students to get instruction and feedback from the teacher and their peers, reducing off-task behaviour and confusion during group work.

Box 5.5 - Misconception 4 Summary

Misconception 4: Every child knows how they learn best, and every child learns differently, so we must teach in differentiated groups.

Resolution: Teachers can harness the shared cognitive architecture of all students by creating effective whole class learning experiences, with built-in opportunities for differentiation and extension. By taking the reins of the learning process, we can ensure students do not choose ineffective learning strategies, nor reinforce misconceptions. While every child is unique, learning needs differ in the amount and level of support, but not usually in the content or style of instruction. All students benefit from excellent teaching together: Some students need additional instruction, with some requiring additional extension. Less time in small, unsupported groups, means more time students can be guided and extended by the teacher.

Concluding thoughts

In this chapter, we have described how findings from the science of learning can change your teaching: including knowing when and how to take the reins as the teacher, the importance of teaching knowledge more than just 21st-century skills, the role of fully guided instruction, and where inquiry and open-ended exploration can still feature.

Table 5.2 Chapter 5 knowledge organiser.

Misconception 1: Students will learn best when provided with a stimulating environment.	***Misconception 2: Be a guide on the side, or risk interfering with learning.***
• The knowledge we need students to learn is often not learnt naturally. • The impact of achievement on motivation is under-rated. • Great teaching is not just edu-tainment. • Materials or the environment are not the main source of learning. • Having students independently discover and try to figure things out neglects what novice earners need: direct and explicit teaching—which does not have to be boring.	• Students do construct their own understandings, but teaching explicitly does not interfere with this. • Fully guided instruction ensures all learners succeed, as opposed to minimally guided, which leaves learning to chance. • Pull back on fully guided when students are more advanced in a particular domain: expertise reversal effect. • Whole class teaching can still be responsive and engaging.

(Continued)

Table 5.2 (Continued)

Misconception 3: Knowledge and basic skills don't prepare students for the 21st century.	***Misconception 4: Every child knows how they learn best, and every child learns differently, so we must teach in differentiated groups.***
• What separates experts from novices is the vastness of their domain-specific knowledge. • We should teach knowledge systematically to build student expertise. • Teaching knowledge and skills well are a pathway (not a preventer) to higher order thinking.	• More time in small groups, means less time with the teacher. • You can cater for difference using effective whole class learning experiences, with built-in differentiation and extension, and adaptive teaching. • Voice and agency come from students mastering the foundations to set them up for future learning, not from choosing what and how they could learn. • Whole class is not 'one-size-fits-all': Use multi-tiered systems of support (MTSS).

We hope you enjoy the subsequent chapter on how insights from science of *reading* can also change your teaching for good.

Where to next?

- De Bruyckere et al.'s *Urban myths about learning and education.*
- Watson and Busch's *The science of learning: 99 studies that teachers need to know.*
- Ashman's *The power of explicit teaching and direct instruction.*
- Sherrington's *The learning rainforest.*
- Progressively Incorrect podcast with Zach Groshell.

Check your indicators – Misconceptions about teaching

On-Track Indicators	*Off-Track Indicators*
• Understanding that students learn best through direct teaching and guidance from knowledgeable others. • Embracing the interactivity, responsiveness of explicit instruction, including opportunities for built-in differentiation. • Providing students with a shared body of knowledge to become independent, free thinkers. • Providing students with ample opportunities for guided and independent practice to master knowledge and automate skills.	• Believing that providing a stimulating environment is the key to optimal learning. • Seeing direct teaching as 'cold' or 'inauthentic.' • Aiming to be a guide on the side. • Worrying that providing too much direct teaching will inhibit students' creative or critical thinking. • Believing that knowledge and basic skills are less important for preparing students for the 21st century. • Assuming that books, the internet, or AI can replace the need for memorisation of knowledge.

(continued)

On-Track Indicators	Off-Track Indicators
• Acknowledging that while independent exploration, critique, and creation are valuable, they are only fruitful when built upon a foundation of sufficient knowledge. • Recognising that while every child is unique, learning needs primarily differ in the amount and level of support, rather than in the content or style of instruction.	• Emphasising independent inquiry without ensuring students have the necessary foundational knowledge. • Believing that every child knows how they learn best, or that every child learns differently. • Trying to cater to children's unique 'learning styles' or 'multiple intelligences.'

Discussion questions

1. What do you currently do to ensure students receive the direct and explicit teaching necessary for them to learn biologically secondary knowledge?
2. How can you optimise the learning environment to minimise distractions and ensure it is conducive to learning?
3. What strategies can you use to ensure that your teaching is engaging and effective without moving towards edu-tainment
4. Based on the chapter, how can you determine when to provide fully guided instruction versus minimally guided instruction?
5. How could your whole class teaching be utilised to create responsive and effective learning experiences?
6. What are some ways you can ensure you meet the needs of all without relying solely on teaching in differentiated groups?

References

Agarwal, P. K., Finley, J. R., Rose, N. S., & Roediger, H. L. (2017). Benefits from retrieval practice are greater for students with lower working memory capacity. *Memory, 25*(6), 764–771. https://doi.org/10.1080/09658211.2016.1220579

Archer, A. L., & Hughes, C. A. (2010). *Explicit instruction: Effective and efficient teaching*. Guilford Publications.

Boushey, G., & Moser, J. (2014). *The Daily 5: Fostering literacy independence in the elementary grades*. Stenhouse Publishers.

Byrne, J., Rietdijk, W., & Cheek, S. (2016). Enquiry-based science in the infant classroom: 'Letting go.' *International Journal of Early Years Education, 24*(2), 206–223. https://doi.org/10.1080/09669760.2015.1135105

Carpenter, S. K., Witherby, A. E., & Tauber, S. K. (2020). On students' (mis)judgments of learning and teaching effectiveness. *Journal of Applied Research in Memory and Cognition, 9*(2), 137–151.

Cowan, N. (2001). The magical number 4 in short-term memory: A reconsideration of mental storage capacity. *Behavioral and Brain Sciences, 24*(1), 87–114.

De Bruyckere, P., Kirschner, P. A., & Hulshof, C. D. (2015). *Urban myths about learning and education*. Academic Press.

Geary, D. C. (2002). Principles of evolutionary educational psychology. *Learning and Individual Differences, 12*(4), 317–345.

Groshell, Z. (2021, January 1). Why the genius hour fad died. *Education Rickshaw.* https://educationrickshaw.com/2021/01/01/why-the-genius-hour-fad-died/

Hollingsworth, J. R., & Ybarra, S. E. (2017). *Explicit direct instruction (EDI): The power of the well-crafted, well-taught lesson*. Corwin Press.

Husmann, P. R., & O'Loughlin, V. D. (2019). Another nail in the coffin for learning styles? disparities among undergraduate anatomy students' study strategies, class performance, and reported VARK learning styles. *Anatomical Sciences Education, 12*(1), 6–19.

Kalyuga, S. (2007). Expertise reversal effect and its implications for learner-tailored instruction. *Educational Psychology Review, 19*(4), 509–539.

Kime, S. (2018). Reducing teacher workload: The 're-balancing feedback' trial. *Evidence Based Education*, March.

Kinder, D., & Carnine, D. (1991). Direct instruction: What it is and what it is becoming?. *Journal of Behavioral Education, 1*(2), 193–213.

Kirschner, P., & Hendrick, C. (2020). Did you hear the one about the kinaesthetic learner: Urban legends. In *How learning happens: Seminal works in educational psychology and what they mean in practice*. (pp. 264–272). Routledge.

Kirschner, P. A., Sweller, J., & Clark, R. E. (2006). Why minimal guidance during instruction does not work: An analysis of the failure of constructivist, discovery, problem-based, experiential, and inquiry-based teaching. *Educational Psychologist, 41*(2), 75–86.

Kirschner, P. A., & van Merriënboer, J. J. G. (2013). Do learners really know best? Urban legends in education. *Educational Psychologist, 48*(3), 169–183.

Knouse, L. E., Rawson, K. A., & Dunlosky, J. (2020). How much do college students with ADHD benefit from retrieval practice when learning key-term definitions? *Learning and Instruction, 68*(April), 101330.

Kohn, A. (1993). Choices for children: Why and how to let students decide. *Phi Delta Kappan, 75*(September), 8. https://www.alfiekohn.org/article/choices-children/

Kruger, J., & Dunning, D. (1999). Unskilled and unaware of it: How difficulties in recognizing one's own incompetence lead to inflated self-assessments. *Journal of personality and Social Psychology, 77*(6), 1121.

Macdonald, K., Germine, L., Anderson, A., Christodoulou, J., & McGrath, L. M. (2017). Dispelling the myth: Training in education or neuroscience decreases but does not eliminate beliefs in neuromyths. *Frontiers in Psychology, 8*(AUG), 1–16.

Manurung, K., & Mashuri, M. (2017). Implementing interest based instructional materials to minimize EFL learners' speaking skills and de-motivating factors. *Theory and Practice in Language Studies, 7*(5), 356.

Martin, A. J., & Evans, P. (2018). Load reduction instruction: Exploring a framework that assesses explicit instruction through to independent learning. *Teaching and Teacher Education, 73*, 203–214.

Mayer, R. E. (2004). Should there be a three-strikes rule against pure discovery learning? *American Psychologist, 59*(1), 14–19.

Mesghina, A., Vollman, E., Trezise, K., & Richland, L. E. (2023). Worked examples moderate the effect of math learning anxiety on children's math learning and engagement during the COVID-19 pandemic. *Journal of Educational Psychology, 116*(2), 173–194.

Mould, K. (2021). *EEF Blog: Assess, adjust, adapt – what does adaptive teaching mean to you?* The Education Endowment Foundation. https://educationendowmentfoundation.org.uk/news/eef-blog-assess-adjust-adapt-what-does-adaptive-teaching-mean-to-you

National Reading Panel. (2000). Teaching children to read: An evidence-based assessment of the scientific research literature on reading and its implications for reading instruction. *NIH Publication No. 00-4769*. https://doi.org/10.1002/ppul.1950070418

Nugteren, M. L., Jarodzka, H., Kester, L., & Van Merriënboer, J. J. (2018). Self-regulation of secondary school students: self-assessments are inaccurate and insufficiently used for learning-task selection. *Instructional Science, 46*, 357–381.

Paas, F., & Sweller, J. (2012). An evolutionary upgrade of cognitive load theory: Using the human motor system and collaboration to support the learning of complex cognitive tasks. *Educational Psychology Review, 24*(1), 27–45.

Parker, R., & Thomsen, B. S. (2019). *Learning through play at school*. LEGO Foundation.

Pozas, M., Letzel-Alt, V., & Schwab, S. (2023). The effects of differentiated instruction on teachers' stress and job satisfaction. *Teaching and Teacher Education, 122*.

Robertson, D. A., Padesky, L. B., & Brock, C. H. (2020). Cultivating student agency through teachers' professional learning. *Theory into Practice, 59*(2), 192–201.

Rosenshine, B. (2012). Principles of instruction: Research-based strategies that all teachers should know. *American Educator, 36*(1), 12–20. https://www.aft.org/sites/default/files/periodicals/Rosenshine.pdf

Rotherham, A. J., & Willingham, D. T. (2010). "21st century" skills: Not new, but a worthy challenge. *American Educator, 34*(1), 17–20.

Schmidt, H. G., Loyens, S. M. M., Van Gog, T., & Paas, F. (2007). Problem-based learning is compatible with human cognitive architecture: Commentary on Kirschner, Sweller, and Clark (2006). *Educational Psychologist, 42*(2), 91–97.

Sold a Story. (2022, March 1). *Sold a Story* [Audio podcast]. https://www.soldastorypodcast.com/episodes

Sweller, J. (2006). The worked example effect and human cognition. *Learning and Instruction, 16*(2 SPEC. ISS.), 165–169.

Sweller, J. (2021). Why inquiry-based approaches harm students' learning. *Analysis Paper (Centre for Independent Studies), 24*(August), 15.

Sweller, J., van Merriënboer, J. J. G., & Paas, F. (2019). Cognitive architecture and instructional design: 20 years later. *Educational Psychology Review, 31*(2), 261–292.

Sweller, J., Zhang, L., Ashman, G., Cobern, W., & Kirschner, P. A. (2023). Response to De Jong et al.'s (2023) paper "Let's talk evidence – The case for combining inquiry-based and direct instruction." *Educational Research Review, 42*(2),100584.

Tobias, S., & Duffy, T. M. (Eds.). (2009). *Constructivist instruction: Success or failure?* Routledge.

Tran, L., Sanchez, T., Arellano, B., & Swanson, H. L. (2011). A meta-analysis of the RTI literature for children at risk for reading disabilities. *Journal of Learning Disabilities, 44*(3), 283–295.

Tricot, A., & Sweller, J. (2014). Domain-specific knowledge and why teaching generic skills does not work. *Educational Psychology Review, 26*(2), 1–38.

Wiliam, D., & Leahy, S. (2016). *Embedding formative assessment*. Hawker Brownlow Education.

Willingham, D., & Daniel, D. (2012). Teaching to what students have in common. *Educational Leadership, 69*, 16–21.

Willingham, D. T., Hughes, E. M., & Dobolyi, D. G. (2015). The scientific status of learning styles theories. *Teaching of Psychology, 42*(3), 266–271.

6 What is the science of reading?

What does it mean for my teaching?

Tanya Serry, Pamela Snow, Eamon Charles and Nathaniel Swain

Many schools begin their science of learning journeys with a transformation of how they teach reading. In recent times, these changes of practice have often been described as aligning with the 'science of reading.'

As already demonstrated, staff in the schools featured in this book make note of the profound results achieved by undertaking such changes. Thus, we are keen to discuss some of the key understandings and clarify any misconceptions as you consider your next moves for the teaching of reading. See the chapter overview in Box 6.1.

Box 6.1 - Chapter 6 Overview

- What is reading?
- What is the science of reading?
- Reading instruction: a highly contested topic.
- Steps to ensure all students succeed.

What is reading?

Reading can be defined in a wide range of ways. In this chapter, we consider reading to be the process by which people 'lift text off the page' *and* arrive at its meaning. What is immediately obvious, is that reading comprises at least two core components:

(1) the ability to decode unfamiliar words or recognise already known words; and
(2) the ability to understand what the text as a whole 'means.'

This can involve us reading everything from single words, such as signs in public places that say 'Exit' or 'Stop,' through to complex works of fiction and/or expository texts. In all

DOI: 10.4324/9781003404965-8

cases along this continuum, readers bring background knowledge to support their comprehension of the text. This knowledge includes an understanding of:

- language (e.g., meanings of words and how these change according to contextual factors);
- sentence structures and their relationship to meaning;
- awareness of **discourse genres** and purpose;
- processing of **idiomatic language**; and
- knowledge about the world around us and how it operates.

Writing systems are human contrivances that are thought to date back around 3,000 to 5,000 years (Robinson, 2007). This is a fraction of the period over which humans have had **oral language** abilities, with estimates on this varying from approximately 150,000 to 200,000 years (Pagel, 2017). For this reason, it is important to remember that innate spoken language has an enormous evolutionary advantage over humans' learned ability to read, write, and spell.

The recency of writing systems for humans means that reading, writing, and spelling have been described as **biologically secondary** skills, setting them apart from oral language skills, which are **biologically primary** (Geary, 2008). Oral language comes first for humans, both in an *evolutionary* sense for us as a species, and in a *developmental* sense, for us as individuals. Children's oral language development begins with vocalisations and crying at birth and culminates typically around age four with the ability to use and understand a range of **discourse genres** (Owens, 2020).

The demands placed by writing systems on the human brain depend on the nature of the written code, with some writing systems being relatively **transparent** (e.g., Italian or Spanish) and others relatively **opaque** (e.g., English).

To understand how reading works several models or frameworks have been proposed in recent decades. In this chapter, we focus on **the Simple View of Reading** (SVR; Gough & Tunmer, 1986) and the **Reading Rope** (Scarborough, 2001). These two frameworks are helpful in informing teachers' understanding of the reading process and the importance of taking the perspective of the novice who is learning to do something complex, that does not come naturally and easily.

Text types in oral or written forms: conversation, narratives, informatives, and persuasive texts for example

Language that is non-literal, including metaphors, similes, idioms, and proverbs, for example

Spoken language across the sound, word, sentence, and discourse levels (c.f. written language)

Knowledge that is acquired through explicit educational experiences, such as reading, writing, and specific academic skills or knowledge

Fundamental knowledge that is innate or develops early in life, such as language acquisition or recognising faces

The spelling system with a small number of patterns and conventions that requires less instructional time and effort to learn

A spelling system that has several layers and is difficult to decipher without significant explicit instruction

A mathematical equation that represents reading comprehension (RC) as word decoding (D) multiplied by language comprehension (LC)

A visual metaphor of the various subskills that need to be mastered over time to reach proficient reading comprehension

The Simple View of Reading

The ability to accurately and fluently convert written words into spoken language by applying knowledge of letter-sound correspondences; a process of efficient word recognition in which readers use knowledge of the relationship between letters and sounds to work out how to say and read written words

The SVR is a mathematical equation that represents *reading comprehension* (RC) as the product (not the sum) of ***word decoding*** (D) and oral *language comprehension* (LC).

Word Decoding (D) X Language Comprehension (LC) = Reading Comprehension (RC)

Importantly, the authors of this model were not suggesting that reading is 'simple.' They were, however, stripping the reading process back to its barest constituent parts so that it can be studied by researchers and understood clearly by teachers. The fact that the mathematical operator in the equation is a multiplication symbol is critical, as anything multiplied by zero is zero. This means that relative strengths on one side of the equation cannot compensate for weaknesses on the other.

Recently, Duke and Cartwright (2021) proposed an 'update' to the SVR named the 'active view,' adding in self-regulatory processes (e.g., motivation, strategy use, attentional control) they saw as absent from the original model of cognitive capacities for reading. In response, Hoover and Tunmer (2021) reviewed the active view's potential utility, cautioning that it is "a weaker, unproven model that could lead education professionals astray if applied in practice" (p. 399), and as such should not be adopted by educational professionals until there is stronger evidence to support any claimed benefits.

Hollis Scarborough's Reading Rope

The *Reading Rope* was published in 2001, some 15 years after the SVR, and provides a more detailed analysis of the core components of the reading process. The Reading Rope is a visual metaphor that outlines the development of complex, interwoven 'strands' that combine together to form a strong reader. As can been seen in Figure 6.1, the lower strands represent the skills needed to identify unfamiliar words and recognise known words. In the upper strands, we can see many skills that are needed to make sense of connected text. Skills in the lower stands need to become automatic as soon as possible, so that students' cognitive and linguistic skills are focussing on the comprehension demands of the text. Students who cannot efficiently decode unfamiliar words by mid-elementary school will not be able to reliably engage with text meanings and are likely to be demotivated about reading (Castles et al., 2018).

As a biologically secondary set of skills, reading, writing, and spelling need to be taught, and this teaching is the responsibility of schools, not parents. This is particularly important in English, which has been described as having one of the most complex alphabetic writing systems in the world (Garrod & Daneman, 2003).

Historically, English has 'borrowed' thousands of words and their spellings from other languages. Over time and geographical locations, pronunciation of many words 'moves around'

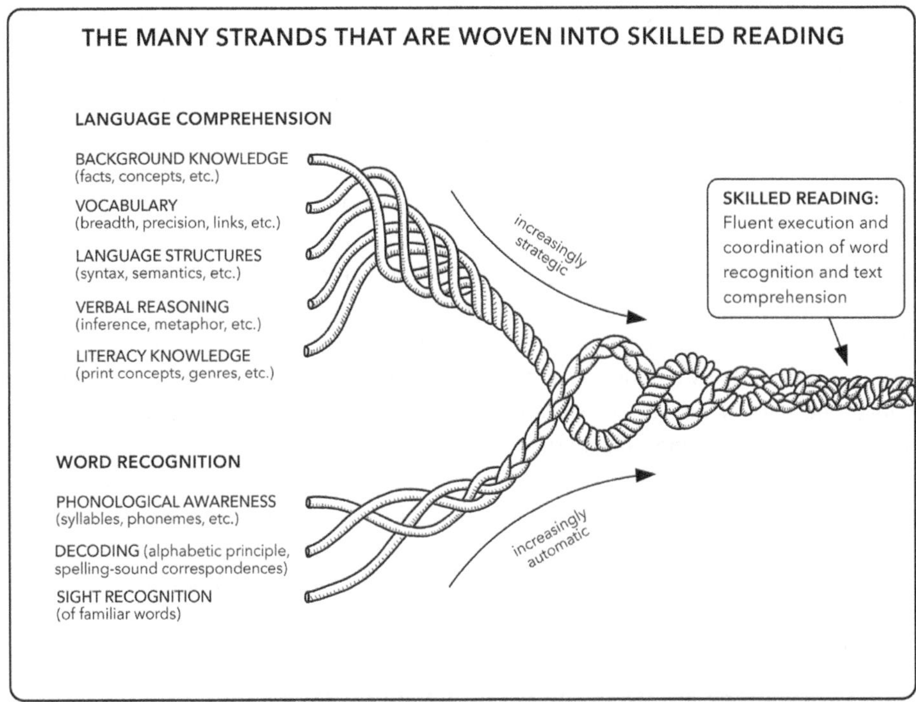

Figure 6.1 Scarborough's Reading Rope (2001).

Image courtesy of Dr Hollis Scarborough.

where spelling remains much more stable. This means that the decoding part of any reading model in English will entail special challenges that also extend to spelling.

A pedagogical philosophy which advocates for immersing children in rich, authentic texts as the main instructional tool. It pushes for the encouragement of students to 'sample' words in texts and to use multiple cues to predict written words

The term for a collection of approaches to teaching reading and writing. These share in common the idea of using a range of methods to teach students; includes elements of phonics and whole language

How to help all children 'read by sight'

Sight words in balanced literacy instruction

A phrase that is often confusing is 'sight word.' In many **whole language** and **balanced literacy** classrooms, sight words have been explained as words that are (usually erroneously) considered too 'irregular' to be decoded ('sounded out') by novice readers. To help students learn in balanced literacy classrooms, children are provided with banks of so-called sight words which they are expected to learn (often at home) as visual wholes, with no guidance for analysing them below the word-level. This approach is problematic because reading is not a process of *visually memorising* words.

How students actually begin 'reading by sight'

Reading words by sight is, in reality, a process of **orthographically mapping** words (Ehri, 2023). This means storing *any written word* in our long-term memory with information about the word's meaning, pronunciation, and spelling bonded together.

When we have successfully decoded a word several times, it can be stored in long-term memory for almost automatic recognition. This process of bonding the letters to sounds and to the word's meaning is 'orthographic mapping'

As renowned literacy educator Jan Wasowicz describes: *Every word wants to be a sight word when it grows up!* This is how students move from laboriously sounding out each letter in a word like /s/ /i/ /t/, to instantly recognising the word. Rather than memorising the letter string 'sit' like a picture, proficient decoders will have orthographically mapped the word so it is instantly recognisable using every letter, and also distinguishable from words that might be visually similar, like 'sip' and 'set.'

With such understandings, teachers and curriculum designers can better support children with the principles from the SVR and the Reading Rope in mind, including a systematic scope and sequence and a focus on early automatising of decoding and word identification. This then creates more space for a strong and increasingly strategic focus on comprehension of a wide and complex range of text types across the curriculum, and for students' reading for pleasure.

Reading proficiency precedes the joy of independent reading

Reading skill paves the way for reading enjoyment (van Bergen et al., 2022), and this is developed through mastery across all strands of the Reading Rope. Teachers cannot bypass this mastery by attempting to foster children's 'love of reading,' e.g., by simply reading to them, or finding them the 'just right' book they are yet to read.

Reading to children is critical for their growth in vocabulary, syntax, and background knowledge development. This is particularly important for students who come from relatively disadvantaged home literacy environments, where opportunistic teaching by adults is less likely to occur and books may be few in number (Snow, 2020). However, this investment in language comprehension and background knowledge *should not* be mistaken for work that needs to occur to explicitly teach children how to decode and then read fluently and meaningfully.

Story Example 6.1 - How we taught reading, then and now - Churchill Primary

Before the instructional change: The school followed a reader's workshop model, including:

- Mini lesson;
- **Guided reading** (e.g., Richardson, 2009) using the three cueing system and levelled readers;
- Teaching strategies such as 'Lips the Fish', 'Tryin' Lion', 'Chunky Monkey', 'Skippy Frog'; and

A popular teaching practice involving small group, or individual conferencing with students, talking about a text, reading a text, or teaching a reading skill

- Independent reading with students reading 'just right' books (even students in their first year of school).

The staff spent considerable time teaching comprehension strategies, and the take home readers were levelled predictable texts.

After the instructional change:

- Phonological awareness is now taught explicitly in junior grades;
- Embedding of Orton-Gillingham (OG; see Sayeski, 2019), phonics and morphology lessons;
- **Decodable texts** are used in class and as take-home readers;
- Literacy daily review used to review spelling, vocabulary, fluency, comprehension, and sentence strategies;
- Explicit teaching of vocabulary, novel studies, and knowledge-rich non-fiction texts;
- Use of shared scope and sequences; and
- Embedding of explicit direct instructional approaches.

Books designed to match the phonics skills (sound-letter patterns) that students have been learning. They are short stories or non-fiction texts that contain only simple sound-letter patterns in them and help develop reading fluency by allowing students to practice word recognition and independent reading

Compared to the underwhelming results and high levels of off-task behaviour before this change, the success and enjoyment of readers and teachers is clear. Combined with the new learning routines, which are explicitly taught, teachers have more time to teach, and students spend their precious time on-task.

So, if that is what we know about reading, what might we mean by the 'science of reading?'

What is the science of reading?

Unlike many areas of science that we are accustomed to hearing about, and whose practitioners have familiar titles (e.g., immunologists, virologists, geologists), there is no discrete group of scientists attached to the science of reading. Instead, people from a range of fields may identify as reading scientists. The Reading League defines the science of reading as:

> *a vast, interdisciplinary body of scientifically based research about reading and issues related to reading and writing.* (The Reading League, 2022)

Their definition, which has gained global traction, privileges the 'scientific process.' In keeping with this, pre-eminent reading scientistic Professor Mark Seidenberg aptly refers to the science of reading as "a work in progress" (Seidenberg, 2022).

Over the last decade, the phrase 'science of reading' has been used (and perhaps overused) as part of a narrative by many educators who are collectively working to reform reading and literacy instruction. This pedagogical reform reflects what cognitive scientists (including many reading researchers) have come to understand about how certain neural networks in the human brain are reorganised when we are taught to read (Dehaene, 2009).

Accordingly, pedagogical practices aligned with the science of reading respect that *learning to read is unnatural*, in the same way that learning to play chess is unnatural (Gough & Hillinger, 1980), and that students need to be *taught* to read.

The science of reading itself is a body of knowledge—not a program or a stand-alone pedagogical practice. It aligns with essential knowledge about how humans learn. The science of reading:

1. highlights the cognitive and linguistic processes necessary for a novice reader to become proficient; and
2. identifies instructional practices that are most likely to optimise reading outcomes for all students (Castles et al., 2018).

Reading instruction: A highly contested topic

For decades, vast evidence has accumulated about the fact that learning to read is not a natural process. Collectively, this body of research indicates that reading and spelling are highly dependent on children's oral language systems on the one hand, but need to be explicitly taught, on the other. Despite this, reading instruction (and intervention) remains highly contested (e.g., Castles et al., 2018; Snow, 2020). Unfortunately, established ideas about literacy pedagogies in our schools have suffered from poor **knowledge translation** from scientific research through to classroom practice. Universities and other institutions that prepare pre-service teachers have neglected to update their recommended pedagogies in light of evolving evidence, and have favoured sociological ideas of reading as social endeavour (e.g., Bloome, 1985).

> The process by which knowledge generated through academic research is utilised in practice

Many English-speaking countries are reporting alarmingly low reading proficiency in their students (e.g., NAEP, 2022). These statistics cannot be attributed to external factors (e.g., screen time, COVID-19, etc.) since this trend has been observable before the penetration of technology into children's lives or the disruption caused by a pandemic. Alas, the evidence housed within the vast body of knowledge known collectively as the science of reading—that can provide educators with a blueprint for best practice when teaching novice readers—remains largely under-utilised.

Whole language, then balanced literacy

One of the original debates about how to teach children to read commenced back in the 1960s. It saw proponents of **whole language** pitted against those who viewed reading as the necessary and cumulative mastery of a set of skills. The latter side was often referred to as 'phonics advocates' at that time, though phonics was not all that they valued.

> A pedagogical philosophy which advocates for immersing children in rich, authentic texts as the main instructional tool. It pushes for the encouragement of students to 'sample' words in texts and to use multiple cues to predict written words

According to the whole language position, children should be immersed in 'rich text' as the primary method of instruction, encouraging 'sampling' of text, using multiple 'cues' to predict what the written words say (e.g., Goodman, 2014). These ideas were well-intentioned, but led to instructional practices that failed too many students who grew up as poor readers and equally poor spellers (Hempenstall, 1997). Their teachers were pushed to move students' attention away from decoding the word itself, and to look for other sources of information (pictures or the sentence/context), thus undermining, no matter how inadvertently, the orthographic mapping processes for many students.

Balanced literacy emerged in the early 2000s as an attempt to address some of the now incontrovertible shortcomings of whole language. Balanced literacy mainly retained aspects the view that reading should 'always be about meaning' from the outset, whilst adding *some phonics* instruction, and a heavy dose of comprehension strategies (Castles et al., 2018; Wheldall et al., 2023). Unfortunately, despite some attempts, there has never been a consistent definition or model of balanced literacy and as such, instruction in one balanced literacy classroom can look quite different to that in the next (Snow, 2020; Wheldall et al., 2023).

Matthew and Peter Effects

In most English-speaking countries, it has been the norm for teachers to miss out on key learning in the linguistic components of written language in their university teaching degrees for several decades (particularly in terms of **phonemic** and **orthographic** knowledge; e.g., Stark et al., 2016). Thus, for the majority of students who *do* require explicit instruction in the writing system, many start school behind and fall further behind—as per the **Matthew Effect**, whereby 'the rich get richer, and the poor get poorer' (see Snow, 2016). For those students who struggle significantly, many receive additional intervention (including the widely-used Reading Recovery® and the Fountas and Pinnell Leveled Literacy Intervention). However, despite their use over several decades, there is a lack of independent, peer-reviewed evidence that these balanced literacy aligned programs sufficiently close the gap in student decoding (May et al., 2023). Readers are referred to Nancy Young's (2021) **Ladder of Reading and Writing** to learn about this phenomenon further.

For students who are behind, their classroom teachers are most likely to have missed crucial university learning in the linguistic and orthographic structure of English, as well as the insights from the cognitive science of reading acquisition and intervention (Buckingham & Meeks, 2019). Therefore, many teachers unwittingly experience **Peter Effects**, whereby they *cannot give what they do not have*. Unless they have begun a journey to rectify this, most teachers are insufficiently prepared to provide effective literacy teaching in the

The term for a collection of approaches to teaching reading and writing. These share in common the idea of using a range of methods to teach students; includes elements of phonics and whole language

Knowledge of how phonemes can be combined and manipulated to create spoken words, and how they can be taken apart

Knowledge of the spelling system, including phonic knowledge, but also spelling rules and conventions

A biblical reference to the notion that the 'rich get richer, and the poor get poorer,' referring to the phenomenon where students without key skills and knowledge at school entry tend to fall further and further behind their advantaged peers as time progresses

An infographic that displays the proportions of students who benefit from structured explicit literacy teaching versus non-research-aligned methods

A biblical reference to the idea that 'one cannot give what one does not have,' referring to the phenomenon where teachers find it difficult to support students struggling with reading or writing because of a lack of preparation regarding the language system and the science of reading sub-components of oral and written language, without *significant* professional learning and support (Snow, 2016).

What can be done to redress these phenomena?

Approaches aligned with the science of reading are characterised by "explicit, systematic, and sequential teaching of literacy at multiple levels" (Spear-Swerling, 2019, p. 202). **Phonics** needs to be taught in a cumulative, bottom-up way, though this is just one element. Other linguistic elements should be explicitly taught, including:

The teaching of sound-letter correspondences

- phonemic awareness;
- vocabulary;
- morphology;
- sentence structure;
- figurative and idiomatic language;
- text structure;
- metacognitive (comprehension) strategies; and
- appreciation of literature across a range of genres and purposes.

Accordingly, several science of reading proponents are now preferring to use the phrase 'structured literacy' instead (e.g., Spear-Swerling, 2019; Young, 2021). This is in part to reinforce the fact that the science of reading refers to much more than phonics instruction alone. These additional linguistic and literary aspects are equally as important, even though code-based instruction remains the most contested (see chapter 7 for more).

Story Example 6.2 - How the science of reading changed our thinking about literacy

Before Riverwood Public School began its science of reading journey, the school's literacy focus was comprehension. The school spent considerable time mapping comprehension skills in a continuum and attempting to classify the kinds of comprehension difficulties their students were having. Once they began looking at models, such as the Simple View of Reading, it was clear that decoding *and* language comprehension were needed for students to proficiently grapple with texts. So, they began using alternative assessment measures such as the Grade 1 phonics check which revealed that the situation with their students' literacy data was dire: 70% of their Grade 3 to 6 students did not pass the Grade 1 phonics check, and therefore lacked basic proficiency in word identification skills.

The leadership team knew they needed to prioritise building teacher knowledge about reading development. After extensive professional learning concerning the Reading Rope, they were able to de-implement certain practices, such as the use of 'Running Records,' predictable texts, three cueing, and extensive drilling of comprehension strategies.

This process made space for the introduction of new teaching practices, including systematic synthetic phonics (SSP), targeted phonemic awareness, word reading and spelling, that encouraged **orthographic mapping** and opportunities for fluency practice. Alongside this, their awareness of comprehension and the role of background knowledge and vocabulary enabled a greater focus on rich texts that connected with one another, shared as a whole class. Over time, their focus on the science of reading stimulated their interest in the science of *learning* and best practice instruction

When we have successfully decoded a word several times, it can be stored in long-term memory for almost automatic recognition. This process of bonding the letters to sounds and to the word's meaning is 'orthographic mapping'

Steps to ensure that all students become proficient readers

Instructional implications

In the following chapter, the authors outline an overview of the key practices and focuses that comprise effective literacy instruction. Here we provide a table to compare typical characteristics of **balanced literacy** (currently the norm in most English-speaking countries), and **structured explicit literacy teaching** that aligns with the evolving science of reading.

The term for a collection of approaches to teaching reading and writing. These share in common the idea of using a range of methods to teach students; includes elements of phonics and whole language

Teaching of reading and writing that is effective, well-sequenced and progress monitored, systematically building students' knowledge and proficiency across word, sentence, paragraph, and text levels, aligning with the science of reading

Multi-Tiered Systems of Support (MTSS), including Response-to-Intervention (RTI)

In the context of reading instruction and intervention, meeting the needs of students with reading difficulties is another key component of operationalising the science of reading.

Response to intervention (RTI), as part of **multi-tiered systems of support** (MTSS), is a framework for ensuring successful and equitable support for all students. **Tier 1 instruction** is the first 'dose' of teaching and should be effective for the greatest number of children. This starts with impactful whole class instruction that incorporates opportunities for additional in-class support and prompting for identified subgroups of students (National Center on Response to Intervention, 2010).

Tier 2 instruction targets small groups who continue to show difficulties despite strong Tier 1 instruction. This may include groupings such as: low progress primary or secondary students, students for whom English is an additional language or dialect who have reading difficulties, and/or neurodiverse students including those with diagnosed specific learning disorders such as dyslexia and dysgraphia.

A tiered framework used in education to provide early, systematic, and targeted support to students who need it, with the goal of preventing long-term difficulties

A framework of multi-levelled systems to support students' learning and behaviour; intended to take a preventative approach

General classroom instruction with the usual teacher

Targeted small group instruction for those who still have difficulty following Tier 1

Table 6.1 Structured explicit literacy teaching and balanced literacy compared.

	Typical characteristics of reading instruction	
	Structured Explicit Literacy Teaching aligned with Science of Reading	*Balanced Literacy (or other whole language derivatives)*
Teacher knowledge	Explicit and detailed knowledge of language and literacy concepts and development in order to properly sequence, explain, model and provide feedback.	Greater focus on teachers' knowledge of literature, than a requirement to understand structures of oral and written language.
Scopes and sequences	Systematic and coherent scopes and sequences are used for at least: phonemic awareness, word reading and spelling, sentence and paragraph writing.	Unlikely to have detailed scope and sequence, or these are focussed on a mix of tangible and intangible skills.
Texts	Literature-focused for oral language. Decodable (phonically-controlled) texts for initial word recognition practice.	Predictable or levelled books for independent and shared reading Limited or no use of decodable (phonically controlled) texts. Emphasis on rich literature over decodability.
Instructional groupings	**Whole class:** Explicit teaching of full range of reading knowledge and skills. Use of call and response, choral and tracked reading, and mini-whiteboards for practice of a range of skills. Checking for understanding and review of prior learning embedded throughout. **Small group:** May include some conferencing during paired reading fluency for example, and some independent reading time, but this is accountable and not unstructured or busy work.	**Whole class**: Mini lesson to emphasise a reading skill or strategy based on students' current errors. **Small group:** Rotations including independent reading and other reading related activities. One group or individual will do conferencing or guided reading with teacher, with a focus on reading from levelled book.
Phonics and orthography	Systematic synthetic phonics instruction focused on blending and segmenting sounds represented by graphemes, and applying increasingly complex spelling patterns and rules. Embedded phonemic awareness in the constant spelling and decoding of words grapheme by grapheme.	May emphasise onset-rime of words, or word families ('analogy phonics,' may incorporate some morphological analysis. May use 'Letter of the Week.' May teach about sounds, but this will not involve a focus on phonics teaching for extended periods. Sounding out words grapheme by grapheme is deemphasised and discouraged as phonics is considered a last resort after meaning and context cues, for word identification.
Memorising word lists	Will emphasise phonics and word structure first and foremost. A small bank of less regular words will be targeted to allow students to access decodable texts and read them fluently.	May require the memorisation of hundreds of 'sight words' without explaining the regularly spelt words as decodable. May use resources such as the Oxford 100 Wordlist, which contain both regular and less regular words.

For those still facing challenges, **Tier 3** offers intensive, individualised interventions (AERO, 2023), often delivered by staff with specialist qualifications.

More specialised intervention, for those who do not make sufficient progress in Tier 2

In RTI, progress should be continuously monitored, guiding data-driven decisions on whether to maintain or adjust the level of support. This aims to proactively identify and address learning difficulties, promote early intervention, and prevent learning gaps from widening (Hall, 2018). Importantly, it is the *dose* and *intensity* of the intervention, not the instructional *approach*, that changes as students access supports from Tier 1 to 2, and into 3.

Story Example 6.3 - Bentleigh West Primary School and Riverwood Public School - How we use RTI and MTSS for intervention

Current principal of Bentleigh West Primary School, Sarah Asome, maintains that the key to success for all students comes down to ensuring high-quality Tier 1 instruction, in every classroom, every day. Before their journey of implementing evidence-based reading instruction, up to one-third of BWPS students required additional support by the end of the first year of school.

Now there remains a small number who access Tier 2 and 3 intervention, but the school leadership are confident that they are the students for whom these tiers were designed. Parents of hundreds of students with additional learning needs and disabilities have been drawn to Bentleigh West, with children with identified learning difficulties now making up more than a quarter of its student body. Despite this, the vast majority of students with diverse learning needs still access their instruction in Tier 1 alone.

Bentleigh West's success–which has supported students who have historically struggled, as well as challenged all students to strive for excellence–has meant their learning *intervention* team underwent a rebrand as the learning *enhancement* team so that specialised educators could better include students needing extension in their remit, in addition to those needing support.

* * *

Staff at Riverwood Public School learnt early on in their science of reading journey that you cannot intervene your way out of a Tier 1 problem. This famous adage from United States MTSS practitioner Terri Metcalf (2018) communicated to Riverwood the core message of RTI. It is essential to have high-quality effective Tier 1 instruction as well as effective screening and assessment processes. Before their science of reading transformation, Riverwood teachers often believed that students would just catch up, and that some children took longer than others to read. It was not until the teachers began increasing their professional knowledge that they could see that their core instruction needed to attend more systematically to the foundations of reading and spelling (phonemic awareness, phonics, and spelling rules, for example), and that without this focus, significant numbers of students would need intervention. Their students showed significant growth when the quality of Tier 1 instruction was lifted.

Since this transformation, Riverwood has developed proactive systems using data collection and early intervention judiciously, even providing oral language and phonemic awareness experiences and supports starting in preschool, as well as screening these important skills upon school-entry. They started by improving their Tier 1 instruction so that it was universally effective, cumulative and systematic; and for Tier 2 and 3, the school has been using a suite of intervention approaches aligned with the science of reading to address and support student needs.

Despite their excellent Tier 1 instruction being the core focus, the staff at Riverwood knew they could not meet the needs of all their students without these additional tiers of support. Decision-making around when and who moves through each tier is always based on reliable, robust data.

This dynamic space and closing thoughts

As we leave this description of what the science of reading is, and is not, we are deeply gratified by the growing awareness and the understanding of the fundamentals of reading science across educator and policymaker communities. The ground-breaking work of investigative journalist Emily Hanford, who created the podcast *Sold a Story*, has shone a spotlight on the problems of reading instruction in the United States and around the English-speaking world. Policymakers globally are beginning to shift priorities and introduce significant disruptions to the ways that reading is taught in our classrooms.

We are also cautious that this energy does not regress into buzzwords, and that schools work to privilege scientific evidence to guide their decisions, over the long haul. We hope that this chapter has helped to demystify the debates about the teaching of reading. See Table 6.2 for a summary of key ideas.

This leads into subsequent exploration into the components of effective literacy pedagogy in chapter 7.

Table 6.2 Chapter 6 knowledge organiser.

1. What is reading?	***2. What is the science of reading?***
• The Simple View of Reading. • Scarborough's Reading Rope. • How to help all children read by sight. • Reading proficiency precedes enjoyment of independent reading.	• A body of scientific knowledge to inform best practices in literacy instruction and intervention. • Not an ideology or a singular pedagogy.
3. Reading instruction: A highly contested topic	***4. Steps to ensure all students succeed***
• Whole language, then balanced literacy. • Matthew and Peter Effects. • Science of reading aligned approaches.	• Instructional implications. • Balanced literacy versus structured explicit literacy teaching. • Multi-tiered systems of support (MTSS).

Where to next?

- Cowan, C. A. (2016). What is structured literacy? https://dyslexiaida.org/what-is-structured-literacy/
- AERO (2023) Introduction to the science of reading.
- Snow, P. (2020). Balanced literacy or systematic reading instruction? *Perspectives on Language and Literacy*, Winter, 35–39.
- Spear-Swerling, L. (2019). Structured literacy and typical literacy practices: Understanding differences to create instructional opportunities. *Teaching Exceptional Children, 51*(3), 201–211.
- Young, N., & Hasbrouck, J. (2024). Climbing the ladder of reading & writing: Meeting the needs of all learners. Benchmark Education.

Check your indicators – Science of reading

On-Track Indicators	*Off-Track Indicators*
• Teachers who are knowledgeable about the linguistic subskills in oral and written language • Informing parents about the nature of the reading process and the importance of early decoding skills. • Use of decodable (phonically controlled) texts for early reading. • Explicit, direct, and systematic instruction of letter-sound relationships. • Use of reliable assessments to identify at-risk readers. • Adequate attention to the upper and lower strands of the reading rope to develop word reading proficiency and language comprehension.	• Teachers who have not been taught key linguistic concepts that account for both oral language and the writing system. • Discouraging parents from reminding their children to 'sound out' unfamiliar words and encouraging the use of guessing/predicting/use of pictures instead • Sending home predictable or uncontrolled texts. • Expecting students to memorise 'sight words' like the Oxford 100 list • Incidental, analytic phonics, or 'phonics in context.' • Use of running records to measure progress and/or identify at-risk readers

Discussion questions

1. How can you apply the Simple View of Reading and Scarborough's Reading Rope in your classroom to enhance students' reading skills?
2. How do principles from the science of reading differ from your school's current practices?
3. What changes can you identify to better align your teaching practices with science of reading principles, and to promote effective literacy development in your students?

References

AERO. (2023). *Multi tiered systems of support snapshot.* https://www.edresearch.edu.au/resources/multi-tiered-system-supports-evidence-snapshot

Bloome, D. (1985). Reading as a social process. *Language Arts, 62*(2), 134–142.

Buckingham, J., & Meeks, L. (2019). Short-changed: Preparation to teach reading in initial teacher education. *MultiLit Pty Ltd.*

Castles, A., Rastle, K., & Nation, K. (2018). Ending the reading wars: Reading acquisition from novice to expert. *Psychological Science in the Public Interest, 19*(1), 5–51.

Dehaene, S. (2009). *Reading in the brain: The new science of how we read.* Penguin.

Dehaene, S. (c.2014). *How the brain learns to read.* https://youtu.be/25GI3-kiLdo

Duke, N., & Cartwright, K. (2021). The science of reading progresses: Communicating advances beyond the simple view of reading. *Reading Research Quarterly, 56*(S1), S25–44.

Ehri, L. C. (2023). Roads travelled researching how children learn to read words. *Australian Journal of Learning Difficulties, 28*(1), 55–71.

Garrod, S., & Daneman, M. (2003). Reading, psychology of. Encyclopedia of Cognitive Science, 3, 848–854.

Geary, D. C. (2008). An evolutionarily informed education science. *Educational Psychologist, 43*(4), 179–195.

Goodman, K. S. (2014). Reading: A psycholinguistic guessing game. In *Making sense of learners making sense of written language* (pp. 103–112). Routledge.

Gough, P. B., & Hillinger, M. L. (1980). Learning to read: An unnatural act. *Bulletin of the Orton Society, 30*, 179–190.

Hall. S. (2018). *10 success factors for literacy intervention: Getting results with MTSS in elementary schools.* Alexandria, VA: ASCD.

Hempenstall, K. (1997). The whole language-phonics controversy: An historical perspective. *Educational Psychology, 17*(4), 399–418.

Hunter, J., Stobart, A., & Haywood, A. (2024). *The reading guarantee: How to give every child the best chance of success.* Grattan Institute.

May, H., Blakeney, A., Shrestha, P., Mazal, M., & Kennedy, N. (2023). Long-term impacts of reading recovery through 3rd and 4th grade: A regression discontinuity study. *Journal of Research on Educational Effectiveness*, 1–26.

Metcalf, T. (2018). What's your plan? Accurate decision making within a multi-tier system of supports: Critical areas in Tier 1. *RTI Network.*

Moats, L. (2007). Whole-language high jinks: How to tell when "scientifically-based reading instruction" isn't. *Thomas B. Fordham Institute.*

Mufwene, S. (2013). The origins and evolution of language. In K. Allen (Ed.). *The Oxford handbook of the history of linguistics* (1st Ed., pp 39–85). Oxford University Press.

NAEP Report Card: Reading. (2022). https://www.nationsreportcard.gov/reading/nation/achievement?grade=4

National Center on Response to Intervention. (2010). *Essential components of RTI: A closer look at response to intervention.* ERIC Clearinghouse.

Ontario Human Rights Commission. (2022). *Right to read: Public inquiry into human rights issues affecting students with reading disabilities.* OHRC.

Owens, R. E. (2020). *Language development: An introduction* (10th Ed.). Pearson.

Pagel, M. (2017). Q&A: What is human language, when did it evolve and why should we care?. *BMC Biology, 15*, 1–6.

Richardson, J. (2009). *The next step in guided reading: Focused assessments and targeted lessons for helping every student become a better reader.* Scholastic.

Robinson, A. (2007). *The story of writing* (2nd Ed.). London: Thames & Hudson.

Sayeski, K. L., Earle, G. A., Davis, R., & Calamari, J. (2019). Orton Gillingham: Who, what, and how. *Teaching Exceptional Children, 51*(3), 240–249.

Seidenberg, M. (2022). The "science of reading" is a work in progress. *Seidenblog.* https://seidenbergreading.net/2022/03/22/the-science of reading-is-a-work-in-progress/

Snow, P. C. (2016). Elizabeth Usher Memorial Lecture: Language is literacy is language-Positioning speech-language pathology in education policy, practice, paradigms and polemics. *International Journal of Speech-Language Pathology, 18*(3), 216–228.

Snow, P. C. (2020). Balanced literacy or systematic reading instruction? *Perspectives on Language and Literacy, Winter*, 35–38.

Spear-Swerling, L. (2019). Structured literacy and typical literacy practices: Understanding differences to create instructional opportunities. *Teaching Exceptional Children, 51*(3), 201–211.

Stark, H. L., Snow, P. C., Eadie, P. A., & Goldfeld, S. R. (2016). Language and reading instruction in early years' classrooms: The knowledge and self-rated ability of Australian teachers. *Annals of Dyslexia, 66*, 28–54.

The Reading League (2022). *What is the science of reading*? https://www.thereadingleague.org/what-is-the-science of reading/.

van Bergen, E., Hart, S., Latvala, A., Vuoksimaa, E., Tolvanen, A., & Torppa, M. (2022). Literacy skills seem to fuel literacy enjoyment, rather than vice versa. *Developmental Science, 26*(3), 1–11.

Wheldall, K., Wheldall, R., & Buckingham, J. (2023). Effective instruction in reading and spelling. MultiLit Pty Ltd.

Young, N. (2021). *Ladder of reading & writing*. https://www.nancyyoung.ca/_files/ugd/ff7f1a_9b604b798f0944f389333823b8c4ebb0.pdf

7 Effective literacy teaching

Nathaniel Swain and Shane Pearson

As explored in chapter 6, literacy teaching is a complex and contentious area of education. While hopefully not as divisive, the task of organising your literacy teaching across the school can feel just as challenging. Here, we have sought to capture key aspects of effective literacy teaching practices, though this is not an exhaustive list or guide, but instead a collection of must-haves.

Background concepts for literacy planning

What is a literacy block?

A **literacy block** is the section of time you spend teaching literacy each day. Below we have provided an overview of suggested components of any literacy block, which also forms the chapter 7 overview in Box 7.1.

The period of time in which literacy is taught each day

Box 7.1 – Chapter 7 Overview – To comprehensively and effectively teach English, you need:

Word reading and spelling instruction

- Phonemic awareness
- Word reading/spelling
- Morphological awareness
- Advanced spelling instruction
- Sentence work
- Reading fluency

Foundational writing instruction

- Explicit handwriting instruction
- Sentence and paragraph teaching

Knowledge building and vocabulary

- Explicit, systematic and incidental vocabulary instruction
- Knowledge rich units

Text level comprehension and writing

- Shared and independent reading, including high-quality literature
- Comprehension strategies
- Modelled, shared, and independent writing
- Genre-level instruction

DOI: 10.4324/9781003404965-9

Your school may organise instructional times differently from what we discuss in this chapter or you may have other constraints or priorities. Nonetheless, we think it is helpful to frame this chapter with two different schools' literacy blocks.

Note about literacy block time recommendations

The recommendations in this chapter are based upon a fully implemented science of learning-informed literacy approach. If you are just starting to implement some of these practices, look at earlier year levels for indications of how much time might be needed to provide adequate focus for each literacy component.

Story Example 7.1 - Example literacy block

Bentleigh West Primary

Table 7.1 Bentleigh West literacy block.

Component	*Daily Time* *First year of school-Grade 2*	*Daily Time* *Grades 3-6*
Literacy Skills		
Phonemes: sound/phonogram cards	5 min	-
Spelling mastery (Grades 1-4)	15 min	15 min
Morphology	10 min	10 min
Handwriting/Paired fluency	10 min*	10 min*
Dictation/learned words	15 min*	15 min*
English review (inc. vocabulary)	20 min	30 min
New Content		
English Lesson incorporating: • The Writing Revolution™; • Questioning the Author; • Core Knowledge™ units; and • (+ Novel studies Grade 1 onwards).	30-40 min	40 min (+15 min Grade 5 onwards)

*Not usually daily, three times a week.

Notes:

- Individual times are approximate. Daily literacy for 2 hours at all year levels.
- Friday is a content review across the school which is a review with a weekly content carries out for assessment purposes.
- Knowledge rich curriculum content, adapted from Core Knowledge® is taught throughout the literacy block.

Story Example 7.2 - Example literacy block

Brandon Park Primary

Table 7.2 Brandon Park literacy block

<table>
<tr><th>Component</th><th>Daily Time First year of school-Grade 2</th><th>Daily Time Grades 3-6</th></tr>
<tr><td>Literacy Skills</td><td></td><td></td></tr>
<tr><td>Phonemic awareness (without letters)</td><td>3-4 min</td><td>1-2 min (if needed)</td></tr>
<tr><td>Word reading and spelling review</td><td>15 min</td><td>10 min</td></tr>
<tr><td>New spelling, morphology, and vocabulary lesson (PhOrMeS)*</td><td>15 min</td><td>20 min</td></tr>
<tr><td>Handwriting/keyboarding (in upper grades)</td><td colspan="2">10 min</td></tr>
<tr><td>Morphological awareness/Tier 2 vocabulary (linked to texts)</td><td>10 min</td><td>5 min</td></tr>
<tr><td>Sentence decoding and spelling (dictation) - (2 days per week)</td><td>6 min</td><td>2 min</td></tr>
<tr><td>Paired fluency reading</td><td colspan="2">10 min</td></tr>
<tr><td>Read to Learn (r2L: Listening and Reading Comprehension)</td><td></td><td></td></tr>
<tr><td>Reading comprehension lesson incorporating:
• Humanities and Sciences texts adapted from Core Knowledge® units and created in r2L project;
• Questioning the author; and
• Fiction/novel/poetry units.</td><td>30-40 min</td><td>50 min</td></tr>
<tr><td>Write to Learn (W2L; Oral and Written Expression)</td><td></td><td></td></tr>
<tr><td>W2L Lesson incorporating:
• Oral syntax development (first year);
• The Writing Revolution®;
• Writing about content from r2L units including Core Knowledge® units; and
• Genre level work including narrative, expository, persuasive, and creative writing.</td><td>35 min</td><td>40 min</td></tr>
</table>

*PhOrMeS is a free word reading and spelling curriculum which also includes morphology in Grades 3-6, developed by this chapter's second author, Shane Pearson.

Notes:

- Individual times are approximate. Daily literacy for 140-150 min per day.
- In the first year of school, the components of the literacy block are introduced incrementally to these students so that it is fully implemented by around end of term 2.

Whole class nearly always

As you may have noticed, a strong theme in this book is the untapped potential of whole class instruction as a cornerstone of your teaching. Sometimes shunned and relegated to 'mini-lessons' in past decades, interactive whole class instruction is one of the secrets to becoming an effective teacher. When implemented with responsiveness, pace, and fidelity, whole class teaching can dramatically improve student outcomes in literacy.

What should we teach or review next?

Scopes and sequences

Before we begin, it is important to flag that nearly all the below components need to be taught explicitly, systematically, and sequentially. Also, the role of daily and monthly review cannot be overstated. Clear and logical **scopes and sequences** are critical for this work.

Curriculum maps

Curriculum maps are like scopes and sequences but have a unit-by-unit focus and may be modular (the units can be swapped or reordered depending on the flow of the term or year). They differ from scopes and sequences, which are more linear as they progress from one set of skills/knowledge to the next.

Table 7.3 Scopes and sequences and curriculum maps.

Area	*Recommendation*	
	Scope and Sequence	*Curriculum Map*
Morpheme awareness + Tier 2 vocabulary (link to texts)	✓	
Word reading and spelling to Grade 3, including phonemic awareness	✓	
Spelling and vocabulary through morphology, from Grade 3		✓
Knowledge rich units		✓
Sentence and paragraph writing	✓	
Genre level writing	✓	

Note: We do not recommend schools start from scratch with their own scopes and sequences or curriculum maps. Adapt and adopt resources to make them work for your setting.

Word reading and spelling instruction

The below section includes areas critical for decoding and spelling instruction across a school: phonemic awareness, phonics, irregular words, orthography, morphology, etymology, and sentence reading and dictation.

Phonemic awareness instruction

The role of **phonemic awareness** in learning to read and spell is almost universally acknowledged even among balanced literacy advocates (Castles, Rastle, & Nation, 2018). However, teachers implementing structured literacy often spend time teaching students to identify and create rhymes and count or isolate syllables and words. This **phonological awareness** work is well-intentioned. However, there is only weak evidence that these syllable-level and 'word part' tasks are necessary to improve decoding or spelling proficiency (Brady, 2020).

> The ability to hear, identify, and manipulate individual sounds (phonemes) in spoken words

> The broad umbrella term which includes phonemic awareness of individual speech, sounds in words, as well as broader skills, like syllable, rhyme and word awareness

On the other hand, the evidence for *phonemic* awareness training–that is blending and segmenting individual speech sounds in words–is robust and also works to address the core phonemic challenge faced by many children at risk for dyslexia (Castles et al., 2018). We recommend that nearly all phonemic awareness work should be embedded within your core phonics and word reading/spelling lessons and that daily phonemic awareness warm-ups should be short and swift (2–3 min maximum; Erbeli et al., 2024).

Pro tip: Continuous blending

Some students show difficulty bridging the gap from 'sounding out' letters to blending words when learning to decode. They can label the individual sounds in a word, but struggle to blend them together. A tip to help such students is **continuous blending** (i.e., sat is sounded out as *sssssssaaaaaaaaat)*. When we model continuous blending (with no breaks between the phonemes in a word), it allows students to 'hear' the words they are trying to decode. This likely works because continuous blending mimics the coarticulation that happens when we say complete words.

> A way of sounding out the sounds in a word where the sounds blend into one another, making it easier to hear the target word

Decoding, spelling, and word recognition

Code knowledge

Explicit and systematic phonics teaching is critical for ensuring that *all* children learn to decode and spell words. Children should receive explicit instruction in **grapheme-phoneme correspondences** (GPCs). Graphemes should be introduced at a rate somewhere between two to six per week and follow a sequence of simple single-letter graphemes to more complex graphemes. These correspondences should be taught both ways–from letter to sound and sound to letter–so that children can use them to read and spell words.

> Sound letter patterns, for example the letters CH makes that /ch/ sound in <chip>

Phonics: Blending and segmenting words

Initial introduction of graphemes must be complemented by explicit instruction in the phonemic awareness skills of blending and segmenting. Using these skills, children learn to reliably decode short words by sounding out graphemes and blending them. Likewise, systematic phonics allows students to begin phonic spelling by breaking up spoken words into sounds and representing each sound with a grapheme (see Table 7.6).

As children's code knowledge and blending skills become automatised, they begin a process of remembering strings of letters, avoiding the need to laboriously sound out and blend. This process is called **orthographic mapping** and is required to read efficiently. In this way, early phonics teaching paves the way to improved reading fluency and comprehension over time.

When we have successfully decoded a word several times, it can be stored in long-term memory for almost automatic recognition. This process of bonding the letters to sounds and to the word's meaning is 'orthographic mapping'

What about words that don't fit the phonics sequence? – Irregular words

How do we get students reading and spelling words like 'was,' 'said' and 'are' when they don't follow simple phonics patterns? Additional brief, daily instruction and review of **irregular words** are also needed. Do not try and teach irregular words as wholes. Decode the parts of the word you can with students, and then highlight the 'weird' part that doesn't fit the rules/patterns they have been taught so far. We find that teaching two new irregular words every week is about right. A selection of these words should be reviewed daily via decoding and spelling as a group.

Words that do not confirm to basic sound-letter patterns. Note: Few words are truly irregular. Many irregular words are often explained later using advanced spelling conventions or by morphological pattern later in the sequence

Table 7.4 Example of irregular words

Example of irregular words with the weird part underlined	*When explained in some phonics sequences**
was	Grade 1
talk	Grade 1
their	Grade 2

*Source: PhOrMeS Word Reading and Spelling Curriculum.

Practice, practice, practice (the right things)

One of the biggest tasks missing from many literacy blocks is sufficient practice of decoding and spelling words. We are not referring here to copying out words, rainbow writing, or look-cover-write-check (these do not work). We are recommending modelling and practising the decoding and spelling of individual words.

The **mini-whiteboard** for practice is your friend. We need many, many words read and spelt by students every lesson, via sound-by-sound decoding and also spelling of individual words. It is this constant opportunity to decode and spell words in your phonics lessons that will move your students from novice to intermediate decoders and spellers.

A small dry erase board that can be used for individual responses to tasks

Morphological awareness and advanced spelling instruction

Spelling proficiency generally develops more slowly than decoding due to its more complex nature. To recall the spellings of tens of thousands of words, children require knowledge about phonics along with orthographic spelling patterns/rules and morphological awareness.

> The study of word forms and the rules for creating and understanding words. It involves knowledge of prefixes, suffixes, root words, and how they combine to form different words

Morphology relates to the underlying structure of meaningful word parts, or morphemes, in words. Morphology has a secondary role to *phonics* in learning to read words, so it is useful to introduce and review the most common prefixes and suffixes to early readers from the first year of school onwards.

Morphology is important for *word reading*, but it plays a *major* role in spelling development (Levesque et al., 2021). To teach morphology, explicit teaching of prefixes, suffixes, and base words is recommended. **Etymology**~ complements morphology teaching and should play a later role in any good spelling program.

> The study of word origins

Additionally, morphology assists *vocabulary development*. As an example, knowing that repayment consists of three morphemes re (again) + pay + ment (noun-forming suffix) will assist in both spelling and understanding this multi-syllabic word and many others like it.

Advanced spelling rules

Teaching orthographic spelling rules and patterns is another area that must be covered in a spelling curriculum. As English spelling has many layers, instruction in the orthographic conventions that govern spelling is essential to master this writing system (Stone, 2021). These advanced spelling patterns should be taught and practised (see Tables 7.5 and 7.6).

Table 7.5 Example of spelling rules and conventions from PhOrMeS curriculum.

Rule	*Example*
Spelling conventions	ck vs. k, using ck directly after a short vowel (lick vs. leek, pick vs. pink)
Silent final e (various types)	lik**e**, hav**e**, clu**e**, chanc**e**, larg**e**, littl**e**
Suffixing conventions	111 Rule: hop + ing → hop**p**ing Silent final e dropping rule: hope + ing → hoping vs. hope + ful → hopeful

Table 7.6 Literacy block component – Word reading and spelling (phonics plus)

	Daily Time Recommendation		
	First year of school-Grade 1	Grades 2–3	Grade 4 onwards
Review*	10–15 min	10 min	10 min
New lesson	15–20 min	15–20 min	15–20 min⁺

*Including irregular word reading and spelling.
+Includes morphology for spelling and vocabulary.

Table 7.7 Literacy block component - Sentence reading and spelling (writing from dictation).

Grade Levels	*Time Recommendation*	
	Sentence Decoding	*Sentence Spelling*
First year of school	1-2 min (2 days a week)	3-4 min (2 days a week)
Grades 1-2	1-2 min (3-4 days a week)	1-2 min (5 days a week)

Sentence reading and dictation

Practising decoding and spelling at the sentence level is another under-utilised teaching opportunity. Get your students decoding sentences and spelling sentences via dictation *within phonics lessons* at least weekly. This allows students to practise reading and spelling both regular and irregular words, as part of increasingly fluent reading and writing. This includes both *sentence decoding*, allowing students to transition from single word decoding to more fluent reading (Mackay et al., 2021), as well as *sentence spelling* (writing to dictation), where students generalise their spelling knowledge from the word level the sentence and paragraph (Robinson-Kooi & Hammond, 2020).

In dictation, start with short sentences. Along with spelling, students practice basic writing conventions without the cognitive load of idea generation (see Table 7.7).

Reading fluency

Reading fluency bridges the path from decoding to comprehension (Pikulski & Chard, 2005). Early decoding is extremely taxing work for children and leaves very little cognitive energy left for comprehending text (Hoover & Tunmer, 2022). As students become more proficient at decoding, they can spend more effort on reading with fluency and comprehension.

Box 7.2 - Reading fluency is a combination of accuracy, rate, and prosody

As an equation, we see it like this:

reading fluency = (accuracy + rate) + prosody.

Reading **accuracy** is improved by early phonics teaching and later practice learning more about morphologically complex words. Reading **rate** improves as words are increasingly orthographically mapped (automatically recognised).

To achieve **prosody**, students must have **syntactic awareness**, understanding of vocabulary and punctuation and adequate comprehension (Chan et al., 2020). Knowing

The ability to correctly read words and sentences

The speed at which words can be read accurately

The way in which a text can be spoken out loud with expression and clarity

The awareness of how words can be combined correctly to form different types of sentences and the ability to monitor and understand the order of and relationship between words, during reading and writing where to raise or lower pitch, place stress in a sentence, and pause and break sentences into phrases is connected to their language and reading comprehension.

A reading teaching practice where students take turns reading excerpts of a shared text aloud with a partner, and listen to each other read for 1-2 minutes at a time for a period of 10-15 minutes

Classroom routines for fluency

A practical classroom-based fluency technique is **paired fluency reading**. Reading **decodable text** (also known as phonically-controlled text) in paired fluency reading is recommended for early readers.

Books designed to match the phonics skills (sound-letter patterns) that students have been learning. They are short stories or non-fiction texts that contain only simple sound-letter patterns in them and help develop reading fluency by allowing students to practice word recognition and independent reading

For accurate decoders, this routine typically uses passages or whole texts from the reading content being studied in class. Before students can read words and sentences accurately, fluency can still be practiced in paired fluency, albeit, at the grapheme and single word level. A bridging practice is the use of fluency triangles, where fluency is practised from the single word incrementally up to phrase and sentence (see the text *Reading Pathways*, by Dolores G. Hiskes).

A teaching practice in which students read the same texts multiple times to improve their reading fluency

A reading fluency teaching practice in which students repeat segments of text. After hearing a fluent reader read each segment

Additional techniques like **repeated reading** and **echo reading** can also boost reading fluency for some students, including on prosody (Kuhn, 2014).

Story Example 7.3 – Reading fluency at Challis Community Primary

Early in Challis' science of reading journey, reading fluency was never taught or practised strategically. Staff were aware that many students were slow, inaccurate, and dysfluent readers but had no reliable method to change this. In years gone by, guided reading was a big feature of the literacy block with 'carousel-style' rotations between groups at different 'levels,' with groups doing what could have been described as 'busy work' when they were not with the teacher.

After Challis began using a systematic and science of reading-aligned approach to phonics, word reading, and spelling, there was an improvement in fluency; then paired fluency reading was introduced as a whole class instructional strategy. Fluency routines were taught and coached, and running the daily routine as a whole class meant all students benefitted.

When teaching fluency was rolled out across the school, teacher and student buy-in was instant, and it very soon became a highlight of the day. Challis Primary now ensures all students access the same text; and these passages or excerpts often have content links to another curriculum area (e.g., reading of poetry, humanities, or sciences topics). Both confidence and results have improved over time, as have the school's use of assessment methods for better identification of students at risk (e.g., DIBELS® passage reading fluency).

Foundational writing instruction

Learning *oral* language is a naturally acquired, biologically primary process. Learning to write, however, is not. Writing can be difficult due to the complexity of spelling. Also, constructing sentences using the more grammatically complex **syntax** found in written expression is heavy work for most children and also requires explicit instruction (Hochman & Wexler, 2017).

Refers to the rules and structure of how words are combined to form meaningful sentences in a language. It involves understanding the order of words, the use of grammar, and the relationships between different parts of a sentence

While the end goal is to assign children open-ended writing tasks that challenge them to use their creativity and develop unique ideas, children also need mastery of the written sentence skills required to express such ideas as they intend.

Explicit handwriting instruction

Explicit handwriting instruction is beneficial for spelling and writing development. The end goal of handwriting teaching is accurate, efficient letter formation. Handwriting is primarily a task-specific **fine motor skill** (Suggate et al., 2023), which means that children should do specific practice *handwriting letters and numerals with pencil in hand on paper* as opposed to doing other activities that are 'about' handwriting (e.g., making letters with playdough).

Skills involving the movement and control of small muscles, such as fingers and hands

Daily handwriting routines

We recommend that handwriting should be taught and practised in isolation for 10–15 minutes daily, until students exhibit mastery. Correct pencil grip and handwriting posture must be taught and reinforced. Explicitly teaching and executing the movements required for correct formation and sizing for every letter is critical, as is reinforcing neat, legible handwriting during all writing tasks.

Sentence and paragraph modelling and teaching

Writing is one of the most complex skills we ask students to complete (Hochman & Wexler, 2017). In typical classrooms, students are asked to write authentic, whole pieces early, even before they have gathered much proficiency in handwriting or spelling. This method of

Table 7.8 Literacy block component - Handwriting practice.

Grade Levels	*Daily Time Recommendation*	
	Explicit modelling and guided practice on mini-whiteboards	*Monitored, independent handwriting practice on sheets or exercise books*
First year of school	3 min	7-12 min
Grade 1	1-2 min	8-9 min
Grades 2-3	1 min print handwriting OR 3-4 min cursive	9 min print handwriting OR 7-10 min cursive
Grade 4 onwards	2-3 min cursive + Remedial modelling and time for students who need it	8-12 min cursive

'assigning' whole text writing comes from a belief that students learn to write by doing lots of writing. Assigning writing tasks without providing appropriate instruction in sentences and paragraphs can promote poor writing habits that become embedded and difficult to remediate. These can include run-ons (unpunctuated sentences), stream-of-consciousness writing, and repetitive sentence structures.

There are therefore intermediate steps between ideation and full text composition. The sentence is the crucial building block and could be analogised as doing for writing what phonics does for reading comprehension. Organisations like The Writing Revolution® have helped to emphasise the importance of sentence level instruction as a building block towards paragraph and text level composition. Any strong writing curriculum should consider how to improve students' sentence level composition.

Box 7.3 - Key example sentence writing strategies from The Writing Revolution®.

- Sentence expansion, and completion (e.g., because, but, so);
- Sentence types;
- Sentence combining;
- Subordinating conjunctions (e.g., if, when, after, even though);
- Appositives (e.g., 'Maria, a strong-spirited woman, rose to the challenge'; and
- Transition words (e.g., however, for instance, nevertheless).

One of the greatest benefits of an increased focus on improving the command of sentences is the reduction of cognitive load. Students with better sentence-writing ability can better articulate and express their ideas in academic language as their working memory is allowed to focus on the *complexity of the content*, rather than the mechanics of foundational skills.

Paragraph planning and writing

Regarding paragraphs, there are numerous paragraph structures and planning processes that can **scaffold** students to write cohesive paragraphs. The single paragraph outline (SPO) is a *revolutionary* concept outlined in the Hochman method (Hochman & Wexler, 2017), which involves the explicit teaching of crafting and revising **topic sentences**, including relevant **supporting details**, and constructing **concluding sentences** that succinctly re-state the main idea of the paragraph.

Support provided to learners to enable them to complete learning tasks; intended to be faded out over time

The opening sentence of a paragraph which contains the main contention of that section of writing

Explanations, examples, and evidence that support the topic sentence

The final sentence in a paragraph, closing the ideas in this part of the text

Story Example 7.4 – Sentences are the phonics for writing – Churchill Primary

A few years into their science of learning transformation, Churchill Primary turned their attention to student writing. They had seen massive improvements in decoding, spelling, and fluency so far, and the staff wanted their successes to transfer to writing. Student writing at Churchill had traditionally focussed on freeform, personal narratives, and a largely Writer's Workshop approach.

Previously, there was not much explicit attention to the syntactical or genre structure or quality, and it was not until the teachers undertook The Writing Revolution® training that they realised that most of their students did not have the awareness or command of a basic sentence. Most student compositions were riddled with fragments (unfinished sentences) and run-ons (unpunctuated sentences), making them difficult pieces to read.

Like many other early adopter schools of The Writing Revolution® (TWR) in Australia to undertake this incredibly useful professional learning, the staff at Churchill had to get up at 2 or 3am on a weekly basis to access it on Zoom. (One staff member at Brandon Park who also did this work pattern came down with shingles in this month-long endeavour.)

Despite the pressures on health and wellbeing, what Churchill learned when undertaking this new approach (that aligns well with the limits of student working memory) that sentences are like the *phonics of writing*, and without mastering how to craft useful, meaningful, and well-structured sentences, it was pointless to send students off to write narratives or persuasive texts at length. After training all their staff in the method, Churchill developed a scope and sequence from school entry to Grade 6, and began to explicitly teach and embed the sentence strategies, ensuring they applied them to the content they were learning in literature, humanities, and science units.

They began retrieval practice of these in daily reviews, and also incorporated the strategies in checking for understanding (CFU) questions in every subject.

The school, alongside similar work at Brandon Park and Bentleigh West, began using comparative judgement via No More Marking to assess writing more objectively, and used these data to drive further improvement at the sentence, paragraph, and then whole text (genre) level. The school has seen a distinct jump in its writing standardised testing data, especially from 2019 to 2021 following the TWR training and implementation in 2020 onwards.

Knowledge and language building

Vocabulary

Teaching vocabulary explicitly improves reading comprehension and writing outcomes for students. Knowing the meanings of words in a passage gives students a good chance of comprehending the passage; while the possession of large vocabularies allows them to increase variety and specificity in their writing.

Vocabulary is best learned in context rather than as an isolated list of words. In selecting vocabulary targets, knowledge of the three tiers of vocabulary words is important (Beck et al., 2013). In this book, the authors describe three different tiers of words. Simple **Tier 1 words** are found in everyday language and need not be taught explicitly unless there are concerns with English language exposure, that is when you have a high number of students speaking English as an Additional Language or Dialect (EAL/D). **Tier 2 words** will be best taught within English lessons from narratives or literature being studied, as well as through targeted review and application activities after their initial introduction with texts (see Beck et al., 2013). **Tier 3 words** are best tackled as they occur in specific content areas like science, geography, and history.

Every day, commonplace vocabulary that should be picked up by nearly all students through socialisation

Academic or lower frequency vocabulary that has broad applications across many subject areas

Curriculum specific terminology that is tied to a narrow set of domains or single subject

The following activities are likely to assist children in retaining new vocabulary.

Box 7.4 - Vocabulary building tasks and practices

- Practice pronouncing the word multiple times;
- Read the printed word;
- Spell the word;
- Link it to morphological word families;
- Encounter and read the word in multiple instances within different contexts;

- Link the new word to other words that are related or distinct in meaning;
- Ask students to engage in meaningful activities where they actively use words (see Beck et al., 2013);
- Systematically review newly and previously taught words.

Once students learn to read, most of their new vocabulary learning occurs implicitly while reading. Teaching children how to infer meaning of unknown words in text using context is also important so that children learn to *self-teach* new vocabulary.

As we will review in the next section, vocabulary is best learned and remembered during knowledge building when connected to concepts and ideas being taught systematically. This is because words need to be connected to a developing **schema** in students' long-term memory.

A mental representation or framework for understanding an area of learning

Pro tip: Teach fewer words and review

It is easy to get ambitious, but with vocabulary teaching, less is indeed much, much more. In our initial vocabulary sequence at Brandon Park, we tried teaching five to ten Tier 2 words every week. Successfully reviewing that many words was difficult. Children learned target words in the moment, but often did not retain them later.

We recommend *three to four specific words a week* (most should come from and be reinforced within the rich texts you are reading). The important point here is that this allows for lots of review (yesterday, last week, last month, last term) to dull the effects of the **forgetting curve** (see Table 7.9).

The phenomenon in which learners tend to immediately forget most of what they have learnt previously, with sharp declines over time, unless content is reviewed

Knowledge-building and comprehension strategies

An under-utilised area of literacy teaching is knowledge building. Connected to vocabulary teaching, we should not just be *activating (background) knowledge*, but *actively building (new) knowledge* with students (Cabell & Hwang, 2020). We need to think hard about how we can systematically build students' knowledge of the world and word (see chapter 9).

Table 7.9 Literacy block component – Vocabulary teaching and review.

	Daily Time Recommendation		*Incidental Teaching*
Focus	New vocabulary teaching	Previous review (yesterday, last week, last month, and last term).	See if students recall it (turn and talk, then cold call). Draw attention to it. Link it.
How much?	5 min (3–4 new words a week)	Only do 3–4 words per review.	Whenever the word comes up. In conversation, discussion, or text reading/writing.

We want students to inquire about and critique into many areas of the curriculum, but fundamentally they should *inquire from a place of knowledge*. By building up students' knowledge of rich subject content, we ensure that their independent reading and investigation is fruitful (see chapter 4).

Comprehension strategy instruction

There is strong evidence for the use of **comprehension strategies** (e.g., Sun et al., 2021). However, the evidence is for relatively short bursts of intervention. In many classrooms today, strategy instruction has taken over as *the* main form of instruction to embed in balanced literacy activities (e.g., reading rotations and guided reading groups). Time is limited. If we fill all our explicit teaching and practice time with the strategy of the week/month, what is being left out?

Metacognitive strategies for comprehension such as predicting, summarising, inferring, connecting, and monitoring comprehension

Box 7.5 – Learning to infer for the sake of inferring

One of the lightbulb moments I had many years ago working with students with reading difficulties after school is that the focus of their main literacy lesson was on the wrong things. When I took students for after school tutoring, every session I would ask them what they learnt about in literacy that day. Here is how many of these conversations went.

Tutor: What did you learn about today?
Student: umm. We did inf . . . inferring.
Tutor: Awesome. I love practising inferring. What were you inferring about?
Student: umm.
Tutor: Do remember what you were reading about?
Student: umm. I remember that we needing to practice inferring.
Tutor: I see.

We know that students' working memory is limited. If we focus their attention too much on the **meta-cognition** of reading (the strategy), and not enough on the cognition (the content about which we read), then we lose the very meaning in comprehension teaching.

The ability to think about and reflect upon one's own thinking and learning processes

What is typically left out is the chance to build concepts and understandings about the actual texts we are reading and the knowledge bases that sit behind them. Always bring the focus back to the meaning in the text.

Table 7.10 Literacy block component - Comprehension strategies introduction and modelling.

What	*Key comprehension strategies:* *Inferring, Predicting, Summarising, Connecting, Monitoring Comprehension*	
Two modes	**Explicit modelling and practice**	**Incidental teaching and practice**
When	Aim for one new model a few times every term (15 min short lesson).	Whenever you can—during read-alouds and shared reading, and independent reading.
How	• Explicit explanation, model; • Guided practice on example text (all on same or similar text/topic).	• Model and demonstrate; • Think aloud using strategy; • Show how to comprehend portion of text.
Caveats	• Don't stay on the same strategy for a whole term; • Don't make the focus on 'predicting' (for example) for the week/fortnight; • Introduce it and then model incidentally (see right).	• Keep the focus on the actual content; • The goal is to comprehend text, not to go through the motions of the strategy.

Pro tip: Introduce and explain, then model and demonstrate during actual reading

After the initial introduction of a comprehension strategy, incidental modelling and practice is the most important way to get students reading with understanding. And we need students to keep in mind *what* they are reading about, not just *what skill* they are trying to practice.

Text-level comprehension and written expression

The powers of whole class text-level instruction

In the reading space, **whole class reading** experiences are often reduced to mini-lessons, or distracted with long discussions about the front/back cover, or predictions about the text. When teaching writing, many teachers make use of mentor texts, asking students to use authorial elements from the text in their own written expression.

A teaching practice in which the whole class participates in the reading and unpacking of a text together, facilitated by the teacher

The overall structure of the text, for example, narrative genre has a story grammar macro structure, whereas an information text may have a compare and contrast macro structure

However, deep, whole class facilitation of comprehension and guided practice in the composition of texts is often missing from instruction. We can exploit whole class instruction to support *all* students' understanding and use of the **macro-structure** of texts, along with micro-language features such as vocabulary choice, metaphor, simile, and onomatopoeia to name a few.

What about guided reading?

A mainstay of balanced literacy classrooms, **guided reading** may be a fundamental practice at your school (Richardson, 2009). There is nothing problematic about working with individuals or small groups on reading fluency or comprehension). However, it is arguably difficult to ensure that students are spending their time wisely when we are not working directly with them (e.g., long periods doing independent reading, or literacy rotations/groups). So, if your literacy block predominantly features group rotations, consider how you can spend more time supporting students in larger groups, or at the whole class level.

A popular teaching practice involving small group, or individual conferencing with students, talking about a text, reading a text, or teaching a reading skill

Read-alouds, shared reading, and independent reading

What is crucial for teaching students' text-level reading comprehension? Reading language-rich and knowledge-rich texts as a whole group. This is important, as the teacher needs to facilitate students' understanding of complex text by:

- explaining new vocabulary;
- showing relationships between sentences;
- completing checking for understanding tasks; and
- being responsive to students' understanding in real-time.

This will allow students to begin to access more challenging and enriching texts. Over time, this propels competency in their own reading. In **read-alouds**, teachers can harness students' innate abilities to engross themselves in stories, and learn from the knowledge sharing of an expert reading to them.

A teaching practice where the teacher or a student reads a shared text out loud so that it can be understood and discussed by the group

In **shared reading** experiences, teachers and students take turns reading or chorally reading texts together, interspersed with checking for understanding, pair shares, discussions, and short written tasks. Practices for whole class comprehension, like in Questioning the Author (QtA; Beck et al., 2020) or Reading Reconsidered (Lemov et al., 2016), provide techniques for rich engagement with text and scaffolding by the teacher and peers.

A teaching practice where teachers and students share a text, taking turns reading segments and discussing the text

Using *high-quality literature* is crucial here, and your curriculum map should include a range of:

- picture books and/or graphic novels;
- short stories;
- novels;
- poetry; and
- non-fiction (these can relate to or can be drawn from your knowledge-rich units for science, humanities, and the arts).

Table 7.11 Literacy block component - Read aloud, shared reading, and close reading (see Such, 2021) including knowledge-rich and literature units.

Grade Levels	*Daily Time Recommendation*
First year of school	20 min
Grade 1	25 min
Grades 2-3	30-40 min
Years 4 onwards	40-50 min

A reading practice undertaken by students without peer or educator support

Students reading texts independently followed by short tasks or discussion prompts to assess whether effective reading is actually happening

Ensure students are released to **independent reading** too, but implement **accountable independent reading** practices (see Lemov et al., 2016) including reading partners, groups, or written tasks following periods of reading, to ensure students are actively engaged during these times. As mentioned above, **comprehension strategies** should be instigated, modelled, and reinforced through these text experiences.

Metacognitive strategies for comprehension such as predicting, summarising, inferring, connecting, and monitoring comprehension

Genre and text level writing

Writing practices and the link to subject content

Writing at the text-level is underpinned by foundational spelling, as well as sentence and paragraph writing skills. The following key practices provide an idea of how you might structure your text or genre-level instruction, perhaps the pinnacle of written language teaching.

Genre level teaching

Text types that tell a story to the reader, and may be structured, using a story grammar framework, including characters, setting, problem, plan of action, resolution

An information text, such as a report, explanation, or descriptive piece

For **narrative genres** (stories, recounts), a game-changing and simple framework for macrostructure is **Story Grammar** (Stein & Glenn, 1975), found in free resources like our own Write to Learn, and commercial programs like Story Champs. For **expository genres** (informative, persuasive), the Multiple Paragraph Outline (MPO) is an ingenious way of planning long-form compositions including essays and reports (see Hochman & Wexler, 2017).

Story Example 7.5 - Reading, discussing and writing about rich texts together - Yates Avenue, Riverwood, and Brandon Park

Many schools may feel 'afraid' to disrupt guided reading in their classrooms. Yates Avenue Public School, along with Riverwood and Brandon Park had many staff who were wary about making changes to guided reading. They also did not know how to make whole class reading and writing work initially. The guided reading groups often provided a sense of *safety* for teachers, who enjoyed being able to conference with individuals or small groups regularly. Although the independent reading time or other rotations that took place during conferencing were not always productive for all students, it did create a sense of choice and agency.

When Brandon Park considered moving from a mini-lesson into its fully-fledged Read to Learn (R2L) whole class text reading and responding sessions, there were a core group of teachers who feared what they would lose without that regular check in to ensure students were still reading well.

Despite this, in all three schools, the change to whole class teaching and away from reading or writing workshops provided:

- more time overall with the teacher and the core instruction;
- greater equity of opportunity to hear proficient reading from peers, and how to make sense of and connect with complex texts, instead of just their levelled group and levelled books;
- a deeper understanding of novels and complex texts for all students, with targeted instruction and guided practice in comprehension and writing skills as well as content knowledge;
- more time to introduce concepts and vocabulary from the texts being read and analysed, and a chance to share a text or writing experience together (in contrast to every student pursuing solitary reading or writing);
- clearer connections between reading and writing lessons;
- richer discussions about content within texts, and application of comprehension and writing strategies for authentic reasons; and
- instruction and practice in reading and writing (and oral language, including vocabulary) as mutually reinforcing skills, thereby strengthening comprehension and written instruction.

While there is less individualised conferencing in all three schools now, there is greater teacher knowledge of the role of vocabulary, content knowledge, syntax, and vocabulary instruction for proficient reading and writing. This knowledge has led to school-wide reading and writing practices that ensure coherent teaching of rich texts.

In these schools, teachers still hear individual students read and support them as they used to during guided reading, but this is in a more targeted and needs-based way. Also, they no longer expect that 10–15 minutes of conferencing could replace the high-quality hours of teaching reading and writing as a group. Now the choice and individualisation for students happens in what they *make* of texts, and what they do with their *own writing*. Each student is afforded an *equality of opportunity* to access instruction and support to analyse and create rich and complex texts—not just the levelled book or open-ended writing task they used to get.

Classroom practices for text-level writing

Modelled writing and **shared writing** can be helpful to bridge the gap between mentor texts and students' own writing choices. Whenever facilitating such writing experiences, it is important to **think aloud** the steps and decisions you are making. Break down the entire text-writing process by modelling example segments of writing, and then provide time for guided practice on mini-whiteboards or paper where students practice this same step. In doing so, you can monitor, highlight, and support students as they learn the intermediate steps towards drafting full pieces.

A teaching practice in which the teacher demonstrates an aspect of writing, or the writing process for students

A teaching practice in which teachers and students construct a written text together

Involves the teacher saying out loud the thinking processes used by a proficient learner as they go about a task (e.g., reading, writing, or solving a problem in mathematics). The teacher's goal is to show the students how to undertake the task or skill themselves

Crucially, you want students to work towards completing cycles of ideation, planning, drafting, and revising (see Self-Regulated Strategy Development; e.g., Salas et al., 2021). Hochman and Wexler (2017) maintain that the two most important stages are not drafting, but planning and revising. It is your job to ensure your students are supported to engage in all these phases of writing with care and adequate prior knowledge.

After students have completed guided practice of these small steps and are therefore ready for independent writing tasks, teachers should circulate, monitor, and troubleshoot when students are stuck.

In Table 7.12, we have provided an indication of average weekly minutes to be spent at sentence, paragraph, and genre level across the primary school years.

Concluding thoughts

Above we have synthesised some key ideas on how reading and writing can be taught to align with the sciences of reading and learning, as well as our own recommendations for managing

Table 7.12 Literacy block component - Sentence, paragraph, and genre level oral and written expression.

	*Time Recommendation in Average Minutes per week**			
Grade	*Sentence level*	*Paragraph level*	*Genre level*	*Total on oral and written expression***
First year of school	100 min	20 min	15 min	135 min per week
Grade 1	115 min	35 min	30 min	180 min per week
Grades 2–3	90 min	50 min	60 min	200 min per week
Grade 4 onwards	45 min	70 min	120 min	235 min per week

*These times are indicative only and may equate to a daily session, a few sessions a week, or distinct units through a term, depending on the grade level and activity. The times are intended to show and increase in the amount of writing over the grade levels, and also the move from more sentence, then more paragraph, then more genre level writing over the grades.

**This time could be used in distinct lessons on writing at these levels, or in writing tasks embedded within reading comprehension, humanities, sciences, etc.

Table 7.13 Chapter 7 knowledge organiser.

1. Word reading, spelling, and fluency instruction	***2. Foundational writing instruction***
• Explicit and systematic instruction of letter-sound relationships. • Systematic, synthetic phonics teaching for decoding unfamiliar words. • Advanced spelling and morphological awareness.	• Mastering handwriting. • Sentence level work. • Paragraph planning and writing.
3. Knowledge and language building	***4. Text level comprehension and written expression***
• Vocabulary teaching that is explicit, contextualised, and reviewed. • Comprehension strategies explicitly introduced and then modelled and practised in shared texts.	• Read-alouds, shared reading and independent reading. • Genre features for fiction and non-fiction.

your time and efforts. By taking a pragmatic and research-informed approach to English curriculum and instruction, teachers can ensure each student becomes a lifelong reader and writer.

Where to next?

Phonics and morphology

- PhOrMeS (a free resource for teaching **Ph**onics, **M**orphemes, **O**rthography, **E**tymology and **S**emantics) by Shane Pearson
- *University of Florida Literacy Institute (UFLI)* teaching resources
- *Effective instruction in reading and spelling* by Wheldall, Wheldall & Buckingham
- *Let's decode* by Lorraine Hammond
- *Reading for life* and *Spelling for life (2nd Ed.)* by Lyn Stone
- *Beneath the surface of words* by Sue Hegland
- *The morphology project*, now on Ochre Education

English and writing

- *The Writing Revolution®* training and book
- The Syntax Project, now on Ochre Education
- *Write to learn*, nathanielswain.com
- *Language for life*, by Lyn Stone
- *Bookworms K-5 reading & writing*

English literature

- *Reading reconsidered*
- *Questioning the author*
- English Novel Study units on Ochre Education
- *Core Knowledge*¨ English Language Arts

Check your indicators - Effective literacy teaching

On-Track Indicators	*Off-Track Indicators*
• Explicit systematic synthetic phonics instruction based on scope and sequence. • Teaching advanced spelling conventions and morphological knowledge. • Effective whole class modelling and practice, and paired fluency practice, including one-on-one conferencing during this time. • Explicit teaching and mastery of handwriting. • Sentence-level instruction focus. • Explicit vocabulary teaching with frequent review. • Explicit modelling of comprehension strategies and guided practice on texts. • Analysing and composing texts using genre features.	• Teaching phonics and word structures mainly as part of shared reading, guided reading, or independent reading. • Significant time on independent reading, or in group rotations. • Assigning writing tasks of texts before students have command of sentences and paragraphs. • Infrequent review and application of vocabulary. • Limited or no use of read-alouds and shared reading with high-quality literature.

Discussion questions

1. Why is explicit and systematic instruction of letter-sound relationships essential in word reading, spelling, and fluency instruction?
2. How does the mastery of handwriting, sentence-level skills, and paragraph planning contribute to overall writing proficiency?
3. How could your comprehension strategies and other elements above be more effectively introduced, modelled, and embedded to enhance understanding and engagement with rich texts?

References

Beck, I. L., McKeown, M. G., & Kucan, L. (2013). *Bringing words to life: Robust vocabulary instruction.* Guilford Press.

Beck, I. L., McKeown, M. G., & Sandora, C. A. (2020). *Robust comprehension instruction with questioning the author.* Guilford Publications.

Brady, S. (2020). A 2020 perspective on research findings on alphabetics (phoneme awareness and phonics): Implications for instruction (expanded version). *The Reading League Journal, 1*(3), 20–28.

Cabell, S. Q., & Hwang, H. (2020). Building content knowledge to boost comprehension in the primary grades. *Reading Research Quarterly, 55*, S99-S107.

Castles, A., Rastle, K., & Nation, K. (2018). Ending the reading wars: Reading acquisition from novice to expert. *Psychological Science in the Public Interest, 19*(1), 5–51.

Chan, J. S., Wade-Woolley, L., Heggie, L., & Kirby, J. R. (2020). Understanding prosody and morphology in school-age children's reading. *Reading and Writing, 33*, 1295–1324.

Erbeli, F., Rice, M., Xu, Y., Bishop, M. E., & Goodrich, J. M. (2024). A meta-analysis on the optimal cumulative dosage of early phonemic awareness instruction. *Scientific Studies of Reading, 28*(4), 345–370.

Hochman, J. C., & Wexler, N. (2017). *The writing revolution: A guide to advancing thinking through writing in all subjects and grades.* John Wiley & Sons.

Hoover, W. A., & Tunmer, W. E. (2022). The primacy of science in communicating advances in the science of reading. *Reading Research Quarterly*, *57*(2), 399–408.

Kuhn, M., Rasinski, T., & Zimmerman, B. (2014). Integrated fluency instruction: Three approaches for working with struggling readers. *International Electronic Journal of Elementary Education*, *7*(1), 71–82.

Lemov, D., Driggs, C., & Woolway, E. (2016). *Reading reconsidered: A practical guide to rigorous literacy instruction*. John Wiley & Sons.

Levesque, K. C., Breadmore, H. L., & Deacon, S. H. (2021). How morphology impacts reading and spelling: Advancing the role of morphology in models of literacy development. *Journal of Research in Reading*, *44*(1), 10–26.

Mackay, E., Lynch, E., Sorenson Duncan, T., & Deacon, S. H. (2021). Informing the science of reading: Students' awareness of sentence-level information is important for reading comprehension. *Reading Research Quarterly*, *56*, S221-S230.

Pikulski, J. J., & Chard, D. J. (2005). Fluency: Bridge between decoding and reading comprehension. *The Reading Teacher*, *58*(6), 510-519.

Richardson, J. (2009). *The next step in guided reading*. Scholastic.

Robinson-Kooi, S., & Hammond, L. S. (2020). Using sentence dictation to practise and assess taught spelling and punctuation skills: A Year 2 explicit instruction intervention. *Australian Journal of Learning Difficulties*, *25*(1), 83-108.

Salas, N., Birello, M., & Ribas, T. (2021). Effectiveness of an SRSD writing intervention for low-and high-SES children. *Reading and Writing*, *34*(7), 1653-1680.

Scarborough, H. S. (2001). Connecting early language and literacy to later reading (dis)abilities: Evidence, theory, and practice. In S. Neuman, & D. Dickinson (Eds.), *Handbook for research in early literacy*. Guilford Press

Stein, N. L., & Glenn, C. G. (1975). A developmental study of children's recall of story material. *SRCD Conference*. Denver, Colorado.

Stone, L. (2021). *Spelling for life: Uncovering the simplicity and science of spelling*. 2nd Edition. Routledge.

Such, C. (2021). *The art and science of teaching primary reading*. Corwin.

Suggate, S. P., Karle, V. L., Kipfelsberger, T., & Stoeger, H. (2023). The effect of fine motor skills, handwriting, and typing on reading development. *Journal of Experimental Child Psychology*, *232*, 105674.

Sun, Y., Wang, J., Dong, Y., Zheng, H., Yang, J., Zhao, Y., & Dong, W. (2021). The relationship between reading strategy and reading comprehension: A meta-analysis. *Frontiers in Psychology*, *12*, 635289.

Wheldall, K., Wheldall, R., & Buckingham, J. (2023). *Effective instruction in reading and spelling*. MRU Press.

8 Effective mathematics teaching

David Morkunas, Toni Hatten-Roberts and Nathaniel Swain

We now turn to the specific body of knowledge and practices which teachers can use to ensure all students become budding and proficient mathematicians. As with reading, there is indeed a science of mathematics (Science of Math, 2023), a body of scientific knowledge concerning how the brain masters this incredible human creation.

The term *mathematics* shall be used here, rather than *numeracy*. While numeracy serves a useful role in describing how number sense can be used to benefit our daily lives and work, mathematics is a stronger term, which allows us to talk particularly about the knowledge and skills we want students to master. This section is broken into six main components (see Box 8.1) which represent key actions for mathematics teachers to better make use of the under-utilised insights from the science of learning.

Box 8.1 - Chapter 8 Overview - Key aspects of improving mathematics teaching in line with the science of learning

- Teaching concepts through well-learned procedures and facts;
- Laying the foundations for number sense;
- Teaching standard algorithms for the four operations;
- Scaffolding problem solving using visual representations;
- Using precise mathematical vocabulary;
- Review and retrieval practice.

Teaching concepts through well-learned procedures and facts

Current popular thinking in mathematics education is dominated by a 'concept before procedure approach' (Kamii & Joseph, 2004), where teachers should ensure students have **conceptual understanding** *before* they are ever introduced to procedures or **algorithms** to solve problems. In this view, teachers expect students to come up with their own **informal strategies** and to seek multiple methods for solving problems, usually before they have ever seen a worked example (Van de Walle et al., 2019).

A term often used in mathematics referring to understanding of the key underlying concepts of an area of study

In mathematics, an algorithm is a step-by-step procedure or set of rules used to solve a mathematical problem or perform a calculation

Strategies aside from formal algorithms, such as drawing or visualising the problem

DOI: 10.4324/9781003404965-10

Despite the popularity of this 'conceptual first' approach, the evidence suggests that conceptual understanding and **procedural fluency** develop together via a two-way relationship (VanDerHeyden & Codding, 2020). When students can recall mathematical facts and procedures fluently from memory (e.g., for the **four operations**), new concepts are more easily attained and teaching mathematics becomes efficient and effective (Fuchs et al., 2021). In this way, teaching conceptual and procedural knowledge together can help strengthen both aspects over time.

Knowledge and competency in performing mathematical procedures

Addition, subtraction, multiplication, division

> *Algorithms are like phonics skills in reading. They work because of mathematical laws. They can be proofed and unpacked.*
>
> (VanDerHeyden & Codding, 2020)

Use manipulatives with care: Manage extraneous load

The default position in recent years has been a conceptual understanding first approach, pushing away procedures (algorithms) or learning of mathematical facts (NCTM, 2023). A big focus on **manipulatives** may be the norm, for example, showing mathematical relationships using teddy bears. This is without ever daring to have students write or view a standard algorithm (e.g., 4 + 5 = 9).

Hands-on resources used in mathematics education

However, manipulatives, when not managed well, can become a potential distractor for learning—as the students incorporate them into imaginative play rather than *use* them for a mathematical purpose. We know that manipulatives can help with certain concepts, but teachers should not forget the potential **extraneous load** involved with these materials (Vassar, 2017). Teachers today are likely to try to develop students' conceptual understanding alone in the early years, and avoid procedures or number facts.

Instead, when procedural and conceptual knowledge is taught in tandem, these two areas can mutually strengthen one another. **Algorithms**, for example, are the step-by-step procedures that add to the scaffolding needed to break down mathematical ideas necessary for solving any problem.

The kind of cognitive load that takes students' cognitive energy away from the task at hand. This is to do with the manner or structure of instruction

In mathematics, an algorithm is a step-by-step procedure or set of rules used to solve a mathematical problem or perform a calculation

Story Example 8.1 - Bentleigh West - Concepts supported by procedures, and vice versa

As one of the top performing primary schools for mathematics in the state, Bentleigh West knows a thing or two about getting students proficient with conceptual understanding. Their results have not always been like this. Before their science of learning journey, students spent more time working through less specific, more open-ended approaches; some became masterful mathematicians, and other students did not.

One aspect that has supported Bentleigh West's shift to an excellent and equitable delivery of mathematics education is the debunking of the myth that the memorisation of mathematical procedures and facts interfere with students' understanding of concepts. Instead, the school has found that ensuring a firm foundation of procedures and fact fluency *facilitates* understanding of the concepts behind them, which in combination then furthers students' abilities in problem solving.

The school has observed that ensuring students are procedurally fluent has also allowed for greater attention to the structure of problems and how best to identify potential solutions. With a firm focus on daily review, explicit teaching, and guided practice of the building blocks of mathematical concepts *and* algorithms and facts, Bentleigh West have seen their standard of mathematics attainment shift, so that Grade 2–6 students are being taught around 18–24 months ahead than stipulated in the curriculum. This is because teaching at the typical level would be dead-boringly easy. Diversity amongst learners always exist (though all but a handful of students perform at or above grade level for mathematics). However, by using **'built-in differentiation'** (see EDI; Hollingsworth & Ybarra, 2017) as well as **adaptive teaching** (see chapter 11), students are given additional support (or extension) where needed, during the flow of the lesson. At Bentleigh West the energy around mathematics is palpable—fun, exciting, and a challenge worth the effort. Students reached this position following the explicit instruction and daily practice for concepts *and* procedures, and much less initial time focussed on letting students struggle to figure things out.

Embedding differing levels of challenge and support into the main, whole-class lesson, to allow students to experience success at various levels

An alternative to differentiated lessons; in adaptive teaching, whole class teaching is planned, and teachers make real-time adjustments for learners based on checking for understanding tasks

Deep conceptual understanding is reinforced by procedural and fact fluency

Mathematical concept knowledge is crucial for accessing understandings within this subject. Students need to understand these concepts deeply, and not just by rote. However, deep understanding is predicated on the accumulation of pertinent facts and procedures in long-term memory (Willingham, 2002).

Students who have well-rehearsed facts and processes can deploy these quickly and accurately, but they can also use such pieces of information to generalise to other areas of mathematics understanding (see Torbeyns & Verschaffel, 2016). By modelling the **think aloud** for algorithms (with precise mathematical language), teachers can support conceptual understanding and procedural fluency simultaneously (see Figure 8.1).

Involves the teacher saying out loud the thinking processes used by a proficient learner as they go about a task (e.g., reading, writing, or solving a problem in mathematics). The teacher's goal is to show the students how to undertake the task or skill themselves

Visual representation

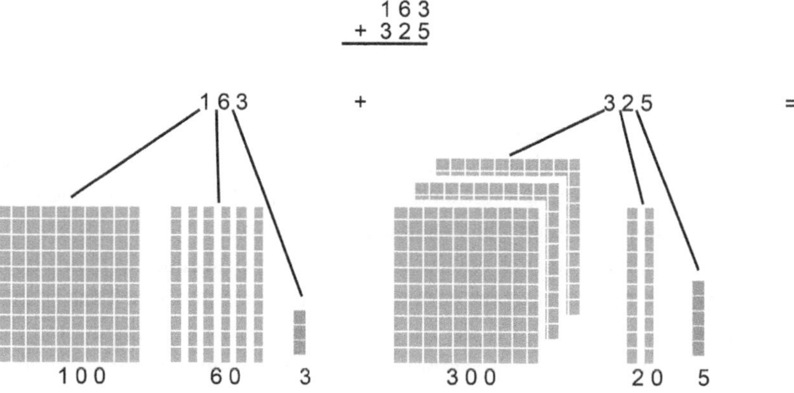

Think Aloud Script

Step 1: Starting from the ones, what's the ones problem?

$3 + 5 = 8$

Step 2: What's the tens problem?

6 tens + 2 tens = 8 tens

Step 3: What's the hundreds problem?

1 hundred + 3 hundred = 4 hundred

Figure 8.1 Addition with hundreds, tens, and ones.

Algorithms, including step-by-step procedures that are 'thought-aloud' by the teacher, are the **worked examples** students can work from to become successful. Students' effective use of an algorithm is underpinned by automatic recall of the order of operations (e.g., **BODMAS/PEDMAS**) and mathematical facts. By ensuring the mastery of mathematical facts and procedures, as well as the explicit teaching of the standard algorithms, students can simultaneously build their conceptual understanding for key mathematical concepts.

A fully-worked problem which has already been solved for the student, showing each step explained clearly

Brackets, Orders/Exponents, Division, Multiplication, Addition, Subtraction

PEDMAS is the same, but the P stands for Parentheses

Laying the foundations for number sense

Symbolic number knowledge is critical for students to develop a good understanding of mathematics. This is built upon students' developing **number sense** (approximate representation of magnitude). Students need to be able to assign a collection to the written symbol and know this with automaticity (i.e., **transcoding**). This ability has been directly linked to future mathematical outcomes for students (Ansari, 2023). This relates to key foundation skills such as **trusting the count** where students can hold the count through the consistent practice of symbolic number knowledge.

The ability to flexibly estimate and judge magnitude in multiple representations

A mental process by which we translate numbers from one form of representation to another (e.g., a collection to a symbol)

When counting a set of objects, knowing the number you say last represents the number of items in the set

The use of **number lines** as the bridge between concrete and pictorial representations is also well documented. Number lines can be used with students for both teaching magnitude as well as addition and subtraction in the early years, and also support a wide variety of mathematics content from fractions to problem solving later. It is always important to draw and display number lines with arrows at each end to consolidate the understanding that the line is not finite. Additionally, the space from 0 to 1 should be represented as a 'segment' not just a line that is one.

Lines on which numbers are marked at intervals, used to show numerical operations or relationships

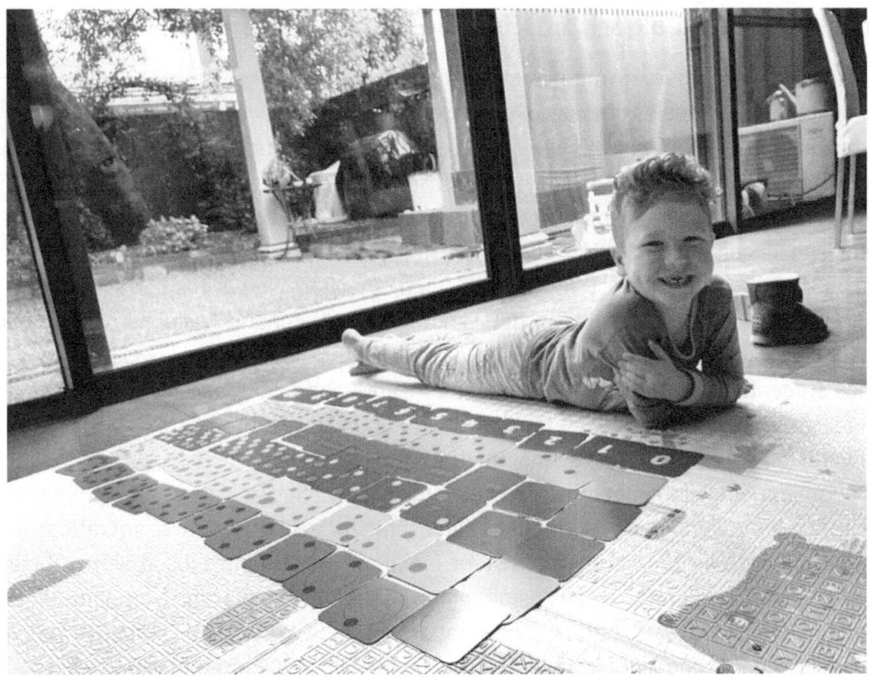

Figure 8.2 Multiple representations of the numbers 0–10.

The concept of **place value** can be supported with both facts and procedures when we focus on the knowledge that underpins the concept. We will demonstrate this principle using the skill of **partitioning**–a way of splitting numbers into smaller parts. This is useful for later addition and subtraction as it makes numbers easier to manipulate. Partitioning, or **regrouping**, requires students to regroup numbers from the next place value. Students need significant practice on this skill, but their understanding can be supported by their memory of the underlying mathematical facts. Fluency with mathematical facts and key procedures is critical for the development of mathematical understanding. Other fluency facts and procedures that support conceptual learning include:

> The value of each digit of a number; e.g., the 5 in 450 represents 5 tens, or 50; however, the 5 in 5,007 represents 5 thousands, or 5,000
>
> Thinking about numbers as made up of component parts e.g., 10 is 8 and 2, or 21 is 20 and 1
>
> Previously termed borrowing or carrying, e.g., the ones place totals 13, three is recorded in the ones place and 10 is renamed as 1 in the tens place; similar term: renaming

- Teaching **rote counting** before **rational counting**; and
- Using **place value** charts as early as Grade 1 to read and write numbers before bringing in manipulatives of place value.

> Children demonstrating that they can recite numbers in order from memory (as opposed to using this process to count a collection)
>
> When children are able to allocate numbers to the objects that they're counting
>
> The value of each digit of a number; e.g., the 5 in 450 represents 5 tens, or 50; however, the 5 in 5,007 represents 5 thousands, or 5,000

Teaching standard algorithms for the four operations

A lot of the current discourse in mathematics emphasises an approach involving informal strategies often as part of open-ended or so-called '**rich tasks**' (Boaler, 2015). In this view, novice learners are usually expected to discover the most effective way of solving problems by themselves. This approach, which we see as simultaneously time-wasteful and inequitable, should be abandoned in favour of teachers providing students with the best and quickest methods of arriving at the correct answer. This develops student conceptual and procedural knowledge simultaneously and harnesses the evolutionary pre-disposition to learn effectively via others' explanations (Geary, 2008).

> Complex, open-ended problems, often with multiple entry points, that require students to apply multiple strategies to find a solution

Once students are introduced to number concepts and begin learning their basic facts, teachers should develop students' familiarity and fluency with the **four operations**. Addition, subtraction, multiplication, and division are the foundational elements of problem solving in mathematics.

> Addition, subtraction, multiplication, division

Providing instruction in using standard algorithms for each of the four operations is fundamental. Algorithms should use consistent language and be introduced with substantial modelling and guided practice (e.g., using mini whiteboards) to maximise students' success. By directing students towards these consistent processes, we reduce the cognitive load associated with students choosing from an internal bank of informal or ad-hoc strategies.

As students become proficient, we acknowledge that they may construct a range of methods to solve a problem. However, we hold that it is adequate for students to have mastered *one* standard and reliable method initially. This is certainly better than novice students trying to choose between a myriad of inefficient or convoluted strategies (Torbeyns & Verschaffel, 2016).

Story Example 8.2 - Brandon Park - From multiple or invented strategies to standard algorithms

At Brandon Park Primary School, recent work has focussed on ensuring a consistent approach to solving problems with the four operations. Historically, a common approach to teach addition to Grade 2 students, for example, would involve a discussion of many different strategies (and invented algorithms) for solving addition problems. There were also high levels of variance in the language and methods used when more formal algorithms were taught from grade to grade. This inconsistency meant that students were often unable to build upon prior knowledge from year to year, and some students lacked a reliable and efficient strategy or algorithm for tackling different kinds of problems.

In recent years, the school's revised mathematics approach has increased in consistency in process and language within and between grade levels, providing greater chances to consolidate their previous learning. This has developed mastery in the most efficient ways to compute problems and the conceptual understanding of how such problems work.

Combined with a much greater emphasis on practice and mastery of algorithms and methods for solving problems using mini-whiteboards (and retrieval practice for fluency with mathematical facts), the momentum in students' attitude and confidence with mathematics is improving; the excellent results are also testament to this school-wide shift.

A progression for introducing algorithms

To begin, students need to be exposed to **number stories** that help them understand what happens when we add, subtract, multiply, or divide numbers (Booker, et al., 2020). A typical early example for addition might go as follows:

Simple descriptions of either real or imagined events that provide a story about a mathematics problem

There were 4 sheep in a field. 3 more sheep joined in. How many sheep altogether?

From here, materials should be used to represent these stories. For single-digit problems like the one above, we would model the use of counters or Unifix blocks on a ten frame (see Figure 8.3).

Once students can reliably construct this modelling on the ten frame or another visual representation, we can move to representing problems using symbols and a standard recording process (see Figure 8.4).

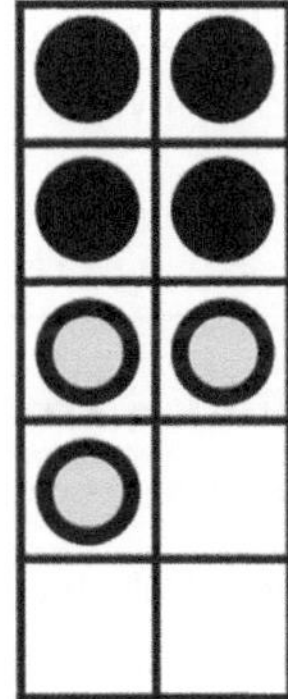

Figure 8.3 Ten frame showing 4 + 3.

$$\begin{array}{r} 4 \\ +\ 3 \\ \hline 7 \end{array}$$

Figure 8.4 Vertical algorithm for 4 + 3 = 7.

This schema can then be built upon and a common strategy (in this case the standard algorithm) can be learned which then will allow students to solve addition problems in any context.

Modelled and guided practice for each step

When solving problems using algorithms, students must be given practice in describing each step using correct **place value** language. Consider subtraction with regrouping in Figure 8.5, which often represents the first significant jump in complexity for primary students.

With a consistent **think aloud** script, this process is simplified to a binary 'if-then' or 'yes-no' process. If we cannot subtract, we must regroup from the next place value (see Figure 8.5), a binary procedure that can also be used with addition with regrouping.

The value of each digit of a number; e.g., the 5 in 450 represents 5 tens, or 50; however, the 5 in 5,007 represents 5 thousands, or 5,000

Involves the teacher saying out loud the thinking processes used by a proficient learner as they go about a task (e.g., reading, writing, or solving a problem in mathematics). The teacher's goal is to show the students how to undertake the task or skill themselves

SCRIPT	RECORDING
	4 3 - 1 5 ———
I have 3 ones, can I take away 5 ones? No, regroup.	3 13 ~~4~~ ~~3~~ - 1 5 ———
I have 13 ones, can I take away 5 ones? Yes, do it. 13 ones take away 5 ones equals 8 ones.	3 13 ~~4~~ ~~3~~ - 1 5 ——— 8
I have 3 tens, can I take away 1 ten? Yes, do it. 3 tens take away 1 ten equals 2 tens.	3 13 ~~4~~ ~~3~~ - 1 5 ——— 2 8

Figure 8.5 Subtraction with regrouping, featuring the 'think aloud' and written recording.

Scaffolding problem solving using visual representations

Problem solving is not a stand-alone skill per se, but rather an application of various forms of conceptual and procedural knowledge towards an end goal (Sweller et al., 2011). In the current mathematics educational zeitgeist, problem solving is touted as a key *pedagogy* for developing mathematical proficiencies: students learn by solving problems collaboratively or independently (Boaler, 2015).

We hope at this point in the chapter you would foresee our scepticism towards this approach. In line with insights from the science of learning, students cannot be equitably expected to lay down the deep mathematical content knowledge they need at the same time as they are attempting to apply this knowledge (Koponen et al., 2007).

Yes, some students will cope with this challenge, but our teaching should be set up so that *all* students benefit, not just those who can already teach themselves. Most students need the mathematical understandings and fluency in hand and from there they will *use* their mathematical knowledge *in order to* solve problems (Tricot & Sweller, 2014).

Sets of generic 'strategies,' 'guess and check,' 'draw a picture,' 'work backwards,' 'look for a pattern,' do not support students well in solving worded problems (Ashman, 2017). Students need experience with solving problems through repeated exposure and deliberate practice of 'sets of problems.'

And now for an exercise. Try working this problem any way you can.

Box 8.2 - Example mathematics problem

Jackson spent three times as much as Duke. Sien spent \$14 more than Duke. Altogether, they spent \$94. How much did each of them spend?

Typically, for this problem we would tell students to underline the key words. But, for a novice what words are these? Alternatively, students may have been taught that 'altogether' is a key word for addition; however, this *will not* help with this problem.

Firstly, students should be guided to understand what the problem is about and is asking. This is where the use of the **bar model** is a preferred way to work through worded problems. By drawing bars to represent what they know, do not know, and what they need to find out, they can scaffold their understanding of the problem. The use of bars is not a strategy in and of itself, but rather a system for representing the variables in a problem. When students have a common visual representation, it reduces their cognitive load.

> A visual representation used to solve mathematical word problems. It involves drawing rectangular bars to represent quantities and relationships

Back to our problem, the question prompts us to find out what each person spent, so we draw bars to represent each variable. We give Duke one part and Jackson three times as many. Then we give Sien \$14 more than Duke. We already have the total of \$94 and this is represented with a bracket totalling our variables.

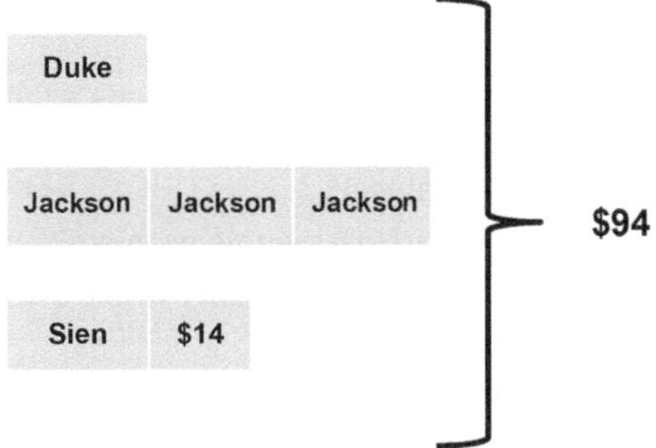

Figure 8.6 The problem represented as a bar model.

Box 8.3 - Solving the problem using the bar model

Step 1: We subtract $14 from $94 = $80.

We now have 5 equal bars that total $80.

Step 2: $80 ÷ 5= $16.

Therefore, each bar is worth $16.

Step 3: Review how many each person has using bars.

Duke has $16.
Jackson has 3 x $16 = $48.
Sien has $16 + $14 = $30.

The bar method consists of two types of problems: **Part-part-whole** and **comparison** problems (see Table 8.1). This scaffolding using a consistent visual representation builds up students' knowledge of different kinds of problems and allows the students to visualise and share what they are thinking. Having students practice labelling bars that are proportionate to the information and then identifying which type of problem initially is part of the explicit teaching and modelling in the early introduction of its use.

Problems involving a whole and its parts, in which there is a missing value. Could involve any of the four operations

A type of problem in which a learner must figure out the differences between sets

Table 8.1 Two main types of problems.

Part-part-whole (usually Grades 1-3)	• Relate to the relationships between parts and the whole. • Using the bars to represent the four operations. • e.g., if one part is missing but we have the total and other part, then we subtract.
Comparison problems (introduce Grade 3 onwards)	• Comparing quantities before and after a change has been made. • Solving single and multistep problems with quantities across all four operations.

The following tasks can be practised to give students a logical series of actions to attempt a problem:

- Underline the question;
- Identify the 'who and/or what' (variables);
- Is this a comparison problem or a part-part-whole problem?;
- Draw unit bars to represent the variables (part-part-whole or comparison); and
- Solve using known procedures.

In the middle years we can use a mix of both comparison and part-part-whole problems.

Story Example 8.3 - Increasing fluency and understanding for later problem solving - Bentleigh West

As discussed above, Bentleigh West's shift in mathematics teaching was followed by profound changes in students' approaches to this subject. For example, the increase in fluency and knowledge of problem structures has allowed students to demonstrate flexibility in thinking, and encourage quick and fluent retrieving of multiple relevant algorithms in order to select efficient ways to solve problems. Students can be seen using their knowledge of algorithms to try alternative methods, so they can check and prove their answers and thinking. Even the elegance of certain formulae and algorithms (e.g., the circumference of circles) has been enjoyed by students, as well as the fun of estimating, experimenting, and playing with formulae. In this way, mathematics has become appreciated and used as an authentic tool for thinking and discovery, not just a subject to be studied. However, in stark contrast to popular approaches that forgo explicit teaching for rich, open-ended tasks or 'productive struggle,' the culture of mathematics at Bentleigh West has changed because of genuine student success in the fundamentals and the guided (and later unguided) application of this mastery to tasks and novel problems.

Precise mathematical vocabulary

In his principles of instruction, Rosenshine (2012) identifies that the use of clear and concise language supports all learners. This is particularly important in mathematics. Using mathematical vocabulary gives consistency in naming of concepts, providing students with the language they need to communicate their mathematical thinking (Powell & Driver, 2015). Mathematical vocabulary can be taught like any vocabulary routine, with verbal rehearsal, definitions and examples, gestures (e.g., hands to make the plus symbol), and even morphology (<fract> mean to 'break apart').

The precision of this language is key, as per the following selection of examples:

- Avoid suggesting the word 'equals' to mean the 'answer' (equal means same as);
- When reading fractions (e.g., 27/100), we say 27 hundredths, not 27 over a hundred, to support the concept of decimal place value; it is also worth over-articulating the /th/ sound for decimal fraction language;

- Never use the word *borrowing* or *carrying* - use *regrouping* or *renaming*;
- Understand the different terminology for digit as opposed to a numeral, understanding that the digit is just the name of symbol (0, 1, 2, 3, 4, 5, 6, 7, 8, 9) to which you are referring (see Figure 8.7).

Figure 8.7 Digits versus number/numerals.

Review and retrieval practice

If reading practice is the driver of fluent decoding, then **daily review** is the driver of mathematical mastery. Research into memory and forgetting demonstrates that humans rarely master something upon their first exposure (see chapter 4). To counter this, daily review in mathematics consists of quick, regular sessions that allow students to revisit past material and consolidate their knowledge.

A short, daily session of practice of previously taught material, including concepts and skills that ensure students consolidate their learning and avoid forgetting

A typical daily review should consist of skills and concepts taught in the last week, last term, or even previous school years. It should cover a wide variety of topics in quick succession, with topics taken out and reintroduced as the need arises (typically, topics are reintroduced just as students are beginning for forget them; Jones, 2019; see Table 8.2).

Regular review allows for purposeful **formative assessment** (Wiliam, 2011): teachers can scan student answers and quickly correct misconceptions or determine foci for future lessons. Review sessions also provide vital consolidation of the basic mathematical facts students need to solve problems and master the algorithms.

Work undertaken by teachers (and students) that provide information or feedback to inform changes to teaching

The mathematical facts themselves need to be built systematically and then practiced to the point of **overlearning** before moving on. Care should be taken when building students' knowledge of the multiplication facts, as these are considered among the more difficult sets of knowledge for students to internalise comprehensively.

The process of rehearsing a skill even after you have reached your peak level of performance on the task

Pro tip: When reciting a multiplication fact, students should be encouraged to say 'five sevens are thirty-five' rather than 'five times seven equals thirty-five.' The former is quicker and it links more strongly to the conceptual idea of multiplication as 'groups of.'

Include built-in differentiation in your review materials

Teachers should ensure that problem sets increase gradually in difficulty within and between sets, catering for students at their level of need. To achieve this, we recommend building materials in advance of review sessions (or using this suite of mathematics review materials offered by Ochre Education). Consider the difficulty gradient across the set of multiplication problems in Figure 8.8.

Table 8.2 Daily review - Non-negotiables from David Morkunas and Toni-Hatten Roberts.

Grade Level	*Daily Non-negotiables*
First year of school-Grade 2	Counting (rote counting vs. rational counting) Subitising Regrouping/renaming Place value Standard algorithms (addition, subtraction) Fact fluency (addition, subtraction)
Grades 3-6	Four standard algorithms Fraction and decimals Worded problem with bar model Fact fluency (all operations)

Note: This is not a definitive list, and your review should also touch on other strands of mathematics including geometry and measurement, as well as statistics and probability.

$$\begin{array}{r} 12 \\ \times\ \ 3 \\ \hline \end{array} \qquad \begin{array}{r} 24 \\ \times\ 13 \\ \hline \end{array} \qquad \begin{array}{r} 67 \\ \times\ 84 \\ \hline \end{array} \qquad \begin{array}{r} 368 \\ \times\ \ 79 \\ \hline \end{array}$$

Figure 8.8 Multiplication problems increasing in complexity.

At first glance, the problems in Figure 8.8 appear simply to increase in difficulty by the number of digits being multiplied; however, they also grow in complexity due to the digits themselves. The first problem requires simply that students know 2 x 3 and 3 x 1, whereas the second introduces 4 x 3, the answer to which is above 10 and therefore requires regrouping.

Problem sets with a gradual increase in difficulty across the examples allow students to practice the same fundamental skill whilst also catering for the differing ability levels that exist within the classroom.

Concluding thoughts

In this chapter, we have attempted to capture the most fundamental insights aligning with the cognitive science that are mostly under-utilised or de-emphasised in classrooms around the world today. While many criticise the value of considering teaching efficiency (as well as effectiveness; e.g., Biesta, 2015), we know that instructional time is always short. If teachers are empowered to choose instructional approaches that work for the greatest number of students, this will allow them to consolidate and build upon firm foundations, and later *apply* this to sophisticated, open-ended tasks and applications.

A key theme of this book is that teachers can make a significant impact when they manage students' cognitive load. The end goal in mathematics is that we want students to spend cognitive energy to grapple with the intricacies of a given problem itself and the strategies required to solve it, rather than spending precious working memory struggling with the foundational skills required. See the chapter knowledge organiser in Table 8.3.

Table 8.3 Chapter 8 knowledge organiser.

Teach concepts through well-learned procedures and facts	**Laying the foundations for number sense**
• Conceptual understanding mutually reinforced by procedural fluency. • Use manipulatives with care; reduce extraneous load.	• Number lines. • Place value and partitioning. • Securing fluency of facts and procedures.
Teaching standard algorithms for the four operations	**Scaffolding problem solving using visual representations**
• Algorithms as reliable first strategies. • Model and guide practice for each step.	• Problem solving is an application of conceptual and procedural knowledge. • Bar modelling.
Precise mathematical vocabulary	**Review and retrieval practice**
• Consistently model and expect correct mathematical terminology.	• Review is spaced, interleaved retrieval practice and is driver of mathematical mastery. • Include built-in differentiation in review materials.

We know that many students around the world report 'not loving' mathematics, and even experience anxiety about this subject (Lau et al., 2022). Nevertheless, we cannot expect students to feel comfortable, or even in love, with an aspect of learning that they lack the confidence and skills with which to contend. By consolidating and mastering mathematical understandings over time, students can be empowered to apply their mathematics knowledge to unknown, unstructured problems, ideally enjoying what this incredible subject has to offer. The sciences of learning and mathematics have many more insights for you to utilise to improve your mathematics instruction, and this is merely a short introduction.

Where to next?

- *Teaching primary mathematics* by Booker et al.
- Centre for Independent Studies papers on Mathematics Education.
- Ochre Education's Free Mathematics Resources.
- *Teaching and learning fundamental mathematics* by Stephen Norton (see videos).
- *Assisting students struggling with mathematics: Intervention in the elementary grades* from What Works Clearinghouse.

For high school

- *How I wish I'd taught maths* by Craig Barton.
- Vic Maths Notes website from Alex Blanksby.

Check your indicators - Effective mathematics teaching

On-Track Indicators	*Off-Track Indicators*
• Conceptual understanding is reinforced by procedural and fact fluency (including algorithms). • Problem solving is broken down and supported using visual representations like bar modelling. • Daily review is embedded and ensures mastery of content. • Students of all learning needs are given explicit instruction and guided practice.	• Invented strategies are encouraged, and formal algorithms are discouraged. • Rich or open-ended tasks are launched, with extended period of time to engage in 'productive struggle.' • Mathematical terminology is inconsistently used across the school. • Topics are taught in pre-test and post-test cycles, and are not routinely returned to for review and consolidation. • Students are streamed into high, medium, and low ability groups.

Discussion questions

1. How do you currently teach fluency of procedures or concepts? What is your view of the explicit teaching of algorithms?
2. How can number lines and/or bar modelling provide scaffolded and sequential representations of numerical relationships and problem solving?
3. Why is review and retrieval practice crucial for mathematical mastery, especially in reducing the forgetting curve?

References

Biesta, G. J. (2015). *Beyond learning: Democratic education for a human future*. Routledge.

Boaler, J. (2015). *Mathematical mindsets: Unleashing students' potential through creative math, inspiring messages and innovative teaching*. John Wiley & Sons.

Booker, G., Bond, D., & Seah, R. (2020). *Teaching primary mathematics. 6th Edition*. Pearson Education.

Fuchs, L. S., Bucka, N., Clarke, B., Dougherty, B., Jordan, N. C., Karp, K. S., . . . & Morgan, S. (2021). Assisting students struggling with mathematics: Intervention in the elementary grades. *Educator's Practice Guide*. WWC 2021006. What Works Clearinghouse.

Geary, D. C. (2008). An evolutionarily informed education science. *Educational Psychologist, 43*(4), 179–195.

Hartman, J. R., Hart, S., Nelson, E. A., & Kirschner, P. A. (2023). Designing mathematics standards in agreement with science. *International Electronic Journal of Mathematics Education, 18*(3), em0739. https://doi.org/10.29333/iejme/13179

Hollingsworth, J. R., & Ybarra, S. E. (2017). *Explicit direct instruction (EDI): The power of the well-crafted, well-taught lesson*. Corwin Press.

Jones, K. (2019). *Retrieval practice: Resources and research for every classroom*. Hachette UK.

Kamii, C., & Joseph, L. L. (2004). *Young children continue to reinvent arithmetic–2nd grade: Implications of Piaget's theory*. Teachers College Press.

Koponen, T., Aunola, K., Ahonen, T., & Nurmi, J.-E. (2007). Cognitive predictors of single-digit and procedural calculation skills and their covariation with reading skill. *Journal of Experimental Child Psychology, 97*(3), 220–241. https://doi.org/10.1016/j.jecp.2007.03.001

NCTM (2023). Procedural fluency: Reasoning and decision-making, not rote application of procedures. Position Statement. *National Council of Teachers of Mathematics*. https://www.nctm.org/uploadedFiles/Standards_and_Positions/Position_Statements/PROCEDURAL_FLUENCY.pdf

Norton, S. J. (2015). *Teaching and learning fundamental mathematics.* https://mathematicseducation.vhx.tv/products/teaching-and-learning-fundamental-mathematics

Powell, S. R., & Driver, M. K. (2015). The influence of mathematics vocabulary instruction embedded within addition tutoring for first-grade students with mathematics difficulty. *Learning Disability Quarterly, 38*(4), 221–233. http://www.jstor.org/stable/24570111

Rosenshine, B. (2012). Principles of instruction: Research-based strategies that all teachers should know. *American Educator, 36*(1), 12.

Sweller, J., Clark, R. E., & Kirschner, P. A. (2011). Teaching general problem solving does not lead to mathematical skills or knowledge. *Mathematics Education Newsletter*, (March), 41–42.

Sweller, J., van Merriënboer, J. J. G., & Paas, F. (2019). Cognitive architecture and instructional design: 20 years later. *Educational Psychology Review, 31*(2), 261–292. https://doi.org/10.1007/s10648-019-09465-5

The Science of Math. (2023). https://www.thescienceofmath.com/

Torbeyns, J., & Verschaffel, L. (2016). Mental computation or standard algorithm? Children's strategy choices on multi-digit subtractions. *European Journal of Psychology of Education, 31*, 99–116.

Tricot, A., & Sweller, J. (2014). Domain-specific knowledge and why teaching generic skills does not work. *Educational Psychology Review, 26*(2), 265–283. https://doi.org/10.1007/s10648-013-9243-1

VanDerHeyden, A. M., & Codding, R. S. (2020). Belief-based versus evidence-based math assessment and instruction. *Communique, 48*(5).

Van de Walle, J., Karp, K., Bay-Williams, J. M., Brass, A., Bentley, B., Ferguson, S., . . . & Wilkie, K. (2019). *Primary and middle years mathematics: Teaching developmentally*. Pearson Australia.

Vassar, A. (2017). *The use of manipulative materials in early place value instruction: A cognitive load perspective* (Doctoral dissertation, UNSW Sydney).

Wiliam, D. (2011). *Embedded formative assessment.* Solution Tree Press.

Willingham, D. T. (2002). Inflexible knowledge: The first step to expertise. *American Educator, 26*(4), 31–33.

9 Coherent, knowledge-rich curricula

Bypassing working memory by laying lots of Velcro®

Nathaniel Swain and Reid Smith

Content knowledge is a key driver of reading comprehension and learning in all subject areas. But this fact has mostly been unknown to teachers and school leaders (Hirsch, 2019; Wexler, 2020). The acquisition of knowledge has often been analogised to be like laying Velcro®, allowing more understandings and learning to better adhere in students' minds, and thus overcoming the limitations of **working memory**.

> Our mental workspace, which can hold a limited number of items at any time

In this chapter, we will unpack the nature of curriculum and knowledge, and examine how you can adapt your school curriculum approach so it is knowledge-rich and coherently builds knowledge and skills across the school grades.

> **Box 9.1 - Chapter 9 Overview**
>
> - What is the curriculum?
> - Why knowledge? What knowledge?
> - What is a knowledge-rich curriculum?
> - What makes a coherent curriculum?

What is the curriculum?

The curriculum of a school is the sum of the learning experiences that are planned for students in an educational setting. Curriculum includes both what students are learning about and how teachers will structure their teaching to build student understanding.

It is useful to separate curriculum into two broad categories:

- The **intended curriculum** is that which is documented within a school or system; the teaching and learning we plan to undertake; and
- The **enacted curriculum** is what actually occurs in the classroom.

> The curriculum which we plan to teach, and which is written in our curriculum documentation
>
> How the curriculum is actually taught and learned

DOI: 10.4324/9781003404965-11

Ideally, the enacted curriculum should be closely related to the intended curriculum, notwithstanding adaptations to curricula in response to formative assessment.

Of course, schools must also meet curriculum *framework* requirements set by their jurisdiction. In the USA, this may be the Common Core State Standards, in England the National Curriculum, and in Australia the Australian Curriculum or its state variations. These frameworks constrain what can be taught in schools to some extent, but in general, do not contain the level of specificity required for school-level curriculum maps and materials.

School curriculum variation

Curriculum variance describes the difference in the enacted curriculum between classrooms. Schools can sit anywhere on a continuum of variation from a school that has very little similarity in the content and instruction between classrooms (high variance), to those schools that have great similarity in instruction (low variance).

In a **high variance school**, class teachers would have very few shared outcomes that would be more specific than 'we are teaching *Romeo and Juliet*' or 'we are learning about the solar system.' Teachers would not have a common understanding of what it takes for the learning to be successful.

A **low variance school**, on the other hand, will have groups of teachers who are very clear about what the students should know and be able to do after teaching. Often teachers' clarity of understanding is achieved through developing detailed teaching and learning plans as part of the intended curriculum.

> An approach to curriculum in which teachers have a high-level of variability in what they teach, and how they teach it and may plan in silos rather than collaboratively
>
> A school in which teachers collaborate and have a shared understanding of what and how to teach the curriculum

Story Example 9.1 - High variance in mathematics teaching - Challis Community Primary

Challis Community Primary began its science of learning journey in a similar state to most schools: with a high variance curriculum, with very little of the 'what' or 'how' of teaching and learning specified in detail. For example, for the different strands of mathematics, there was a distinct lack of specificity or consistency, even within the same grade level: Different terminology was used on topics, as well as different end points in the teaching/review cycle. Unsurprisingly, this created gaps in the skills and knowledge of students as they passed through.

To look at how two-dimensional (2D) shapes were taught in the first year of school: Some teachers would only teach square, circle, rectangle, and triangle. Others would instantly extend to pentagon and hexagon, a choice completely determined by individual teachers. This lack of specificity and variability fuelled gaps in student understanding. The work of the school to improve consistency and collaboration was paramount to implement practices that aligned with the science of how students learn. The school needed to lower the variance from grade to grade and class to class.

Why a low variance approach?

1. *To provide an opportunity for teachers to share good practice.*

Engaging in a collaborative approach to the development of a knowledge-rich unit requires all teachers to negotiate the *what*, *why*, and *how* of teaching: the content that will be included and why, and how that content will be delivered in classrooms.

2. *To increase the quality of instruction over time.*

A common curriculum anchors teachers' instruction and provides a foundation for continuous improvement. A low variance intended curriculum codifies our 'best bets' for teaching a unit which can help teachers to increase instructional quality over time. Reflections on its enactment in classrooms helps teachers to make modifications and increase the quality of instruction each year of delivery.

3. *To provide students with a consistent experience between classes.*

Within each grade, students need consistent experiences between classes, in routines and classroom set ups for example. Secondly, and probably more importantly, they should have consistent experiences over time. As students move through school, learning should accumulate to construct shared understandings from the curriculum.

4. *To reduce the planning and preparation loads on teachers.*

When we plan collaboratively, year on year, it reduces teachers' preparation load. This allows teachers to use their time more effectively, including thinking about the needs of the students in their classes.

5. *To build a strong instructional culture.*

The idea of **instructional culture** imagines schools as *organisations* rather than collections of co-located private practices. In a school with a strong instructional culture, there are common expectations around what is taught and how. These expectations and decisions move from being idiosyncratic to collective.

> A shared understanding and way of working to deliver effective curriculum and pedagogy

Why knowledge? What knowledge?

There are no shortcuts to knowledge

E. D. Hirsch Jr., American educator and theorist, has argued against long-standing movements towards what he dubs 'how-to-ism'—attempts to de-emphasise detailed subject knowledge that must be taught and remembered by students (Hirsch, 2013). Such movements have argued that, instead of actual knowledge, students need 21st-century or transformative skills or competencies (e.g., OECD, 2019).

However, research makes it increasingly clear that knowledge does in fact matter, and forms the foundation for the development of so-called 'generic' or 21st-century skills. Education thought leader Daisy Christodoulou says the best way to think of knowledge is "as a pathway to skill. You teach knowledge, and skills are the end result" (Christodoulou, 2023). Students need to think about and grapple with the content to be learnt. Ensuring students have the knowledge and space to do this mental work is key.

As laid out in chapter 4, experts have expertise because of their stores of **declarative** and **procedural knowledge**, which is specific to their particular domain (Frensch & Sternberg, 2014). The research shows that they do not perform anything like an expert when outside of their domain (see Willingham, 2006). So, to get our students off their 'training wheels' and begin to have expertise on a given task, we need to teach them the knowledge they require. How can we hope to develop the students we educate into critically and creatively thinking, well-rounded citizens of tomorrow? By ensuring they have buckets of rich, interconnected, well-sequenced knowledge.

Knowledge of facts, terminology and key ideas and the connections between them; 'knowing that'

Knowledge of how to complete a task or demonstrate a skill; 'knowing how'

Teach students systems of (substantive) knowledge, not disconnected facts

The **substantive knowledge** of a particular subject includes all the knowledge that defines it as a domain: the big ideas, details, facts, dates, locations, and concepts. Teaching students the substantive knowledge from the humanities, sciences, arts, and literature, for example, is critical to their development of elaborated subject-specific **schemata**. These schemata in turn are essential for students' ability to read and write texts, and to solve problems and create solutions.

The facts, concepts, big ideas, and the substance of the subjects we teach

A mental representation or framework for understanding an area of learning

After all, learning more of the substantive knowledge of a range of subjects increases the complexity of the chunks of information with which we can grapple during any task (Hirsch, 1996). Far from meaningless facts, knowledge is the beautiful stuff that we think *with* (Didau, 2018).

What separates strong and weak readers is not just how well they can decode the words or follow the structure of the language, but what they know about the topic. Illustrated in the work of E. D. Hirsch as well as journalist and knowledge-rich curriculum advocate Natalie Wexler, numerous scientific studies show that content knowledge has significant impact on the students' understanding of what they are reading (Wexler, 2020; see the Baseball Study: Recht & Leslie, 1988).

To take the example of vocabulary, Hirsch (2013) argues that knowledge building allows for a more systematic and effective method to maximise the chances of mastering new language: "Knowledge of a word is a memory residue of several meaningful encounters with the word in diverse contexts." By building language and vocabulary teaching into meaningful texts, we ensure all students develop sophisticated linguistic and subject knowledge.

Story Example 9.2 - Teaching *Treasure Island*, Bentleigh West Primary

Before considering a knowledge-rich approach, most Grade 4 teachers at Bentleigh West Primary would never have chosen a classic title like *Treasure Island*. Having learnt about the importance of knowledge for student comprehension and enjoyment of text, Bentleigh West teachers set out to use existing high-quality materials (Core Knowledge®) and adapt them using effective teaching practices (Questioning the Author; Beck, McKeown, & Sandora, 2020).

Once they had built students' background knowledge about the time of pirates in the 18th century, the Grade 4s at Bentleigh West were able to engage with a rich text written in complex and, at times, archaic language. In fact, students were hooked by the captivating story, brought to life by the teacher read-alouds and class discussions. The excitement was palpable.

Teach students how *that knowledge comes to be: Disciplinary knowledge*

Disciplinary knowledge is that knowledge specific to domains, like the Arts and Science, that offers students different ways of inquiring about and understanding the world (see Ashbee, 2021, for example). It is critical here that we emphasise that knowledge *should not* be taught unquestioned, or purported to be definitive or absolute.

> The way in which knowledge within a particular subject is developed, investigated, questioned, and valued. For example, scientists gather information through experimentation and theorisation, whereas historians might work more on analysis and interpretation of various sources

Knowledge as imperfect, dynamic, and up for negotiation

Students should be taught that the knowledge they are being asked to learn is fallible (is up for debate), and may be proven wrong one day. Our curriculum should invite students into the discussions and debates about what knowledge is valued in one discipline but less important in another. They can then learn how historians, scientists, and artists continue to debate, shape, and re-construct the knowledge in their subject areas. Students still get the cognitive benefit of moving towards mastering a domain of expertise, but are not limited by thinking such knowledge is irrefutable or unquestionable.

What is a knowledge-rich curriculum?

Knowledge has until recently been sidelined by many 'progressive' education discussions of curriculum. Learning facts about the world, pre-determined by an authority, has been cast down as 'old-hat' (Karseth & Sivesind, 2010). Many contemporary curriculum documents have become more about the *skills* students can demonstrate than the *content* they can master (Wexler, 2020). There is also the intuitive, but erroneous, conception that:

> Since you can google anything, or get AI to write anything, why would you need to know anything by heart? Surely, you just need to know how to think creatively, critically, collaboratively, in a way that computers cannot (yet) do?

The untruth of the idea that knowledge is irrelevant is plainly revealed by the science of how we learn. Below, we highlight the work being undertaken to bring knowledge back to centre stage in the curricula that guide our teaching, namely the concept of a **knowledge-rich curriculum** approach, and the potential it holds for learning excellence and equity in our schools.

An approach to curriculum design in which knowledge, well-structured and specified in detail, provides an underpinning philosophy for learning

How knowledge helps

Knowledge is hardly an unnecessary step towards higher order thinking as some would claim. Knowledge is the fuel that drives all our thinking and paves the way to collaboration, creation, and critique (see Table 9.1). As Bernstein (2000) notes, it is knowledge that allows students to "think the unthinkable and the not yet thought."

Table 9.1 How rich content knowledge fuels learning and thinking.

Knowledge helps students understand and think more	• Knowing about a topic means students can piece together ambiguous or incomplete information (make adequate inferences).
Having knowledge allows you to gain more knowledge	• New knowledge is built upon prior knowledge. • Students can make sense of more complex information when they can recognise larger, familiar chunks within it.
Knowledge helps you automate tasks and solve problems	• Novel information takes up more space in working memory, so when content is familiar, there is more cognitive capacity to tackle the task at hand.
Knowledge building closes gaps between haves and have-nots	• Knowledge takes students outside of their immediate experience (Young et al., 2014). • Knowledge enables students to access the discourses of power no matter their home lives and privilege of their parents.

Adapted from Willingham (2006).

Whose knowledge?

In the 1980s, E. D. Hirsch Jr, the somewhat notorious pedagogue who has long spearheaded the teaching of content knowledge in American schools, worked up a list of the essential knowledge for students to learn. In attempting this task, he fell short. *Cultural Literacy* was not seen for what Hirsch intended: that American children needed to have a shared cultural knowledge to learn and communicate as a society. Lambasted by the (mainly liberal/progressive) educational establishment upon its release in 1987, instead the harsh critiques centred on what knowledge he had left out of his example list. Particularly, Hirsch's list was seen as an attempt to push a White, middle-class, Western perspective of the world onto children, leaving out diverse voices, histories, and cultures. While this was not Hirsch's intention, it raised the important question regarding whose knowledge should we be teaching, and how can we avoid reproducing the past.

How can a knowledge-rich curriculum avoid simply reproducing the status quo?

Students from diverse backgrounds have home and community literacy practices and ways of knowing that are invaluable but are often distinct from that which is valued in school or in public civic life. The language and knowledge of school is different from, but not superior to, that of many diverse families and communities.

There is growing consensus that school curricula should change to become more **culturally responsive** or **culturally sustaining** (e.g., Ladson-Billings, 1995; Paris & Alim 2017). A culturally responsive curriculum is one that is actively designed to reflect the diversity of voices, perspectives, and stories of the community it serves, as well as seeking to redress the traditional ignoring of ideas from historically marginalised groups. This is important work for all schools and systems.

> Pedagogy grounded in teachers' practice of cultural competence, and may involve ensuring students' languages and cultures are reflected in the curriculum and sustained through this work
>
> Pedagogy that utilises diverse students' culture and language to positively impact diverse learners' achievement
>
> Attempts to ensure students' experiences and identities are reflected; they can see themselves in the curriculum
>
> Attempts to include diverse perspectives and ideas that seek to take students out of their own experiences in the curriculum; they can see into other 'worlds'
>
> Topics, areas of study, or ways of discussing ideas that conform with prevailing dominant ideas. Such discourses are not necessarily better but happen to be useful to access discussions that have socio-political utility (e.g., language used for job interviews, university education, or civic engagement)

Curricula as mirrors to within, and windows to beyond

The concepts of **curricula as mirrors** and **curricula as windows** (see Pondiscio, 2022) are useful when discussing the problem of 'whose knowledge?' When choosing the knowledge taught in your curriculum, you must consider how much of it reflects and validates the experiences of your students, and how much it aims to take them *beyond* their immediate experience.

Indeed, Lisa Delpit (2016), American educational researcher and advocate, implores all teachers to enact culturally relevant curricula. However, she also says that this alone is insufficient to ensure excellence and equity, especially for children of colour. Delpit argues that without teaching students the knowledge (and currently dominant discourses) of history, geography, science, and politics, teachers can inadvertently deny students access to **discourses of power** which they will need to navigate the world as it is today.

We may seek change to such dominant discourses through education, but we must also ensure all students, no matter their background, achieve their potential by giving them the knowledge and language they need to access conversations outside their immediate, home experiences.

When factoring in the importance of rich, content knowledge for learning, attempts to allow students to find themselves in the curriculum alone (just mirrors), without ensuring they have access to knowledge and language within the civic, legal, and academic conversations of society as it functions today (windows), could be described as foolish at best, and negligent at worst. Because of these issues, the question of which knowledge to teach also plagues contemporary curriculum theorists (e.g., Paraskeva, 2021). In short, choosing what or *whose* knowledge to teach is complex.

Not deciding is an indefensible position

If we are to give up and determine that it is too controversial to decide on the knowledge to be taught in our curriculum, then students miss out on access to cumulatively scaffolded knowledge and the opportunity to master it. Hirsch argues, in line with the science of learning (Smith et al., 2021; Dehaene, 2020), that all children need to have mastery over an important body of essential knowledge to ensure educational success and civic engagement. The controversy surrounding *which knowledge* does not circumvent this.

A pragmatic course of action is for schools and systems to do their best to choose knowledge which is beneficial to students' learning and important to the school and wider community.

Powerful knowledge

Johan Muller and Michael Young's (2019) theory of **powerful knowledge** is also useful here (though not without its critics; see Miedema, 2023). This concept refers to the kinds of knowledge that take students *beyond their experience*, that is usually inaccessible or uncommon in the home or community. It is *powerful* knowledge as it opens up understanding and conversations that depend upon the traditions of human inquiry (e.g., through the academic disciplines like history, geography, science, and the arts), and is critical to gain access to full civic and societal engagement.

> Young's notion of the kind of knowledge that addresses inequities between students, and allows them to go beyond their own experiences

Most importantly, the knowledge taught should be rich, distinct from common sense, systematic, specialised, and sufficiently challenging/ambitious: the very qualities of a *knowledge-rich* curriculum (Ashbee, 2021).

What makes up a knowledge-rich curriculum approach?

While there are different definitions of 'knowledge-rich curriculum,' Tom Sherrington, UK teacher, writer, and instructional coach, has outlined in his Teacher Head blog (2018) four useful principles:

(1) **Knowledge provides a driving, underpinning philosophy**. Recall that knowledge building is far from the memorisation of meaningless facts. In this approach, knowledge is taught in both its substantive and disciplinary forms. Here, skills are never generic but are contextualised and understood as emerging from the accumulation and application of rich knowledge.

(2) **Knowledge specified in detail.** Explicit links between disciplinary knowledge and the substantive knowledge that comprise it support students to inquire in a productive way. The emphasis on *disciplinary* knowledge (how the subject works) in contemporary curriculum frameworks in the English-speaking world sometimes fails to make the required links with *substantive* knowledge (what we want students to know in this subject). This means that students are often asked to inquire into and analyse phenomena or content without the underlying knowledge required to do this reliably (García-Carmona, 2020).

When we do not specify the knowledge in detail, generic and fruitless student inquiries can be common, as the focus is not on the new knowledge, but on the student engagement in the activity instead.

(3) **Teaching knowledge to be remembered, not just encountered**. Teachers plan so students are not just *exposed* to knowledge and information, but that they are given every opportunity to remember and consolidate their rich understandings. Also, we must not forget that children (like adults!) are prone to forgetting, and that retrieval and review should strongly feature in any attempts to build up students' knowledge from the curriculum (see chapter 4). In a knowledge-rich approach, we do not expect novice students to jump into the role of expert historian, artist, designer, or scientist roles without building stores of substantive and disciplinary knowledge as foundations for current and future learning.

(4) **Teaching knowledge should be well-structured.** By ensuring students develop knowledge within and across various subjects, teachers support students with a much richer cognitive framework or schema, in each domain. These schemata act as a mental structure (or Velcro®) for organising and connecting new information. Then, when faced with complex problems, students can draw upon these knowledge frameworks in their long-term memory to make connections, identify patterns, and generate potential solutions (see Hirsch (1998) and Wexler (2020). See Table 9.2 below for an example.

Table 9.2 Example of knowledge-rich unit from Core Knowledge – Grade 1 Mesopotamia.

Previous Connecting Units (First year of school-Grade 1)	*Current Unit*	*Future Connecting Units*
First year of school Geography: Plants Geography: Farms English Language Arts: Kings and queens Grade 1 Geography: Continents, countries, and maps	Grade 1 Mesopotamia - Land between the rivers; soil rich in nutrients - Farming and changes to society - How civilisations work and how first appeared - Development and importance of writing - Religion and beliefs	Grade 1 - Ancient Egypt - Three World Religions Grade 2 History Units - Ancient India - Ancient China - Ancient Greece

Adapted from Core Knowledge Foundation (2023).

Story Example 9.3 - Making reading a knowledge-building endeavour – Brandon Park Primary

Nothing surprised Brandon Park teachers more on their science of learning journey than seeing how a shift in focus in reading lessons suddenly activated the 40% of students who were previously under-engaged. Under the old ways of teaching reading, students were always polite and respectful perhaps due to the norms and routines that were well-embedded across the school community. However, it was not until suddenly the topics in reading lessons became captivating, and rich in knowledge, that the teachers realised just how much *more* engaged their students could be.

As in nearly all English classrooms, the focus of reading lessons had historically been the drilling of comprehension strategies through mini-lessons and release of students into reading groups or rotations. The challenge here was that the students at Brandon Park could be reading about anything; all that was common across the classrooms were that students were practising to infer, summarise, question, or make connections.

In the Grade 3 classrooms, where teachers piloted their first knowledge-rich units, adapted from resources such as the Vikings from Core Knowledge®, the energy in reading sessions transformed, with one student literally exclaiming to his teachers: "I love reading . . . [pause] now!"

From the sheer cliffs of Scandinavian fjords, to fearsome raids and epic sea voyages, this rich unit stimulated discussion, creative writing, and independent inquiry. Even the at-risk students in the class were entranced and invested. The students' fascination extended to fact-checking details in documentary clips, some of which had depicted Vikings as having horned helmets—which to the Viking-aficionados were preposterously unwieldy and would never have been worn (according to the students' independent research).

This shift in their students' engagement and expertise prompted a lot of reflection amongst the teachers about how students must have felt about their reading lessons before. While calm and busy classrooms may seem to reflect genuine engagement, perhaps it is more often politeness. Brandon Park teachers (and students) were hooked, and could not go back to the old (knowledge-sparse) approach.

Where does inquiry and exploration fit?

As set out in chapter 5, inquiry and open-ended exploration have a place within a knowledge-rich approach, so long as these investigations are facilitated as applications and extensions upon an already developed body of knowledge. While attempting to teach primarily through inquiry can be seen as the norm in many classrooms, the evidence suggests it unlikely that students benefit as much as they would with initial clear, explicit instruction about the underlying knowledge they need to develop (Oliver et al., 2021).

Let's take the example of the 'whirly-bird' experiment—a popular, cheap activity for early science where pieces of paper are folded and cut into a specific shape, resembling helicopter blades. When students drop the paper from a height, it spins as it descends, demonstrating forces of gravity and air resistance. If students undertake such an experience too early in their learning, before they have any background knowledge to connect with the task, then it is more likely that students will be dazzled by the intricacies of the whirly-bird flying machines, rather than the underlying forces at play.

We want students to be engaged with the actual knowledge at hand, and then to come to such captivating experiences with a proper background to see the understandings embedded within.

When considering how to balance sequenced knowledge building and inquiries or explorations into such areas, one of the biggest questions to ask yourself is: *What will students be thinking about when doing the task you set?* Harvard educational researcher, Elizabeth City et al. (2009) reminds us that 'task[s] predict performance.' During an open-ended inquiry where students are producing a poster, portfolio, or presentation, what will the students be focussing on? Will it be:

- The key content to be mastered and explored and the nuances therein; or
- How to choose the best font, design the best slide, and which images to copy from a Google® image search?

What makes a coherent curriculum?

Curriculum maps

Most often, as teachers, we think of our work on the scale of lesson by lesson. But Bodil Isaksen (2015) notes that: *the lesson is the wrong unit of time* for curriculum quality. To develop high-quality curricula, we must think about units or sequences of learning, comprising several connected and cohesive lessons.

A **curriculum map** shows a sequence of learning in one or more learning areas over the course of multiple years of schooling. A curriculum map is intended to be a high-level planning document; therefore, it usually contains only the:

> A high-level document showing the units to be taught and the key ideas and skills within

- Unit name;
- Unit purpose (Big Idea);
- Brief overview of lessons; and
- Schedule in the year and grade level (where it is taught and for how long and in what subject).

The map is constructed so that teachers and school leaders can, at a glance, get a sense of what students will know as a result of the teaching in their school (see tips in Box 9.2).

Box 9.2 - Tips for constructing a curriculum map

Start with one subject or grade level.

Audit the current curriculum.

- Agree on the criteria for inclusion/exclusion before the audit.
- Decide on which units are to be removed from the curriculum based on the criteria.
- Analyse the remaining units.

Construct the desired curriculum.

- Determine new units needed.
- Be pragmatic throughout this process.

Sometimes as your curriculum map is coming together, it is fine to deliver a unit in two different grade levels in the same calendar year. This reduces the planning load in the first years of implementation, and allows the team to get ahead of the planning requirements.

Building a curriculum map is a big job, but a worthwhile one. If you are a school leader, nothing will help you gain a better understanding of what is happening in classrooms as much as being able to put your finger in the curriculum pie, to be able to see what it is that we intend to teach, even if that is not exactly what is enacted.

Story Example 9.4 - Curriculum mapping reflection - Canberra Goulburn Diocese Catalyst

Prior to Catalyst, it was 'choose your own adventure' for mathematics in this group of 56 catholic schools. The Australian and state curriculum frameworks determined what was to be taught, but it fell to schools how this would be realised. After reflecting on previous failed attempts, the Catalyst team realised that previous documents had been too vague and open to interpretation to enable delivery with fidelity.

To address this, the Catalyst team needed to focus on the instruction first, to establish buy-in by building the case for change. This first step of professional development into the science of learning behind effective mathematics instruction (see chapter 8) fostered the desire for change and created the space for a more prescriptive scope and sequence and curriculum materials.

The team worked with educational consultants (Shaping Minds) to create a customised scope and sequence for the first year of school to Grade 6, which provided a clear anchor from which teachers could pull content, and which ensured that spaced and interleaved practice could be easily implemented. Initial successes with the trial materials created an appetite to develop more, and the team were able to recruit teachers from some schools to work with non-profit curriculum developer, Ochre Education, to begin creating all the lessons, resources, and instructional materials to deliver the scope and sequence.

In a few short years, the system has gone from the curricular 'wild west' to a group of highly collaborative schools planning and enacting a low variance, high coherence curriculum.

Coherence

One of the key benefits of a knowledge-rich curriculum is the ability to develop coherence. **Coherence** refers to the degree to which a curriculum is logically organised and sequenced, with a coherent curriculum featuring deliberate and systematic connections between the content studied in each subject within a grade and as students advance through the years.

> How well your curriculum connects and comes together as a whole, for example, horizontally (across subjects), vertically (across grade levels)

Claire Sealy (2017) conceptualises this coherence as a three-dimensional curriculum in Table 9.3.

Table 9.3 Sealy's (2017) three dimensional curriculum.

Dimension	*Vertical*	*Horizontal*	*Diagonal*
Links	Between *grade levels* in the *same subject*	Between *subjects* in the *same grade level*	Between *different subjects* in *different grade levels*
Example	Comparing and contrasting fables (Grade 2 English) with fairy tales (Grade 1 English)	Reading and discussing Jackie French's *The Night They Stormed Eureka* (Grade 5 English) after learning about the Eureka Stockade (Grade 5 History)	Developing artworks in the style of the Ancient Egyptians (Grade 8 Art) after studying Ancient Egyptian history (Grade 7 History)

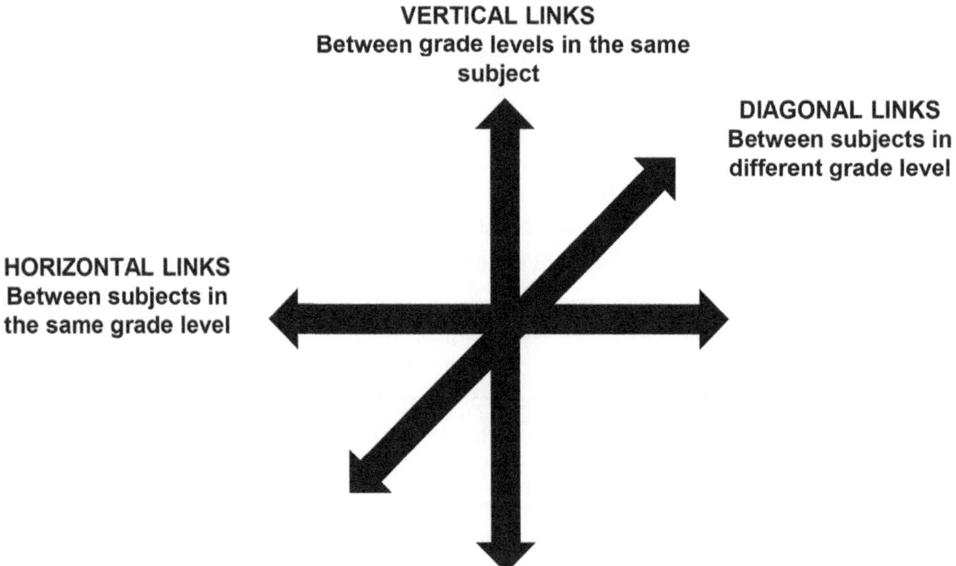

Figure 9.1 Three dimensional curriculum and coherence from Sealy (2017).

It is important to distinguish the idea of a coherent **dimensional curriculum** from a **theme-based curriculum**. The coherent curriculum leverages powerful knowledge that exist in different domains, gradually and carefully builds understanding over time.

Ways of ensuring that subject content meaningfully connects across different subjects and grade levels

A slightly forced way to integrate between multiple subjects where a high-level theme or connection is drawn, but does not reflect and authentic synergy across subjects

This is not the same as having a theme for a period of time. For example, we do not want an equivalent of 'apple month,' where in Maths we are counting apples, in Art we are drawing apples, and in English we are writing a persuasive essay on apple eating. Thematic sequencing tends to force ideas and applications, while a coherent curriculum purposefully uses natural links within the curriculum.

Closing thoughts

The decisions we make as curriculum planners and enactors have far-reaching ramifications on students' lives. Ashbee (2021) contends that curriculum is a matter of social justice, as how we spend the limited time in school can dictate what is taught and how well it is learnt, with shortcomings and lost opportunities affecting the educationally 'at-risk' to a far greater degree.

In this chapter, we hope we have provided a solid introduction to the key drivers of your curriculum decision-making, and have made a case for moves towards knowledge-rich and coherent curricular approaches across the subjects of school.

See knowledge organiser in Table 9.4.

Table 9.4 Chapter 9 knowledge organiser.

What is curriculum? • Intended vs. enacted curriculum. • Low vs. high variance. • Benefits of low variance curriculum.	***Why knowledge? What knowledge?*** • There are no shortcuts! • Substantive vs. disciplinary knowledge. • Knowledge as imperfect, dynamic, and up for negotiation.
What is a knowledge-rich curriculum? • How knowledge helps. • Whose knowledge? • What makes up a knowledge-rich curriculum approach? • Role of inquiry and exploration.	***What makes a coherent curriculum?*** • Curriculum maps. • Current curriculum → desired curriculum. • Vertical, horizontal, and diagonal coherence. • Coherence vs. theme-based curricula.

By including coherent and knowledge-rich curricular changes in our work to harness the science of learning, we can turn every school subject into an equalising opportunity for the social, intellectual, cultural, and political enrichment of our students. We hope the resources we also provided below assist you in this work.

Where to next?

- Hunter, J., Haywood, A., & Parkinson, N. (2022). *Ending the lesson lottery: How to improve curriculum planning in schools.* Grattan Institute.
- *Building a Coherent Curriculum.* Think Forward Educators presentation by Reid Smith. https://thinkforwardeducators.org/meetings-for-members/reidsmith-apr-2021
- *Getting Started with a Knowledge-Rich Curriculum.* Think Forward Educators presentation by Brad Nguyen. https://thinkforwardeducators.org/meetings-for-members/reidsmith-apr-2021
- Jensen, B., Ross, M., Collett, M., Murnane, and Pearson, P. (2023). *Fixing the hole in Australian education: The Australian Curriculum benchmarked against the best.* Learning First.
- *Core Knowledge®* curriculum.
- Wit & Wisdom® curriculum.
- EL Education curriculum.
- Knowledge matters campaign.
- Steiner (2017), *Curriculum research: What we know and where we need to go?*
- Ollie Lovell's *Tools for teachers.* See curriculum chapter.

Check your indicators – Curriculum

On-Track Indicators	*Off-Track Indicators*
• Low variance in curriculum implementation to ensure consistency. • Knowledge taught as imperfect, dynamic, and subject to negotiation. • Developing a curriculum that is rich in content knowledge across various subjects. • Incorporating inquiry and exploration as extensions and applications to deepen students' understanding.	• Big difference between planned and enacted curriculum. • Lack of emphasis on the building student knowledge systematically. • A focus on generic or transferable skills, e.g., creativity, collaboration, critical thinking, communication. • Teaching a theme-based approach where subjects are integrated in a forced or arbitrary way. • An absence of clear knowledge-rich curriculum maps or scope and sequences of learning.

Discussion questions

1. Is there a big difference between the intended and enacted curriculum in your teaching?
2. How do you currently ensure that what you teach is rich in content knowledge, and is built and remembered over time?

3. How can you balance the teaching of powerful knowledge with culturally responsive curriculum practices?
4. Would an audit of your current curriculum identify areas for improvement?

References

Ashbee, R. (2021). *Curriculum: Theory, culture and the subject specialisms.* Routledge.

Beck, I. L., McKeown, M. G., & Sandora, C. A. (2020). *Robust comprehension instruction with questioning the author*. Guilford Publications.

Bernstein B (2000). *Pedagogy, symbolic control and identity: Theory, research, critique*. Rowman & Littlefield.

Christodoulou, D. (2014). *Seven myths about education*. Routledge.

Christodoulou, D. (2023). *Skills vs. knowledge: 13 years on*. No More Marking blog. https://substack.nomoremarking.com/p/skills-vs-knowledge-13-years-on

City, E. A., Elmore, R. F., Fiarman, S. E., & Teitel, L. (2009). *Instructional rounds in education: A network approach to improving teaching and learning*. Harvard Education Press.

Core Knowledge® Foundation (2023). *Core Knowledge History and Geography (CKHG) program*. Core Knowledge® Foundation. https://www.coreknowledge.org/curriculum/history-geography/

Dehaene, S. (2020). *How we learn: The new science of education and the brain*. Penguin UK.

Didau, D. (2018). *Making kids cleverer: A manifesto for closing the advantage gap*. Crown House Publishing Ltd.

Frensch, P. A., & Sternberg, R. J. (2014). Expertise and intelligent thinking: When is it worse to know better? In *Advances in the psychology of human intelligence* (pp. 157–188). Psychology Press.

García-Carmona, A. (2020). From inquiry-based science education to the approach based on scientific practices: A critical analysis and suggestions for *science teaching. Science & Education, 29*(2), 443–463.

Hirsch, E. D. (1987). *Cultural literacy: What every American needs to know.* Houghton Mifflin Harcourt Publishing.

Hirsch, E. D. (1998). *The schools we need: And why we don't have them*. Anchor.

Hirsch, E. D. (2013). A wealth of words: The key to increasing upward mobility is expanding vocabulary. *City Journal (Winter)*. Houghton Mifflin Harcourt Publishing.

Hirsch, E. D. (2019). *Why knowledge matters: Rescuing our children from failed educational theories.* Harvard Education Press.

Isaksen, B. (2015). *A lesson is the wrong unit of time*. Red or green pen? https://redorgreenpen.wordpress.com/2015/01/29/a-lesson-is-the-wrong-unit-of-time/

Karseth, B., & Sivesind, K. (2010). Conceptualising curriculum knowledge within and beyond the national context. *European Journal of Education, 45*(1), 103–120.

Mccrea, P. (2017). *Memorable teaching: Leveraging memory to build deep and durable learning in the classroom*. John Catt.

Miedema, S. (2023). Knowing and the Known: A philosophical and pedagogical critique on the concept of 'Powerful Knowledge.' *Social Sciences, 12*(10), 578.

Muller, J., & Young, M. (2019). Knowledge, power and powerful knowledge re-visited. *The Curriculum Journal, 30*(2), 196–214.

Oliver, M., McConney, A., & Woods-McConney, A. (2021). The efficacy of inquiry-based instruction in science: A comparative analysis of six countries using PISA 2015. *Research in Science Education, 51,* 595–616.

Organisation for Economic Co-operation and Development (OECD). (2019). *OECD future of education and skills 2030: OECD learning compass 2030*. OECD.

Paraskeva, J. M. (2021). *Conflicts in curriculum theory: Challenging hegemonic epistemologies.* Springer Nature.

Paris, D., & Alim, H. S. (2017). *Culturally sustaining pedagogies: Teaching and learning for justice in a changing world*. Teachers College Press.

Pondiscio, R. (2022). Wanted: A Science of Reading Comprehension movement. *Flypaper.* Thomas Fordham Institute. https://fordhaminstitute.org/national/commentary/wanted-science-reading-comprehension-movement

Recht, D. R., & Leslie, L. (1988). Effect of prior knowledge on good and poor readers' memory of text. *Journal of Educational Psychology, 80*(1), 16.

Sealy, C. (2017) The 3D curriculum that promotes remembering. *Primary Timery*. https://primarytimery.com/2017/10/28/the-3d-curriculum-that-promotes-remembering/

Sherrington, T. (2018). What is a knowledge-rich curriculum? Principle and Practice. *Teacher Head*. https://teacherhead.com/2018/06/06/what-is-a-knowledge-rich-curriculum-principle-and-practice/

Smith, R., Snow, P., Serry, T., & Hammond, L. (2021). The role of background knowledge in reading comprehension: A critical review. *Reading Psychology, 42(3), 214–240.*

Wexler, N. (2020). *The knowledge gap: The hidden cause of America's broken education system—and how to fix it*. Penguin.

Willingham, D. T. (2006). How knowledge helps: It speeds and strengthens reading comprehension, learning—and thinking. *American Educator* (Spring).

Young, M., Lambert, D., Roberts, C., & Roberts, M. (2014). *Knowledge and the future school: Curriculum and social justice*. Bloomsbury Publishing.

10 The science of learning implementation piece

Pursuing sustainable school-wide change

Simon Breakspear, Nathaniel Swain and Katie Roberts-Hull

Implementation in schools is complex, messy, and deeply human work. School leaders often know 'what' they want to improve but may lack clear models for 'how' they can lead change. We now have codified evidence-based practices that provide a good starting point for school improvement goals. But how can leaders mobilise science of learning research in busy schools with overloaded educators?

Bridging the gap between the scientific research and daily classroom practice is a core leadership challenge. Effective implementation will require ongoing learning and *un*learning of teaching practices as well as the development of new organisational structures, routines, and working cultures. This chapter outlines a structured implementation model designed with insights from implementation science research (e.g., Langer et al., 2016; Sharples et al., 2019) to provide a systematic approach for this work. The four-stage model offers practical guidance to school leaders and their teams about the processes that support effective science of learning implementation across diverse school settings.

Box 10.1 - Chapter 10 Overview - The 4E Implementation Model

1. Exploring
2. Experimenting
3. Expanding
4. Embedding

The complexity of implementation

> *Ultimately, it doesn't matter how great an educational idea or intervention is in principle; what really matters is how it manifests itself in the day-to-day work of people in schools.*
> (Sharples et al., 2019)

Implementation is best conceptualised as a set of stages in which teachers and leaders engage in collaborative work overtime (Sharples et al., 2019). Occasionally, we can make the

DOI: 10.4324/9781003404965-12

mistake of thinking new practices are implemented after one professional learning session. Deeper change, however, requires more planning and staged execution (Ehlert et al., 2022).

Teacher learning requires multiple opportunities to learn and apply information (Timperley et al., 2007). Different schools may start out with the same goals, but through experimentation and feedback will end up with varied practices based on context. Ultimately, a successful change process involves trialling new approaches, collecting student learning information, and adapting in continuous improvement cycles.

A model for change: The 4E Implementation Model

In our work partnering with schools, we have found that a four-stage framework can provide a helpful mental model for implementation action planning. The 4E Implementation Model includes four stages: exploring, experimenting, expanding, and embedding. The model can support leaders to take the right action at the right time during the right stage of implementation.

The 4E Model can be applied when making both minor and major shifts towards practices that align with the science of learning. With minor practice changes, schools may progress through the stages at a faster rate; and with major shifts, schools may take much longer, especially at the early stages of exploring and experimenting.

After achieving success and sustainability with one practice, leaders may choose another focus and work through a new 4E journey. For example, a school that has worked on formative assessment and questioning techniques for a year and has seen success at the embedding stage (the final stage) may then choose to next focus on cognitive load theory and associated teaching techniques. On their path towards becoming a science of learning informed organisation, schools will likely work through the 4E Model multiple times as they collectively build knowledge and change instructional habits across different prioritised focus areas.

Cognitive load effects for teachers implementing change

Schools implementing the science of learning may find that the processes for implementing different practices often overlap, especially as teachers get more comfortable with their own learning. Many school leaders reading this book would be familiar with the research that knowledge builds on knowledge (Hirsch, 1999; Willingham, 2006). This is true for both teachers and students.

Schools that are more 'novice' with the science of learning may need to separate change processes into manageable chunks, with a single focus on one practice area at a time. The implementation process at novice schools will likely be more school leader driven, with a whole-school or whole-department focus area.

In 'intermediate' or 'expert' schools, there will potentially be many overlapping implementation processes initiated by different leaders and teachers in the school. The principal may have less visibility over the work being done. In this way, the work of the implementation model mimics the scaffolds of explicit instruction (Archer & Hughes, 2010). New knowledge will be introduced with high levels of leader involvement, but leader support can be withdrawn as teachers move toward expertise and independent practice.

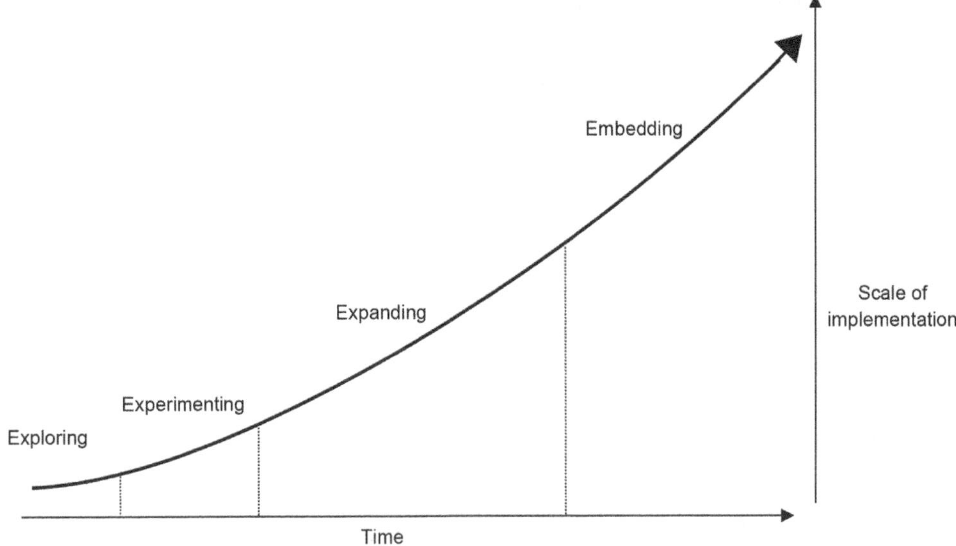

Figure 10.1 4E Implementation Model.

Breaking the change down

The 4E Implementation Model takes leaders through the implementation stages linearly; it is purposely not a cycle. This is to show that leaders can move on to a new focus area when the implementation of one practice is embedded. However, this does not mean that schools should not continue to review and improve practices over time. Ongoing evidence-informed monitoring, reflection and adaptation are crucial across each of the four stages of implementation (Fixsen et al., 2013).

Implementation progress is rarely straightforward, linear, and predictable, and teams must collectively act, monitor, and adjust throughout their journey (Sharples et al., 2019). Early monitoring will provide the opportunity to adjust evidence-based approaches in context. During all stages of the 4E Model, there needs to be a focus on monitoring implementation fidelity, consistency, and outcomes for learners. This is especially true for the later stages when the practice is scaled. The larger the school, the more work might have to be done to ensure new practices are leading to better outcomes for all students across all classrooms (Fixsen et al., 2013).

Stage 1 – Exploring: Lay the groundwork for change

The first stage of the 4E Model is exploring. Exploring is the groundwork of the implementation process where schools build knowledge, define problems, assess organisational readiness, and codify feasible approaches aligned with the science of learning. School leaders should work with a small team to engage in learning, information gathering, and decision-making about the intended evidence-informed teaching approaches and the professional learning and collaborative structures they will utilise to enact change.

Options and readiness for change

School leaders must take time to explore options and decide which new practices will fit their specific context and the problems they are trying to solve. Analysing the current context might involve observing existing practices and instructional methods to check alignment with research-informed approaches.

Leaders can also gauge teacher interests. Even at schools very early in the science of learning journey, there are often small groups of teachers already interested in reforming particular practices. It can work well to start with goals that teachers are already interested in pursuing. Conversely, it is important to understand areas that teachers may be hesitant to change. Individual teacher personalities, previous leaders, and pre-existing resources can all affect school culture and affect how easily you can implement change.

Knowing the culture of the school

Leaders benefit from bringing a spirit of curiosity, openness, and possibility to this searching stage rather than prematurely rushing to a final answer, or rapidly copying what others are doing.

Some leaders might assess the situation and believe it is important to push through the difficult resistance to make a big change in practice. Other times it might be better to start with the lowest-hanging fruit, the easier changes, and build up from there. In our experience, sometimes it takes an expert or external voice to help with this exploration process.

Story Example 10.1 - Exploring stage - Bentleigh West Primary's implementation of systematic synthetic phonics for word reading and spelling

Did you build leadership team knowledge and understanding?

Once then intervention teacher Sarah Asome partnered with Principal Steven Capp to overhaul the teaching of decoding and spelling at the school, they commenced professional learning with instructional expert A/Prof Lorraine Hammond AM. This involved reading government inquiries into literacy teaching and articles on the science of reading. In this initial exploration, the explicit teaching of systematic synthetic phonics appeared repeatedly in their searches.

Did you assess organisational readiness and define problems?

Steven and Sarah identified that the various assessment points they had for reading, spelling, and writing were not providing rigorous and reliable data. In terms of existing programming, teachers used many different spelling programs, with one grade level having five simultaneously. Informally, it was clear that student work had constant spelling errors, and many grade levels had non-readers. The readiness for change was perhaps prepared by the teacher's growing awareness that a more systematic and coordinated approach would make their work easier and more effective, with certain teachers across the school displaying a particular passion to learn how. For Principal Steven this was a real place of vulnerability, as he had few answers for how to teach spelling and decoding himself, and instead leant on the research evidence for guidance.

Did you decide on a specific 'what' and a 'how'?

The 'what' of the change was determined to be the explicit teaching of systematic synthetic phonics, whilst the 'how' of bringing about the change was still being figured out. The school knew they wanted to learn about and implement:

- Explicit teaching (What was the most suitable model?);
- How to be systematic (Did they need a coherent scope and sequence?);
- **Systematic synthetic phonics** from the sounds and codes up, and teaching of decoding/encoding;
- Assessment that could gauge students' **code knowledge**, **phonemic awareness**, word reading, and spelling; and
- How to optimise review of previously learnt material.

Initial methods for approaching staff learning were a lot of shared professional reading, and the modelling of exemplar lessons by Sarah, the most expert teacher at the time (see stage two).

A structured and well-sequenced approach to teaching phonics which involves breaking words down into the individual phonemes and graphemes, and blending them together

Knowing the sound-letter patterns of a language and how they are used to spell/read words

The ability to hear, identify, and manipulate individual sounds (phonemes) in spoken words

Stage 2 - Experimenting: Rapidly learn through trialling the approach in context

In the *experimenting* stage, there is a period in which school leaders work with a smaller sub-section of staff to apply their early thinking on a small scale. The aim is to create successful school-based examples of a science of learning informed practice to make it work in the specific school context.

Leaders should plan to run a series of small-scale prototypes combining the identified evidence-based practices (the 'what') with chosen professional learning approaches (the 'how'). The low-risk testing helps to refine the approach before asking more staff to commit time and effort to change.

Trying out mechanisms for change

Some schools may be utilising existing resources, such as externally created curriculum materials or professional development programs. In these cases, the small school leader group may work on reviewing and adapting materials before involving the wider school community. Other schools may want to adapt their own instructional models in line with science of learning sources. The moves to create **instructional playbooks** at some schools is an example of this. These schools might have a small team designing models, and getting feedback from other teachers on this work.

A bespoke collection of instruction techniques for a school to reference in 'how we teach ___ at our school'

Networking with like-minded schools

During the experimenting stage, it can be particularly helpful to connect with other schools that have already gone down a similar path. These school visits allow for observation of classroom set up, documentation and resources, as well as informal conversations with teachers and leaders at the host school.

Establishing the 'social proof' of the change

By the end of the experimenting stage, leaders should aim to have had multiple teams run several trials using the new approach. Based on early evidence of impact and practitioner feedback, school leaders can make necessary adjustments to their initial approach, enhancing the likelihood of future success. The end goal of the experimenting stage is to have some local school-based successful examples of the teaching approach happening in context. This provides 'social proof' (and some professional envy from the teachers outside the trial) that the approach is feasible and impactful.

Story Example 10.2 - Experimenting stage - Bentleigh West Primary

Did you build a small initial experimentation team?

In the school's journey to implement systematic phonics, there was an unavoidable period where the leadership team worked more intensely with a sub-section of the staff to apply the new model for teaching reading and spelling. Teachers who displayed interest in being 'early adopters' were selected for more intense experimentation while the rest of the school only had a small-scale commitment to two 15–20 minute explicit spelling lessons per week.

How did you refine and sharpen your ideas?

Demonstration lessons were often used to model from one staff member to the rest of the grade level team. These became a springboard for discussion of what was and was not working. Staff meetings became spaces in which the champions modelled example spelling lessons and explained the spelling rules or sounds for the week.

During these collaborative meetings, staff began noticing the effectiveness of whole class instruction, how common explicit teaching routines were enjoyable for students and also helped with student behaviour. Also, previously lower-performing students were gaining spelling and other knowledge more securely with greater review and practice. This built an appetite for change across the school.

If you launched with the whole school immediately, what impact did this have?

Bentleigh West did not hesitate from bringing the learning to the whole school, but focussed much more intensively with certain teams. Spelling improvements were celebrated across the school, making the change appealing and achievable.

Stage 3 – Expanding: Spreading and scaling up improved practice

The expanding stage is about spreading the new knowledge and practices across more of the school. Practical, timely, transparent communication is vital to keeping everyone informed and clear about expectations. The evidence from formative assessment is relevant for the adult learners (teachers) in this part of the process (Wiliam, 2011). This is essentially a time for constant checking for understanding. This communication through the implementation journey should be two-way, with regular feedback channels that welcome early sharing of practitioner concerns or challenges. Leaders need to actively hear and respond to emerging implementation barriers and frustrations and adapt the model accordingly.

De-implementation

Here it is essential to consider any practices that need to be *de*-implemented (Hamilton et al., 2023). It is unreasonable to roll out new initiatives without a gameplan for how they will fit, and what will go to make room. It may be too soon to remove programs or practices to which too many teachers are attached, but there may be some 'low-hanging fruit' your school could reduce or remove. Down the track, once you are firmly embedded, you can circle back to these other practices/programs and fully de-implement as necessary.

Finding and listening to change champions

Throughout this stage, leaders should strongly focus on building teachers' knowledge, motivation, and collaborative ways of working. Drawing on the stories, insights, and advice of educators who successfully engaged in the experimental work is helpful. These 'champions' can help to adapt and spread the new practices and approaches across more classrooms. As more teachers and teams make early progress, school leaders should work to support, celebrate, and showcase the work of those already involved and model what is possible.

Story Example 10.3 - Expanding stage - Bentleigh West Primary

How did you build lead practitioners and champions to spread momentum across teams?

In addition to the first year of school team, selected leaders that were passionate also undertook the initial word reading/spelling training, and they were strategically placed as leaders at Grades 1 and 2 to continue the work as the first cohort of students progressed into these grade levels. Later that year, every leader was trained. A response-to-intervention (RTI) team also worked on creating a set of school-wide scope and sequences for spelling and word reading, which were adopted across the school.

How did you show examples of the desired changes in context?

The school spent considerable time and resources showing videos of core practices that needed to be expanded across the school including:

- review;
- introducing new phonemes and codes;
- words to read; and
- words to spell.

This was coupled with continual work on the theory and key models of how students learn to read (e.g., the Simple View of Reading, see chapter 6).

How did you scale up the professional learning and collaboration?

Staff meeting times continued as professional learning time so teachers could rehearse what they were observing and implementing. The school also set up a small-scale observation and 'learning walk' initiative to gain insight into how change was occurring, allowing teachers to learn from seeing each other in practice.

Stage 4 - Embedding: Form new habits and routines for sustainable change

By the end of the expanding stage there is still a lot of work to do to make sure practices are maintained. Sustaining the work is often a more significant challenge than the initial launch. The final implementation stage, *Embedding*, involves developing instructional habits and sustaining organisational routines. The goal is to avoid returning to default classroom approaches that predominated before embarking on the school-wide implementation.

Developing habits and routines helps reduce the cognitive load associated with executing the new approach in the classroom. When practices become habits, they are less susceptible to being dropped or overlooked during stress or high workload periods.

Ironing out the kinks

The embedding stage might involve a review of the pain points for teachers that have now started to shift practice. The school leadership team can seek out, or create, resources and supports to help teachers embed practice. For some practices, this might mean creating a simple resource like an **assessment rubric**. In other instances, the work required to embed might be more substantial. Leaders might realise they need, for example, a re-development of an existing teaching and learning program to better fit the new direction on which teachers have embarked.

A tool to evaluate and score students' work based on specific criteria

Another key mechanism for embedding practices is planning the ongoing maintenance of professional knowledge and expertise for existing staff, and the training and onboarding of new staff as part of an induction into the approach. This must be built to ensure sustainability over time regardless of any changes in staff.

Monitor maintenance of change

Having established the new approach, continuous monitoring and adaptation are essential. School leaders will know if practices are embedded by observing teaching regularly and reviewing student learning data. It can sometimes be the case that everything looks on-track–the right documentation, strong teaching practices and increased teacher knowledge–but student learning is still lagging. This might be a flag that the implementation has gone astray. Perhaps teachers are spending too little time–or too much time–on a particular instructional method in the classroom. Maybe the current assessments are not properly designed for the new practices. Or, as is often the case, it might take time for changes to teaching practice to show demonstrable changes in student learning.

The goal of embedding science of learning-informed practices is to improve student learning, so school leaders should keep a careful eye on assessment data and try to diagnose potential **implementation fidelity** problems. As teachers and leaders build knowledge of the science of learning and go through implementation processes with multiple practices, they will start developing a better sense of when implementation is going smoothly and where there might be issues.

Rolling out a new initiative in a high-quality way where the things that matter are consistent and effective

Story Example 10.4 - Embedding stage - Bentleigh West Primary

How did you avoid a backslide to default approaches?

Leaders developed a school-wide timetable and work programs with times allocated. Termly low variance curriculum planners detailed what to teach each week. Lesson materials were created, tweaked, and shared, as well as materials for daily review sessions.

How did you embed it into team and organisational routines?

The school allocated time for a structured literacy block for this teaching, and structures to support fidelity of delivery, based upon genuine success the school had already established (e.g., observations, learning walks, and resource provision and refinement). With these structures in place, the new way of teaching word reading and spelling became the Bentleigh West way.

What approaches to monitoring and evaluation are you using?

- **Short cycle assessments:** quick quizzes, short spelling tests linked to scope and sequence;
- **Medium cycle:** Dynamic Indicators of Basic Early Literacy Skills (DIBELS®); and
- **Long cycle:** Progressive Achievement Tests (PAT), Phonics Screening Check, and national standardised testing (NAPLAN).

Immediate checking for understanding tasks that occur during every lesson and inform how the teacher teaches in real time

End of unit assessments and performance tasks like written tasks, oral presentations, or projects

Standardised data including yearly/bi-yearly data collection and high stakes testing

How do you ensure new staff understand and apply the approach?

There is a continual and consistent revisiting and building of knowledge around how the brain learns and a focus on linking to practice. The school's induction handbook features videos of practice from the school's own teachers. Teaching staff have the time and opportunity to continually tweak and road-test lessons, based on the solid set of materials already developed.

How do you continue to adapt and evolve the approaches to respond to changing circumstances?

During professional learning team inquiry cycles, the collected data may indicate areas for improvement. Teams will reflect on practice and current level of attention in the literacy block and make small, but meaningful, adjustments.

This school's case demonstrates that successfully making it to the embedding stage can be a real sweet-spot for teachers, as the cognitive load associated with learning something very new has been alleviated. Staff can focus on small discrete changes to refine their practice even further, based on the short, medium, and long cycle data they collect.

Importantly, Bentleigh West (now a national leader in the teaching of word reading and spelling, among many other aspects) could not have reached this point without the school-wide journey from experimenting to the final stage embedding, managed by the unwavering leadership team.

Table 10.1 Chapter 10 knowledge organiser for the 4E Implementation Model.

1. Exploring	***2. Experimenting***
• Laying the groundwork for change. • Identifying the 'what' and 'how' of the change. • Understanding readiness and any contextual complications.	• Running small scale prototypes for change, with small select teams. • Networking and learning from like-minded schools. • Establishing the 'social proof' that change can work.
3. Expanding	***4. Embedding***
• Building structures to support change (e.g., planning documents, materials, time, training, and coaching). • Consider any urgent de-implementation, or else earmark for later. • Foster change 'champions' to lead collaborative improvement. • Harness feedback loops about what is and is not working.	• Develop instructional habits and routines to make practice easy. • Address pain points and change structures for ongoing learning (including new staff induction). • Monitor maintenance of change to avoid backslides.

Concluding thoughts

This chapter has outlined a simple and adaptable process for guiding school implementation journeys focused on mobilising the insights from the science of learning. Implementation is not a lock-step process and each school's story will be unique. Yet, the 4E Implementation Model provides a helpful heuristic that can reduce the likelihood of getting stuck in common implementation pitfalls (see chapter 10 knowledge organiser).

It is the role of school leadership teams to guide educators through a collective learning journey to adaptively integrate evidence-informed ideas into instructional routines. The end goal should be that the practices informed by the science of learning are embedded without a return to pre-existing default approaches.

Where to next?

- *Teaching sprints: How overloaded educators can keep getting better* by Breakspear & Jones.
- *Cognitive load theory in practice: Examples for the classroom* by Centre for Education Statistics and Evaluation (CESE) (2017).
- *Responsive teaching* by Harry Fletcher-Wood.
- *How learning happens* by Kirschner & Hendrick.
- *Teaching Walkthrus series* by Sherrington & Caviglioli.
- *Understanding how we learn: A visual guide* by Weinstein Sumeracki & Caviglioli.
- *Embedded formative assessment* by Dylan Wiliam.
- *Powerful teaching: Unleash the science of learning* by Agarwal & Bain.

Check your indicators - Implementation

On-Track Indicators	*Off-Track Indicators*
• Conducting thorough research and analysis to understand the need for change. • Engaging stakeholders in discussions about the proposed change. • Establishing feedback mechanisms to gather data on the effectiveness of the small-scale implementation testing. • Developing structures and resources to support the scaling up of successful prototypes. • Monitoring and evaluating the maintenance of the change to prevent backsliding.	• Never quite finishing or fully implementing changes across the school. • Failing to de-implement practices that need to go, to make room for new ones. • Neglecting to build capacity or provide support for the expanded change. • Ignoring or failing to make adjustments based on feedback. • Allowing the change to become stagnant or backslide.

Discussion questions

1. How can we lay the groundwork in our school, ensuring that all stakeholders understand the need for change?
2. How can we network and learn from like-minded schools to gather ideas and establish 'social proof'?
3. How should we approach urgent de-implementation of practices that are not working, and how can we ensure that other changes are earmarked for later implementation?
4. How can we develop instructional habits and routines that support and maintain the changes?

References

Archer, A., & Hughes, C. (2010). *Explicit instruction: Effective and efficient teaching*. Guilford Press.

EEF Blog. (2017). *Untangling the 'Literacy Octopus' - three crucial lessons from the latest EEF evaluation | News.* (2017, December 1).

Ehlert, M., Hebbecker, K., & Souvignier, E. (2022). Implementing evidence-based practices in reading classrooms. *Studies in Educational Evaluation*, *75*(December), 101203.

Fixsen, D., Blase, K., Metz, A., & Van Dyke, M. (2013). Statewide implementation of evidence-based programs. *Exceptional Children*, *79*(2), 213-230.

Hamilton, A., Hattie, J., & Wiliam, D. (2023). *Making room for impact: A de-implementation guide for educators*. Corwin Press.

Hirsch, E. D. (1999). *The schools we need and why we don't have them*. Anchor.

Jones, K. (2020). *Retrieval practice: Resources and research for every classroom.* John Catt Educational.

Langer, L., Tripney, J., & Gough, D. (2016). *The science of using science: Researching the use of research evidence in decision-making*. EPPI Centre, Social Science Research Unit, UCL Institute of Education.

Sharples, J., Albers, B., Fraser, S., & Kime, S. (2019). Putting evidence to work: A school's guide to implementation. *Guidance report.* Second Edition. Education Endowment Foundation.

Sherrington, T. (2019). Rosenshine's principles in action. John Catt Educational, Limited.

Timperley, H., Wilson, A., Barrar, H., & Fung, I. (2007). *Teacher professional learning and development: Best evidence synthesis iteration (BES).* Ministry of Education New Zealand.

Willingham, D. (2006). How knowledge helps. *American Educator (Spring).*

PART THREE

The Takeaways

11 Kickstarting your work with the science of learning

Nathaniel Swain

> *Learning can happen without our teaching; but teaching cannot happen without their learning.*

I penned the above quotation to affix to my office door at La Trobe University, adapted from the famous motto from the father of Direct Instruction, Siegfried Engelmann: *If the children are not learning, we are not teaching.* My small, but significant alteration to the message was that students *can* learn beyond what an educator can teach them directly, as our students continue learning and teaching themselves, no matter what we implement. However, Engelmann's axiom rings true when we consider the role of the educator: not just to facilitate self-guided learning, but to *ensure* that students learn. That is what defines the very act of teaching.

If you take only *some* ideas from the science of learning and implement them in a *piecemeal* way, you are unlikely to observe the potential benefits to teachers and students captured in this book. Instead, to harness the science of learning, we need to completely rethink our understandings of 'great teaching' and seek to develop educator knowledge and expertise in instructional practices that ensure all students benefit. Only then can we begin to level the playing field and stop amplifying the inequities.

Taking the unavoidable insights into account

So, what do teachers, schools, and educational systems need to do to harness the science of learning and thus realise excellence and equity?

You will need to take a position on key tensions revealed by this scientific research, for example:

- How does your instructional approach account for the fact that working memory is so limited?
- How does it account for the fact that nearly all learning students will undertake in schools is biologically secondary, and therefore not picked up naturally?
- How does it systematically account for the forgetting curve, where students forget most of what we teach them unless we review?
- How does it account for the fact that novices benefit from much greater guidance during instruction?

Deciding how you will handle these questions sets up the key mind shifts you need to make to harness the science of learning, including the role of the teacher, ways of ensuring

DOI: 10.4324/9781003404965-14

learning is mastered and retained, structuring groups, and how to cater for all students effectively.

In this chapter, we will explore key changes to be made in light of the gaps between common practice and implications for practice from the science of learning. It will focus on some of the *unavoidable insights* for school-wide instructional planning. See the chapter overview in Box 11.1.

Box 11.1 - Chapter 11 Overview - Key mind shifts in light of the science of learning principles

1. Put student learning at the heart of teaching;
2. Make effective and engaging teaching the norm;
3. Plan curriculum that is coherent, knowledge-rich, and includes regular review;
4. Teach at the whole-class level responsively;
5. Make it easy for your students to participate; and
6. Invest in your professional knowledge.

Brief note: Science of learning ≠ explicit instruction

There is an established science of effective instruction (Archer & Hughes, 2010; see Project follow through: Adams, 1996; Ashman, 2020), which although controversial in many educational circles, remains well-researched. It encompasses teaching approaches that align well with the science of how students learn best (AERO, 2023).

That being said, the science of learning is *not synonymous* with explicit instruction, as learning sciences capture more than just effective teaching, covering all aspects of the learning process.

Can you utilise the science of learning without a form of explicit instruction?

Defined broadly, explicit instruction is any form of direct and clear modelling or explanation, followed by targeted student practice (whether guided or independent) that builds upon the initial modelling or explanation. Such an orientation aligns well with many principles from the science of learning. Although some educational commentators may not like all that explicit instruction entails, I would argue that it is an unavoidable (and also highly beneficial) component of effective teaching.

Key frameworks to support the alignment of your practices with the science of learning have been included in the endnotes of this chapter. These include principles of learning, and techniques for counteracting the **forgetting curve**, as well as some models of fully guided/explicit instruction, including:

The phenomenon in which learners tend to immediately forget most of what they have learnt previously with sharp declines over time, unless content is reviewed

- Anita Archer's (2010) Explicit Instruction;
- Hollingsworth and Ybarra's (2017) Explicit Direct Instruction (EDI);

- Lemov's (2021) Teach Like a Champion techniques;
- Sherrington and Caviglioli's (2019–22) Teaching Walkthrus; and
- Rosenshine's (2012) Principles of Instruction.

Archer and Hughes' Explicit Instruction model which includes an (1) *opening*, (2) *body* (I do, we do, you do), and (3) *closing* of the lesson is an elegant framework to conceptualise teaching that scaffolds and supports learners. Also, Stanislas Dehaene's (2021) four pillars of learning is particularly useful for crystalising the non-negotiables of successful learning, and includes (1) attention, (2) active engagement, (3) error feedback, and (4) consolidation.

1. Put student learning at the heart of teaching

At the centre of our work as educators, we must always prioritise what students need from us to experience successful learning. The science of learning indicates that a novice needs guidance, which includes explicit instruction right from the start, and clear connections to prior learning. If we leave this initial introduction to chance, we can leave many learners behind, particularly those who most need teacher guidance and support.

There is thus an **equity imperative** to break down learning into manageable parts, use explicit instruction techniques, and collect in-the-moment formative assessment (or checking for understanding, see below) to ensure instruction is working and to indicate when to gradually release responsibility to each learner.

The requirement to address the needs for students who are currently under-achieving and who need our support

Get started: Checking for understanding

Hollingsworth and Ybarra (2017) define **checking for understanding** (CFU) as the teacher continually verifying that students are learning *what* is being taught *while* the teaching is still happening. This is real-time **formative assessment,** not at the end of the lesson, or unit, or term, but every 3–4 minutes in the midst of the instruction. Checking for understanding is the secret to making explicit instruction work, as it intersperses questions, prompts and tasks that require students to frequently and actively respond and engage with the learning at hand, while you are breaking it down and putting it back together (Archer & Hughes, 2010).

The teacher checking if students are learning while the lesson is unfolding using short, specific checks of understanding and proficiency

Work undertaken by teachers (and students) that provide information or feedback to inform changes to teaching

CFUs can take the form of:

- pair shares/turn and talks;
- mini-whiteboard tasks;
- cold calling;
- multiple choice or true/false; and
- exit tickets—to name but a few.

Crucially, CFU is *not* a check for opinion or perspective (e.g., *What do you think about ___?*), nor a check for awareness: (e.g., *Everyone got that*?). CFUs, although taking many forms, are illustrated in Hollingsworth and Ybarra's TAPPLE acronym which involves:

- **T**eaching students something first;
- **A**sking a specific questions related to that learning;
- **P**air shares, each student with a set partner;
- **P**icking a non-volunteer;
- **L**istening for a response; and
- **E**ffective feedback through echoing, explaining, or elaborating on the students' answers.

Ever heard the criticism that explicit instruction means you have to 'lecture' students for far too long? Or the idea that students cannot focus for longer than 5-10 minutes at a time? By incorporating CFU every 3-4 minutes, you break up your instruction into manageable pieces. This restarts students' focus by asking them to do something actively, so there is no chance for students to zone out, get off-task, or muck around. When using CFU, explicit instruction is not 'lecturing,' it is interactive and responsive teaching that keeps teachers and students accountable for learning.

Checking for understanding is essential as it allows teachers to identify areas where students may be struggling and adjust the instruction accordingly at the time it counts most– when students can use the feedback you provide to understand and learn then and there. To read more, please turn to Hollingsworth and Ybarra (2017), Archer and Hughes (2010), and Lemov (2021) for the experts in this irreplaceable instructional practice.

How does the science of learning amend what we see as 'great teaching'?

Putting student learning and success at the centre of our work means being intentional and purposeful in all our instructional decisions. It means providing good instruction right from the start, using explicit instruction, and checking for understanding diligently and effectively. By doing so, we can create a more equitable and just educational system that truly serves the needs of all learners.

What shifts in teacher practice are required? Key aspects to consider when making changes in light of the science of learning include:

- building predictable classroom routines;
- minimising extraneous load from the environment and learning materials;
- attending to the prior knowledge of students, and explicitly connecting new learning;
- developing students' knowledge explicitly and systematically;
- guiding students' practice from understanding a model, to sharing the responsibility for completing the task, through to independent execution of the task;
- checking for understanding (CFU) constantly whilst teaching; and
- re-teaching, extending, and supporting learners based on the differential insights gained from CFUs.

If our instruction is haphazard or ineffective, despite well-intentioned, the outcomes can be devastating for our most at-risk. Thus, putting student learning at the heart of our teaching also requires a deep commitment to *equity* to ensure we are meeting the needs of all students, regardless of their background or abilities.

Story Example 11.1 – What does great teaching mean now at our school? Riverwood Public School

Since its overhaul of its literacy program and the introduction of explicit instruction pedagogies for new content, great teaching has taken on a whole new set of meanings. This is based on high expectations and high support for all teachers and students, despite the challenges of the school's complex community.

Now 'great teaching' means:

- a systematic school-wide approach to instruction, intervention, knowledge-building, observation, and coaching;
- supported through a multi-layered approach to professional learning;
- responsive to student need;
- using an explicit and fully guided approach for any content that is biologically secondary, only having students problem solving and inquiring when they have the foundational knowledge to do so; and
- regularly refining teacher practice, based on class-level and school-wide data.

Riverwood's teachers pride themselves on leaving nothing to chance, ensuring their students are learning and thriving. No time is wasted and every instructional minute counts for their students. In some ways, the school is unrecognisable from a handful of years ago. Riverwood also differs from the status quo in its adherence to a more rigorous, research-informed, dynamic learning environment, that still fosters confidence, motivation, fun, and enjoyment in all students.

2. Make effective and engaging teaching the norm

Explicit instruction and responsive teaching help to level the playing field and ensure that all students have access to high-quality learning experiences. By breaking down complex concepts into manageable pieces and providing clear explanations, we can help even the most struggling learners make progress.

Engaging for learning, not entertaining

Far from a boring or rigid approach to instruction, teaching that aligns with how students learn should be fun, inviting, and engaging because of the opportunities for students to respond and actively contribute.

As per Archer and Hughes' (2010) **eliciting frequent student responses** and Hollingsworth and Ybarra's (2017) **engagement norms**, we can ensure that our teaching is truly engaging:

Orchestrating frequent chances for students to participate in the learning through call and response, choral reading, and other checking for understanding tasks

Taught, practiced, and expected routines for student responses and participation (e.g., attention signal, choral or tracked reading, pair shares, mini whiteboards)

- Engaging *not* because we are trying to entertain (or 'hook' students into learning using semi-related content); but
- Engaging because we expect and are making it easy for students to respond and actively contribute to the learning as it happens.

Moving from 20% to 80%

When you build a base of good instruction, curriculum, and assessment, teachers begin to reach a greater proportion of the class in their main teaching delivery.

Often, teachers may be reaching only 20% of the class in explicit teaching, helping the remaining 80% of learners in small-groups or through individual conferencing. Changing your approach to teaching can shift this to 80% of students in the teacher-guided phase, with only 20% remaining for additional small group teaching.

In this way, effective explicit instruction (Tier 1) is one of the best things you can do for students with individual needs. Your school should of course use **multi-tiered systems of support** (MTSS) like Response to Intervention (RTI), but crucially the teacher needs to get Tier 1 as strong as it can be. Teach your students well and, initially, teach them as a whole group (see section on using small groups wisely below).

A framework of multi-levelled systems to support students' learning and behaviour; intended to take a preventative approach

3. Plan curriculum that is coherent, knowledge-rich, and includes regular review

As unpacked in chapter 9, coherent, knowledge-rich curricula set learners up for success, and allow for well-sequenced and ambitious planning with high expectations for what students can learn.

It is critical to remember that students' long-term memory does not discriminate between factual and counter-factual knowledge, so the role of the curriculum and the teacher is to ensure that solid, factual information is taught cumulatively and carefully (substantive knowledge), addressing misconceptions, and ensuring students understand where such knowledge comes from, and how it is put together (disciplinary knowledge; Ashbee, 2021).

Your curriculum decisions should always create a **low floor** (accessible and achievable entry point), and **no ceilings** (a chance for learners to challenge themselves without limits). This means ensuring that:

Providing an accessible entry point to the learning, so that all students can experience some success

Enabling any student to continue to challenge themselves through to application and open ended creation or critique

- students have the foundational knowledge and skills they need to be successful;
- teachers bridge from the *known* to the *new* effectively; and
- solid foundational learning becomes the stepping stone to more advanced learning and expertise.

Not all learners will find it as easy to engage with the planned curriculum. Ensure that the learning progresses logically and takes account of students' prior learning. But then increase the supports for students that need it; or create a challenge for those who need to be extended. However, you should also try to avoid the trap of deciding that some content is just too hard for some students. This is why I advocate **differentiating by the support** we provide to students, rather than **differentiating by curriculum** (e.g., differentiating in the kinds of content to which students get access) (Enser 2019, as cited in Fawcett, 2019, p. 159).

Deciding that all students should get access to the main areas of study. Differentiating by changing the level of support or extension you provide, or the number of exposures needed for particular students to experience success

Deciding that some students will study some things at their 'right level' and others will do easier or harder areas of study. Differentiating by changing what activities and learning some students get access to

Remembering is key

Teachers and leaders have often been convinced that learning is not about memorisation, and that 'deep understanding' is the target of effective teaching. What this truism misses is that a learner cannot understand something they do not recall. To begin to understand something, you have to first know it at a surface level, as a minimum.

This is one of those fundamental mind shifts that need to happen if you are to embark on a science of learning journey. It is an immutable fact that learning involves remembering. It does not have to be boring. Remembering does have to happen, however.

Pursuing understanding without knowledge being taught and built coherently is putting the cart before the horse. Recall that prior knowledge powers future learning, and that being able to remember fluently and automatically frees up working memory to focus on the new aspects of learning.

Review and retrieval practice

Remember that forgetting is part of learning. When you embed daily and monthly review, you take advantage of the benefits of **retrieval practice**, spacing, and interleaving. Plan for your students forgetting by breaking up learning up over time.

Opportunities for students to attempt to remember how to complete previous learning tasks or recall previously learnt concepts, facts, or skills

This fundamentally addresses Dehaene's (2021) fourth pillar of learning: consolidation. By utilising existing review materials and ensuring you can see exemplary delivery of this daily practice, you will notice the change to students' consolidation and retention of prior learning. The schools in this book report that students will find it fun, and that the change in the retention will be rapid.

Your curriculum needs to be low variance (to avoid unnecessary gaps between classes and students, and coherent, including opportunities for retrieval practice/**spaced practice** (see chapters 4 and 9). Just because you taught it, it does not mean it was learnt, nor that it will be remembered and mastered.

Structuring learning, so that it is spaced out over time, meaning there are time gaps between the lessons that allow students to better consolidate their learning

Story Example 11.2 - Example of quick win: Daily reviews - Steven Capp

Former principal Steven Capp commenced at a new school in 2023, and began implementing the seeds of school-wide change, being careful not to put anyone off in the process!

A quick win has been the introduction of **daily reviews.** Steven has worked with grade level leaders to ensure support materials for reviews are available and to ensure very easy implementation of simple starters to begin this work.

A short, daily session of practice of previously taught material, including concepts and skills that ensure students consolidate their learning and avoid forgetting

Reviews are now happening from the first year of school to Grade 6 at Steven's new school with a high rate of consistency. Teachers have reported high student engagement, improvement in learning, as well as increased understanding of mathematical knowledge. The insights gained from this basic practice has led to the realisation that some curriculum design might need to change and teachers are already working on solutions for the year to come; the implementation of reviews is paving the way for bigger and bolder changes.

Steven celebrated these small wins via school communications, walk-throughs, observations, and staff discussion reinforcing the changes.

Create pathways from foundational to higher order learning

When students know and remember more—and less information is new or unfamiliar—the bridge to more complex learning becomes stronger, faster, and can go to many more interesting places. Mastery of prior foundational knowledge provides the pathway to higher order learning.

Story Example 11.3 - Getting the foundations right lifts everyone - Bentleigh West

One could not describe the *primary* focus of Bentleigh West as seeking to raise the bar for gifted and/or talented students. Rather, the school has doggedly pursued the most explicit, systematic, and fully guided instruction it could, and the result has meant that a robust foundation has been laid for core learning in English and mathematics.

Despite a clear focus on closing the gaps for students at risk, there has been an even more stark shift in all students' achievement and capacity for learning. With firm foundations set, the school has needed to raise the curriculum level of mathematics and English, so each student is studying the equivalent of 12–18 months ahead.

By working on the foundations and nailing them, students with the greatest learning challenges have of course benefited (all are now 'at level' as determined by the National assessment benchmark following intervention and classroom instruction). In addition, the results across the school have also shifted significantly upwards (see Table 11.1), meaning that such work not only increases equity, but also general excellence for all.

Table 11.1 Percentage of students achieving exceeding or strong in national standardised testing (values in %).

	Reading	*Spelling*	*Writing*	*Mathematics*	*Grammar and Punctuation*
Grade 3	89	87	99	93	93
Grade 5	95	94	100	98	95

For example, all but five students in a grade level of 50 made it into the state-wide high ability program for English and Maths in 2023. There is also an increasing number of students who require an individualised learning plan for *extension* across all grade levels.

Some may warn against putting so much effort into foundational concepts, or *relying* too heavily on explicit instruction, for fear it will limit the potential of students who need extension. The example of Bentleigh West suggests that exact opposite effect. The work on getting the foundations right benefits all, and raises the bar for what is possible across the board.

4. Teach at the whole-class level responsively, and adapt where needed

By and large, your initial instruction should begin with effective, explicit teaching at a whole class level. During this time, learners needing further support or further extension can be supported in the moment, and later on in the lesson, as responsibility is released to students.

Adaptive teaching has been proposed as an alternative to differentiation (Eaton, 2022) and is focussed more on planning for whole-class success in learning outcomes, with real-time changes to lesson delivery/questioning/tasks based on how students are understanding or performing (i.e., formative assessment). Adaptive and responsive teaching might involve opportunities for effective and efficient **checking for understanding** routines (to know when to go back and re-teach) and additional prompts or supports to provide to students while their peers complete pair shares or mini-whiteboard work.

The teacher checking if students are learning while the lesson is unfolding using short, specific checks of understanding and proficiency

Story Example 11.4 - How we use small groups now - Churchill Primary

Small groups used to be the way Churchill teachers taught most things: guided reading, literacy rotations, and numeracy rotations, for example. In fact, they did not understand any other way to provide that instruction.

Now whole class instruction is the norm. Smaller groups are *mainly* used to go deeper into learning and provide additional instruction and support for those students who happen to need more for that particular lesson. This usually occurs while others go to independent practice.

Some gaps do persist for certain Churchill students, so additional intervention is provided as per **RTI/MTSS** (see chapter 5). These small groups access interventions provided out-of-class and in-class support. Churchill staff pride themselves on effective and responsive whole class teaching. They certainly do not miss having to repeat the same content or student questions across multiple groups across multiple days, which used to be a daily occurrence.

A tiered framework used in education to provide early, systematic, and targeted support to students who need it, with the goal of preventing long-term difficulties

A framework of multi-levelled systems to support students' learning and behaviour; intended to take a preventative approach

How to make it work for all

Could it be that effective teaching that aligns with the science of learning can *benefit high achievers as well as those at risk*? How could something that builds the foundations and introductory skills of students starting from behind, simultaneously work to extend the thinking and abilities of advanced students? It is simple; great teaching is great teaching for all! While students who need more support get the foundational support, stronger students gain an explicit awareness of that which they have only intuited.

Responsively formed small groups, following whole group instruction

If you find yourself repeating learning content to different small groups of students, you should consider providing this initial instruction as a whole class. You can always follow up with additional smaller group instruction based on need. Importantly, when you break learning down into manageable chunks, using checking for understanding to see how students are responding, it becomes clearer who needs this additional support. This avoids making assumptions about what students are ready to learn, based on the group they are in.

A simple way to support students requiring additional support and practice is to run a focus group of particular learners after the main part of the lesson is concluded. Most students may go off to independent practice for this part of the lesson, while your focus group can get targeted and additional instruction and support with a small number of peers.

Story Example 11.5 - How we cater for diversity - Riverwood

Riverwood continues to support a richly diverse school community, in terms of cultural-linguistic, parental occupation, and socio-economic differences. However, the school does not allow diversity to become an excuse for lowered expectations.

The school is guided by the following principles to support and cater for diversity, while keeping expectations sky-high:

- Student growth is the main focus and the school measures it regularly: The school expects all students to make more than a year's worth of growth each academic year;
- Assessment and data are the starting point (a clear assessment schedule and student screening before entry is vital);
- The school also believes in **differentiation by support**, not **differentiation by curriculum**;
- Integration funding for students with medium to high support needs is invested into in-class or small group evidence-based interventions; and
- The school seeks out community partnerships to support their diverse student and community population, including a playgroup partnership and additional services that can be accessed on-site (e.g., school meals, psychology, and social work).

> Deciding that all students should get access to the main areas of study. Differentiating by changing the level of support or extension you provide, or the number of exposures needed for particular students to experience success
>
> Deciding that some students will study some things at their 'right level' and others will do easier or harder areas of study. Differentiating by changing what activities and learning some students get access to

5. Make it easy for your students to participate: Implications for behaviour and engagement

The incredibly good news story here is that the changes that align with the science of learning increase academic achievement, whilst also improving the confidence, engagement, and motivation of students. The stories featured in this book demonstrate that those students who would typically require your attention for behaviour and wellbeing concerns will benefit from a shift to enact the principles from the science of learning. This is because of the virtuous cycle that can start with academic success and continue with relationship building and trust between teacher and student.

As our stories have shown, the changes to implement science of learning informed practices have led to marked decreases in student behavioural incidents including office referrals, suspensions, and expulsions. As emphasised in chapter 4 and revisited in the next chapter, developing and embedding clear and consistent classroom norms and routines helps to ensure all students know how to participate and also reduces the cognitive load of the learning as the environment becomes calmer and more predictable.

Making your instruction pacier, more bite-sized, with more frequent **opportunities to respond** allows your students to feel engaged in the actual learning, not 'hooked' into it by some extrinsic opener. Great teaching makes it easy for students to participate and stay motivated.

> Teacher initiated opportunities for students to respond to prompts or tasks about the learning

Story Example 11.6 - Building bridges to expected learning routines - Challis Community Primary

Needing to motivate and support the wellbeing of its students is a key goal at Challis Community Primary. For all students, there are school-wide expectations and teaching/rehearsal of expected behaviours. The school could have adapted common approaches for attempting to *engage* students by creating entertaining lessons, that cater to their interests. Instead, the school has raised its expectations for what students can learn to do and includes 'behaviours for learning' as a key part of its curriculum.

At Challis, any behaviour the school wants to occur routinely has to be explicitly taught. The teaching of routines for pair shares provides a clear example of the utility of strong routines for making explicit what we mean by engaged, learning behaviours.

Prior to the explicit teaching and rehearsal of the pair-share routine across the school, there were lots of 'group chats' in Challis Community Primary classrooms. Often, students would be seated in groups, and when the teacher said to discuss it was more of a 'free for all.' Classrooms were incredibly noisy and not always on task. Often, the most dominant personality would do all the talking. Some students would not utter a word. If there was a disagreement with what was said, chaos could ensue. In this environment, behaviour would escalate very quickly from a group chat to physical confrontations and high risk, unsafe behaviour. In many ways, these lower expectations and lack of routines for learning made class interactions less predictable, and arguably more dangerous.

This contrasts strongly with how routines and engagement norms are now used, where students are provided a clear seating plan, and are explicitly taught a routine to decide who goes first, how to share responses, how to respond when listening, and how to agree/build on/challenge. As a result, behaviour has improved, and learning experiences have been optimised.

The lesson we can learn from Challis' success is that trying to increase motivation with exciting lessons or activities is insufficient and likely ineffective. Instead, motivation and engagement can be instilled by improving behaviour teaching and support systems, and using excellent instructional methods so that students experience success and enjoyment in their learning. This is key to helping students break the cycle of under-achievement and de-motivation.

6. Invest in your professional knowledge: There is more to learn about the science of learning!

Remember that your own professional knowledge is critical to better harness the insights from the science of how humans learn. In the interest of accessibility, the complex field of learning sciences has been condensed for this book. There are additional theories within the science of learning that are summarised for your further reading in Table 11.2.

Table 11.2 Additional theories or approaches comprising the science of learning.

Theory or Approach	*Brief Description*
Dual coding theory (Paivio, 1991)	Suggests that learning is more effective when verbal/written and visual information is presented simultaneously in a complementary way for all learners.
Meaningful learning theory (Ausubel, 2000)	Emphasises the importance of relating new information to existing knowledge in meaningful ways, promoting deeper understanding and retention.
Generative learning theory (Fiorella & Mayer, 2016)	Focuses on learning strategies that encourage students to generate understandings and their own explanations, or visualisations leading to more active engagement and retention.
Self-regulated learning (Panadero, 2017)	Involves students taking control of their own learning process, including setting goals, monitoring progress, and adjusting strategies to improve learning outcomes.
Concept of Mode A versus Mode B teaching (Sherrington, 2017)	Mode A teaching emphasises direct instruction and explicit teaching methods (80% of time), while Mode B teaching involves more open-ended and exploratory approaches (20% of time).

Closing thoughts

Undoubtedly, there are multiple ways to improve your teaching using the science of learning and each journey will look different, depending on your school, staff culture, and the community you serve. In this chapter, I have explained the mindshifts that offer profound improvement opportunities in both general achievement and engagement of your students and you as a teacher. These are key ideas that we *cannot afford* to ignore any longer.

See the knowledge organiser in Table 11.3.

Table 11.3 Chapter 11 knowledge organiser.

1. Put student learning at the heart of teaching • Check for understanding. • Review and retrieval practice. • Amend definition of 'great teaching'	***2. Make effective and engaging teaching the norm*** • Engaging for learning, not entertaining. • Moving from 20% to 80%.
3. Plan curriculum that is coherent, knowledge-rich, and includes regular review • Remembering is key. • Review and retrieval make it easy. • Create pathways from foundational to higher order learning.	***4. Teach at the whole-class level responsively and adapt where needed*** • Get whole class, adaptive, and responsive instruction working well. • Use small groups wisely. • Make it work for those needing extension as well as those needing support.
5. Make it easy for your students to participate • Implications for behaviour and engagement. • Motivation links to achievement. • Norms and routines.	***6. Invest in your professional knowledge: There is more to learn about the science of learning*** • See table 11.2.

Where to next?

- Australian Education Research Organisation [AERO] (2023). *How students learn best.*
- Australian Education Research Organisation [AERO] (2024), *Classroom management resources.*

The following boxes provide key principles and approaches from the science of learning, and explicit instruction.

Box 11.2 - Four pillars from Stanislas Dehaene

- Attention
- Active Engagement
- Error Feedback
- Consolidation

Box 11.3 - Explicit Direct Instruction (EDI) key components

- Engagement Norms and Checking for Understanding
- Activating Prior Knowledge and Learning Goals
- Teacher Explanation and Modelling (concept development, skill development)
- Guided Practice
- Closure
- Independent Practice

Box 11.4 - TLAC 3.0 teaching practices

- Lesson Preparation
- Check for Understanding
- Academic Ethos
- Lesson Structures
- Pacing
- Building Ratio Through Questioning, Writing, Discussion
- Procedures and Routines
- High Behavioural Expectations
- Building Student Motivation and Trust

Box 11.5 - Rosenshine's Principles of Effective Instruction (2012)

1. Begin a lesson with a short review of previous learning
2. Present new material in small steps with student practice
3. Ask a large number of questions and check the responses of all students
4. Provide models
5. Guide student practice
6. Check for student understanding
7. Obtain a high success rate
8. Provide scaffolding for difficult tasks
9. Require and monitor independent practice
10. Engage students in weekly and monthly review

Check your indicators - Kickstarting the work

On-Track Indicators	*Off-Track Indicators*
• Great teaching is about well-structured lessons, checking for understanding, engagement norms, and daily review. • Pathways from foundational to higher-order learning are understood and student mastery leads to later exploration. • Whole-class instruction is adaptive and responsive to student needs, using checking for understanding and responsive teaching. • The two-way links between motivation and achievement are acknowledged and addressed.	• Student learning outcomes are important but not your central focus. • Great teaching is about engaging students with topics that interest them personally. • Students mainly learn in small group rotations based on need; whole class learning is swift and introductory. • Learning routines are not executed fluently, and considerable time is spent on managing behaviour and ensuring student focus. • Sometimes the goal posts are shifted away from learning as students have significant issues with wellbeing and behaviour.

Discussion questions

1. How do the definitions of 'great teaching' from this chapter compare with your current teaching practices?
2. What practices can you develop to regularly check for understanding and do review/retrieval practice?
3. What steps can you take to emphasise the importance of remembering, incorporate effective practice, and create clear pathways from foundational to higher-order learning?

4. How might you ensure that your classroom is engaging for learning without reducing your work to entertainment?
5. How can you ensure that your whole-class teaching is adaptive and responsive? How can you use small groups wisely to support different learning needs?
6. What specific aspects of the science of learning do you wish to explore further?

References

Adams, G. (1996). Project follow through: In-depth and beyond. *Effective School Practices, 15*(1), 43-56.

Archer, A. L., & Hughes, C. A. (2010). *Explicit instruction: Effective and efficient teaching.* Guilford Publications.

Ashbee, R. (2021). *Curriculum: Theory, culture and the subject specialisms.* Routledge.

Ashman, G. (2020). The power of explicit teaching and direct instruction. *The Power of Explicit Teaching and Direct Instruction*, 1-152.

Australian Education Research Organisation [AERO] (2023). *How students learn best: An overview of the evidence.* https://www.edresearch.edu.au/research/research-reports/how-students-learn-best-overview-evidence

Ausubel, D. P. (2000). Assimilation theory in meaningful learning and retention processes. *The acquisition and retention of knowledge: A cognitive view* (pp. 101-145).

Dehaene, S. (2021). *How we learn: Why brains learn better than any machine . . . for now.* Penguin.

Eaton, J. (2022). *Moving from 'differentiation' to 'adaptive teaching.'* EEF blog. https://educationendowmentfoundation.org.uk/news/moving-from-differentiation-to-adaptive-teaching

Fawcett, D. (2019). *Relearning to teach: Understanding the principles of great teaching.* Routledge.

Fiorella, L., & Mayer, R. E. (2016). Eight ways to promote generative learning. *Educational Psychology Review, 28*, 717-741.

Foreman, P., & Arthur-Kelly, M. (2017). *Inclusion in action.* Cengage AU.

Hollingsworth, J. R., & Ybarra, S. E. (2017). *Explicit direct instruction (EDI): The power of the well-crafted, well-taught lesson.* Corwin Press.

Lemov, D. (2021). *Teach like a champion 3.0: 63 Techniques that put students on the path to college.* John Wiley & Sons.

Paivio, A. (1991). Dual coding theory: Retrospect and current status. *Canadian Journal of Psychology, 45*(3), 255.

Panadero, E. (2017). A review of self-regulated learning: Six models and four directions for research. *Frontiers in Psychology, 8*, 422.

Sherrington, T. (2017). *The learning rainforest: Great teaching in real classrooms.* Hachette UK.

Sherrington, T., & Caviglioli, O. (2020). *Teaching walkthrus: 5-step guides to instructional coaching.* John Catt Ltd.

12 Improving your school as a science of learning leader

Steven Capp and Nathaniel Swain

School leadership is a messy space with often conflicting ideas. There are numerous viewpoints on what makes a good leader and how best to enact school change. We anticipate this chapter, directed mainly at current or aspirational school leaders, may further demystify this important work for you and your colleagues.

Hopefully, you are starting to get excited about the kinds of changes your school could undertake. The following headlines provide the laser-focus you will need to make good decisions as you navigate your science of learning journey:

Your ultimate role as leader is to protect the attention of your teachers and students.

Teaching can be overwhelming. Learning can be overwhelming. These are, by definition, cognitively-taxing undertakings, and distractions away from the successful pedagogy are endless. It can take considerable effort to minimise the interruptions, devices, wellbeing concerns, behavioural issues, and administrative tasks that always seek to steal the attention of students and teachers alike. There is much a leader can change to succeed in this endeavour.

Your penultimate role is to manage the cognitive load of the changes you wish to make.

Change, on the other hand, is nearly *always* overwhelming. So, your job is to support teachers and students to find a resurgence of energy and calm in their work, while extending that sense of flow to the very change process. Change fatigue is real.

The *why*, *what*, and *how* of these changes must be understood and valued by your staff, and should be clearly aligned with your agreed-upon, refreshed school vision; and as the late business theory heavyweight Peter Drucker (2006) argued: leaders can make this vision *clear*, or they can make it *very clear*.

Vision for precision

Upon appointment at Bentleigh West Primary school in 2015, Steven ascertained from discussions with staff members, students, and parents that the school was searching for identity.

DOI: 10.4324/9781003404965-15

Story Example 12.1 - Bentleigh West - Crafting the new school vision, Steven Capp

As the new principal, I could see an opportunity for a new, more sustainable identity: a chance to strip everything back to the core purpose of teaching, learning, and wellbeing.

We sought to confront our current reality, acknowledge it, and collectively identify the changes we could make, informed by evidence. As part of this process, Bentleigh West worked with students, staff, parents, and the wider community to build the school vision, from which the changes at the school were all planned and understood. It was a chance for the school to find its 'why.'

Through this work, I was proud to oversee the school adopting the following vision:

BWPS is committed to:

- fostering knowledgeable, respectful, and caring young people who contribute positively and responsibly to their local and global community.
- being recognised as a high performing school with a reputation of evidence-based best practice that is visible in each classroom.

Make it easier for teachers to improve their teaching, and for students to improve their learning

How best to realise your ambitious vision? Surely, you can go whole-hog and change it all!

Hold up. Remember that human attention and working memory are fragile. We must optimise the **intrinsic load** and minimise the **extraneous**–for teachers and students alike.

Peps Mccrea (2020) describes attention as the 'economy' of the school. Thus, everything that a science of learning leader does, should protect attention: the attention of your teachers and the attention of your students. When considering the changes you wish to make, consider how you can ensure everyone's attention is on the work ahead.

The kind of load associated with the task itself and the level of complexity within it. Intrinsic load will differ based on the background, knowledge and skills of the learner

The kind of cognitive load that takes students' cognitive energy away from the task at hand. This is to do with the manner or structure of instruction

resolve. n. - firmness of purpose or intent; determination

To undertake a science of learning transformation, your school also needs sufficient *resolve*. Make this firmness of purpose possible by dividing up your school improvement plan into distinct but simultaneous parts:

(1) give time, space, and resources for teachers to change their practice and work; and
(2) build structures and buffers to make changes doable and sustainable.

Table 12.1 Chapter 12 Overview - Science of learning school improvement framework.

(1) Provide time, space, and resources for teachers to . . .	
PLAN THE LEARNING	• Optimise the content (intrinsic load)
ENACT THE TEACHING	• Change the instructional practices and environment (extraneous load)
(2) Simultaneously, reshape school structures that:	
BUILD THE SPACE FOR CHANGE	• Make change process smooth • Facilitate professional learning, leadership development, and student support
PROTECT AND PROMOTE THE WORK	• Celebrate successes • Prioritise the 'essentials'; cut the 'extras' • Communicate and network around your success

Some insights into leadership developments for the science of reading are available (e.g., Townsend & Bayetto, 2021). However, we designed our science of learning improvement framework in Table 12.1 based upon on-the-ground experiences of school leaders.

1. PLAN THE LEARNING: Change *what* you are teaching

Based on the insights from cognitive load theory, we know that teachers need to be able to adequately segment the learning into manageable chunks—especially for biologically secondary knowledge that is new. Optimising the intrinsic load means teachers can break down those concepts that are hard to teach. To do this, your teachers need knowledge, guidance, and resources (Sweller et al., 2019).

Explicit instruction that reaches 80% of students the first time

We have worked with several schools that have adopted principles from the science of learning. At all of them, we have seen the power of explicit instruction that works to meet 80% of students' needs upon first teaching.

Archer and Hughes' (2010) 'I do, we do, you do' provides an elegant frame for *how* teachers should *guide* learning across the phases of any lesson. Similarly, the distinction between Hollingsworth and Ybarra's (2017) **concept development** versus **skill development** helps teachers know *what* it is they are *explaining* or *modelling* across the phases of the lesson (see Rosenshine, 2012). The example at Bentleigh West indicates how leaders can promote consistency and high-capacity teaching.

> The teaching of key ideas, terminology, and concepts including bullet-proof definitions, features, examples, and non-examples
>
> Teachers model problems step-by-step using a think-aloud as an example for students to observe

Story Example 12.2 - Planning the learning so no one was lost, Steven Capp - Bentleigh West

As a collective at BWPS, we could see our teaching was inconsistent. The variance between classrooms was impacting student outcomes. The most common occurrence was our teachers doing the 'I do' part of the lesson and then sending the students off to their 'You do,' only to have more than half the class raising their hands because the instruction didn't work for them.

We looked at practices that align with the information processing model, as outlined by Willingham, and sought to adapt a model of teaching from Explicit Direct Instruction (Hollingsworth & Ybarra, 2017). The model allowed us to teach whilst taking into account: attention, working memory, and long-term memory. We then worked collectively on how to break skills and concepts down sufficiently for our students, how to model, and then practice new concepts and skills to be transferred and automatised in long-term memory.

To use the example of sentence writing, our staff worked to understand the difficult parts of this concept. Because of the **curse of knowledge**, we found it hard to think immediately of what makes a simple sentence simple. Given some time, space, and by using excellent resources (e.g., The Writing Revolution®), we found the common pitfalls for students who were struggling with sentences; we then used this to improve our explanations and examples.

A phenomenon where an expert's mastery over a task or area makes it very difficult for them to understand the progression of skills and knowledge that are needed for a novice learner to master this area

And just that small change flipped our success at teaching. For the 'I do' phase of the lesson, our teachers moved from reaching 20% of the students to 50%. By the end of the 'We do' we reached 70% to 80% of students.

Suddenly, we had optimised the intrinsic load so much that nearly all students benefitted, and teachers were freed up to provide additional instruction to the ones who still needed it (typically when the rest of the class moved to independent practice).

Your improvement plan needs to help teachers to have clarity about what they are teaching, and how each lesson and unit helps students along the continuum of learning. **Scopes and sequences** become very important, so the plan is clear and shared.

The overall plan and organisation of content and skills to be taught in a curriculum or educational program. The scope outlines the breadth and depth of the topics and concepts to be covered, while the sequence determines the order in which these topics are taught. It provides a structured roadmap that ensures a logical progression of learning, with skills and knowledge building upon one another in a clear and comprehensive way

Teachers need to move beyond those questions about 'What should I teach next week,' and into discussing 'How should we teach this best?' Whatever they are teaching, it is crucial that teachers break the learning down sufficiently so that a student's working memory is not overloaded.

It can feel like we are learning only one week ahead of the students

You might be implementing *subject-specific changes* like explicit spelling instruction, place value language, paragraph structure, new science units, for example. Some of this content may be entirely new for you and your teachers, and it may feel that they are only just keeping ahead of students.

This is where your school's professional learning and knowledge building needs to intersect directly with your planning.

- *How do I take that great idea we have learnt about and use it in this lesson or unit of work?*
- *Are there exemplar lessons or units from which I can teach first in order to understand how these ideas are meant to work in practice?*
- *What existing curriculum materials can I use or adapt?*

Teaching something new will be overwhelming initially, but as teachers become confident in this new content or in a new practice, their attention will shift and they will start noticing more of what students are doing, whether the intrinsic load is too high and if some students are getting left behind.

The leader needs to ensure teachers have a licence to play and have fun and feel safe to be like a novice before they are expected to be the expert in teaching something new. Leaders can reassure teachers that they are not going to remember all these nuances initially. They are not going to excel at following a more explicit and responsive approach straight away. They are going to muck it up, and sometimes teachers might have to learn it just the week ahead of the students. The battles can be won or lost in whether leaders can build that trust with staff, valuing that the teachers are learning, too, and need time, space, and resources to do it.

Reviews - Counteract the forgetting curve

From our perspective, **daily review** and **retrieval practice** provide the ultimate quick win for both elementary and secondary schools on this journey. Teachers all know how often students seem to forget everything we teach them. Make Ebbinghaus' **forgetting curve** a key focus at your school, and bring in daily and monthly review as soon as you can.

As outlined in chapters 4 and 5, frequent review provides all students with high doses of repeated exposure, modelling, and a chance to take advantage of retrieval practice, which strengthens connections for material they are starting to forget. Another selling point of reviews is that they provide quick and easy formative assessment, to check the impact teachers are having, allowing them to adapt when student understanding is sub-optimal.

A short, daily session of practice of previously taught material, including concepts and skills that ensure students consolidate their learning and avoid forgetting

Opportunities for students to attempt to remember how to complete previous learning tasks or recall previously learnt concepts, facts, or skills

The phenomenon in which learners tend to immediately forget most of what they have learnt the previous day, with sharp declines over time, unless content is reviewed

The long game: Coherent, low variance curriculum

It is not uncommon for schools to have inherited upwards of three or four different programs or approaches to teach the one thing. At Steven's school, there were five different spelling programs before they began their journey. Double up and redundancy like this means that there will be high variance in what students learn from class to class, creating gaps and inconsistencies in students' mastery of the content. Variance can also be in what subjects get 'squeezed out' when the daily timetable is over-run.

Reducing the variance in curriculum planning and enactment is pivotal to improving your school. Over time, your work should aim to build a shared coherent and cohesive way of teaching subjects that is simple to navigate but allows for all the benefits of curriculum alignment outlined in chapter 9: Less time spent searching for what resource to teach next, and more time adapting and refining resources you will use as a team.

Eventually, it is critical that this curriculum planning and refinement occurs in (i) English, (ii) Mathematics, and (iii) knowledge-rich content areas including the humanities, social studies, sciences, and the arts.

Finally, agreement around teaching time of each subject across the week, term, and year becomes critical so that all students benefit from your planning for learning, no matter their grade level or teacher.

2. ENACT THE TEACHING: Change the instructional environment

Teachers need time and expertise to better manage the instructional environment and thereby reduce the extraneous load for students. The learning environment must support how the brain learns and the first step to any learning is attention (Dehaene, 2021).

The learning environment must protect attention.

Box 12.1 - Simple examples to reduce distractions in the instructional environment

As students move past classrooms during learning time, how does a rowdy, inefficient transition compare to a fast-paced, inaudible transition?

Is there a way to change the public announcement (PA) system so that interruptions to class discussions are minimised?

Can outside subjects, like physical education, occur away from classrooms?

Could noisy school maintenance, like leaf blowing, occur outside of scheduled class time?

The instructional environment should be predictable, consistent, free from distraction, and make it easy for students to focus and learn.

School-wide values, expectations and norms

This starts with what you expect of students' behaviour. At many schools, low consistency around behaviour management, class routines, and class expectations is commonplace. There is high variance in the use of learning routines and effective teaching techniques. The result of the inconsistency is most often poor engagement and poor behaviour, as students' working memories are filled with everything but the desired learning.

Uninterrupted learning time must become sacred.

Science of learning leaders need to embed *clear expectations* that work to protect attention (see Positive Behaviour Support: PBS). Your expectations should flow from your school values to your norms and then routines (Bennett, 2020).

You should also use a tiered response as per **Multi-Tiered Systems of Support** (MTSS), which includes Positive Behaviour Support (PBS). For students needing extra support to engage with positive learning behaviours, staff with expertise should utilise functional behaviour assessments to develop behaviour and safety plans in consultation with families (Tier 2 and 3).

Classroom routines and organisation

Tom Bennett's (2020) guide to *Running the Room* provides a clear roadmap for creating, introducing, and rehearsing shared classroom routines with students. These should flow from your values and norms, and should include:

- Lining up;
- Entering the classroom;
- Ways to move around the school quietly during learning time;
- Seating plans for different learning modes;
- Routines around accessing learning materials;
- Consistently displayed timetables.

The importance of well-established routines cannot be overstated. Transitions that are messy or issue-ridden waste precious time and attention.

The classroom organisation of your school can also contribute to, or hopefully minimise, extraneous load. We need to ensure all students can hear and see the teacher and learning stimuli without having to turn or move awkwardly. This is about equity and effectiveness of the environment for learners (see Box 12.2).

Box 12.2 - Teachers should organise the classroom to minimise extraneous load

- Orientate your board, display/projector, and student seating so everyone can see without turning
    - o Implement rows, u-shapes, and/or clusters of pairs that all face the same way
    - o You can always create routines for turning chairs around for group work when the time is right (see **pair squares**; Swain, 2022)

A classroom layout that allows students to sit in pairs, facing towards the front of the room, but turn into squares or groups of four for impromptu group work

- You can have other key visual supports on display like timetables and number charts, but consider rotating them out when they are not relevant or needed (less is more)
- Make decorations clean, neat, and minimalist where possible
- Create sit spots so students know where to go and don't waste time arguing over who is sitting where
- Remove clutter and unnecessary items from front and centre
- Move samples of student work and other artefacts unrelated to the target learning to the back or far sides of room, so they are on display for students, but not in their eyeline during learning
- Make learning materials accessible and easy to find and put away
- Keep desks tidy, organised, and minimalist

Learning routines and effective teaching techniques

When you have the curriculum planning chugging along, it creates time to focus on the *how* to teach rather than just *what* to teach. This can allow for more collaboration between staff and to understand the real professional learning needs of teachers.

As discussed in this volume, **checking for understanding** (CFU) is perhaps the most useful concept to introduce into a school that is harnessing the science of learning. By embedding specific short answer, multiple choice, and true/false questions into every lesson plan, teachers can obtain real-time information about whether the lesson is on track or off the rails.

The teacher checking if students are learning while the lesson is unfolding using short, specific checks of understanding and proficiency

When you plan for these CFU questions as a team, it helps develop a shared understanding of how the practice shapes and supports the flow of the lesson. This is the ultimate, immediate, form of formative assessment (Wiliam, 2011). Do not neglect CFU (see chapter 11 for more).

When you embed key learning routines and teaching techniques, you will see cumulative improvement year-on-year. This is supported by the fine-tuning of teaching and planning via coaching and professional development, rather than 'reinventing the wheel' for curriculum and instruction each year.

Box 12.3 - Key learning routines and techniques for students to get used to, and for teachers to make their own

- Engagement norms (read with me, track with me, no hands up, non-volunteer to promote thinking)
- Attention signals (e.g., eyes on me, 1, 2, 3; knock knock . . . who's there)
- Pair shares/turn and talks

- Use of mini whiteboards (3, 2, 1 chin it, clear your board, park your board)
- Responding to checking for understanding questions
- Using '**Do Nows**' and '**Exit Tickets**'

A quick, quiet activity at the start of a lesson that typically involves no (or minimal) guidance from the teacher, and which reviews or activates prior learning, or pre-teaches vocabulary for example

A short low stakes task, usually on paper, completed at the end of the lesson to detect proficiency or any difficulties with the learning, and collected for analysis by the teacher

There are many more examples of these, but together having strong routines for learning will allow full attention to crucial learning and limit undesirable interactions to give the best opportunity for full engagement in lessons.

Routine is our friend - use novelty with care

A sport coaching analogy demonstrates this point best. When introducing a new way of teaching something (like a new football drill), one knows that it is going to take two to three sessions to get used to the routine. There is a lag involved where the attention of the students (or players) is on *how* the process works, not on what they should be mastering during that process.

So for education, if your teachers are constantly changing the way that the information is being presented or the way learners practice, then students could be spending more time wondering about the process not the learning:

- 'What should I be doing here again?'
- 'What do I need to do in this bit?'
- 'Where do I put this question?'
- 'Do I need this sheet or that sheet?'

This wasted cognitive energy can be avoided when teachers develop learning routines that work for them, and keep novelty to a minimum. Sometimes, teachers can feel like they must come up with a myriad of different activities to cover the same skill. But often the students will not even realise that they have been practising that same skill the whole week, as the novelty of the activity detracts from the learning.

Variety in how we are teaching can be overrated. Keeping the activity consistent can help to ensure the cognitive work is on the new learning, not on the new kind of activity.

All students benefit from *predictability* in the things that can remain consistent. Interestingly, teachers like predictability as well. In the next section, we will argue that it is critical to build predictability and support that allows teachers to focus on the change ahead (see below).

3. BUILD THE SPACE for teachers to change

Vision and professional development

A key tenet from this chapter is that your school's vision should flow into your professional development. Any high performing school must invest heavily in the development of staff, and you should demonstrate to teachers how this work aligns with your school's vision and improvement plan.

Embed frequent professional learning into structures of school

- Reduce administrative meetings;
- Make school meetings opportunities for professional learning, planning, and problem-solving;
- Ensure professional development is not considered an added extra, but an essential part of the week; and
- Develop strong onboarding and induction plans for new staff that address missing required knowledge they need in order teach well at your school.

Also, strategically use partnerships with universities to help mentor and attract new teachers and do the same with casual relief teachers.

Coaching from instructional experts; get the focus on teaching

If you do not have the instructional expertise in your school, bring this in. Teachers cannot enact teaching practices they have never seen themselves. Often staff scepticism and low confidence can be mitigated when you bring in a coach who can model it with your staff members' own class. See Box 12.4 for some key coaching models and providers to consider.

Box 12.4 - Instructional coaching models and providers

- StepLab
- Walkthrus
- Leverage leadership 2.0

Rebuild support structures for teachers' work and re-align around the vision

Another essential output for the leader is to create the best possible learning and working environment for your staff. Optimal teaching from your staff necessitates the best training, support, and accountability measures from you. Having clear professional and behavioural expectations within the vision and strategic plan allow for a culture that promotes inclusivity and safety.

If you need to rebuild your *staff culture*, the whole school investment in professional knowledge and alignment with the shared vision, allows people to see if this workplace is for them. As a principal, Steven frequently conferences with staff around their performance and development plan to set specific goals that aligned with the school vision. This helps to ensure gaps in staffing or professional needs are identified.

Assessment, data, and reporting

Ensure your *assessment data and reporting* aligns with the work of your improvement plan. You need to make it easy to find those initial and sustained 'wins' to share with teachers and students alike. Remove data collection that is unreliable, unused, expensive, or time-consuming. Assess only as much as you need to make a difference to students and teachers.

By focussing on short-cycle **formative assessment** through to high stakes **standardised data**, you can get better information into the hands of teachers. Renowned cognitive scientists Kirschner, Sweller, and Clark (2006) state "if nothing has changed in long-term memory, nothing is learned" (p. 77), and our assessments must ensure learning is secure in long-term memory.

> Work undertaken by teachers (and students) that provide information or feedback to inform changes to teaching
>
> Data that is collected using tools with high statistical validity and reliability

Multi-tiered systems of support - Response to intervention (RTI) and positive behaviour support (PBS)

Build up the systems and expertise around responding to students falling behind in literacy and mathematics and ensure students with additional learning needs, including disabilities, get the support they require. This is additional to the work of the classroom teacher, so invest in staff to manage detailed student profiles and compile evidence for planning and funding applications.

Train up educational support staff (teacher aides) to deliver high-quality Tier 2 and Tier 3 intervention, so those students who need additional instruction receive it more often and more intensively.

Table 12.2 How do you show it is working?

Use the forgetting curve to understand what it means to 'learn' something, and on what scale

Assessment Level	*Time Frame*
Checking for understanding	Minute to minute, lesson to lesson
Reviews and teacher-created tasks	Week to week
Standardised progress monitoring (DIBELS)	6–12 months
Standardised testing (e.g., NAPLAN) and student wellbeing surveys	Long-term trends

This support allows teachers to continue to focus on the classroom and small group level, while much of the administration, data entry, and timetabling of students is reduced. This can increase your school's effectiveness and efficiency in successfully navigating assessment and compliance to secure funding, as well as supporting students in and outside of the classroom.

Ensure you have working systems of school-wide **positive behaviour support**, with systems that give teachers confidence that they are supported when behaviours escalate. When students come into class still reeling from blow-ups or disagreements in the yard, that stress and anxiety impacts their working memory, and that of teachers too. Ensure if students need time to de-escalate and only come into class once they are calm, then teachers have structures that allow that to happen.

> A whole-school framework for ensuring explicit teaching of behavioural expectations and boundaries as part of Multi-Tiered Systems of Support (MTSS)

Always circle back to your expectations and norms to make it easy for students to exhibit positive behaviour, as this work comes from a place of care for each student, and care for their learning (Bennett, 2020).

Sufficient planning and curriculum support

Make it easy for teachers to do their work. If they are overloaded with planning and resource creation, find a workable solution for the short or medium term (use available or adaptable materials, until you can reshape your own). Ensure teachers are not expected to develop content they lack the time and experience to develop.

When you provide your teachers with exemplars of what it can look like in class, including some materials to try the next day, you can build confidence and allay anxiety about 'all the extra work' they will have to put in to achieve the desired change.

Staff and leadership development

Change management

Having clear roles and goals, aligned to the wider school improvement plan, is important for every staff member. Each staff member needs to understand the role they play in focusing or enabling the focus to remain on teaching and learning for improved student outcomes.

What if some staff do not like the changes? Do everything you can to build the excitement and momentum around the changes and initial wins. All leaders know, however, that some changes will not be everyone's 'cup of tea.' When you bring disquiet or performance issues back to the vision for the school, staff can often find a way of self-selecting if a change is or is not for them.

Ensure all staff members in positions of leadership have sufficient knowledge and wherewithal to take on roles that will form part of the transformation. Your fellow leaders cannot always please everyone when there are changes to be made.

Leadership development

Sustainable school change requires *future leader development* and succession planning. Steven has overseen scaffolded development through a 'school leadership pipeline,' where staff are mentored to lead teams for a 12-month period as a team leader through to a 2-to-4-year period as a middle leader to principal. The principal would engage these leaders in various programs and build experience within the school or in partnerships with other schools if required.

Promoting out is another useful idea for schools consolidating their practice, as a deliberate extension of this pipeline for emerging leaders. Leaders are developed and promoted to take that expertise to other schools. A lot of schools may be unwilling to let go of those qualified teacher leaders. However, if you keep all that expertise (and resources) at the top then you could potentially find yourself short on the funding for professional learning and intervention. Promoting out is also a mechanism to spread those great ideas to other schools. This can turn your school not just into a place to deliver great outcomes for students, but somewhere for teachers to develop their skillset and resumes for future leadership.

> Creating opportunities for middle leaders to apply for higher roles in other schools so as to ensure opportunities of current teachers to become future leaders

4. PROTECT AND PROMOTE THE WORK of teachers and students

Look for successes and wins; identify gaps and opportunities to improve even further. Reduce distractions of 'the next shiny thing.' Stay true to the vision.

As previously mentioned, a shared vision of high expectations, supported by science-informed practice provides the basic requirement of the science of learning leader. The principal needs clear systems and structures to ensure the school's focus can remain on core business: improving teaching and learning.

Gather your evidence of impact and celebrate the wins

Use your quantitative and qualitative data to measure the extent of your impact as a school. The change in outcomes for all case study schools in this volume have been profound and are often readily observable. Look for such outcomes to celebrate quick wins.

Monitor student behaviour, wellbeing, and engagement indicators. When things are working well, this success should flow through to the non-academic realm and should be a great source of pride and inspiration.

Governance and engagement with school community

Effective, efficient, and student-safe governance, as well as fundraising and connection to the school community, are the lifeblood of a successful school. The parents and families associations or equivalent and student leadership have a role to play in realising the school vision, and creating and executing the school improvement plans.

It is part of your job to communicate and share the work you are doing and the progress in improving academic and wellbeing outcomes. This will help to educate parents as to how they could support with the highest impact. Highlight the changes to teaching structure and content via newsletters, assemblies, social media, information nights, and school tours. Also be active in talking to parents and carers, and celebrating important events and milestones that promote your school vision and values.

Work to ensure that extra-curricular events complement not conflict with core learning and teaching. Strategise within your school governance structures to ensure that you oversee an inclusive and culturally safe environment, continuing the work to support strong curriculum and teaching that supports wellbeing and personal growth.

Finance

Ensure you have adequate funds for the initiatives and changes you seek to make. You may need to decommission and realign certain roles and programs to move into a healthy financial position. Resources should be dedicated to invest in teacher development, quality resources and increased efficiency to get better at teaching our students as the school requires.

Sometimes this means a prioritisation of programs. You may need to *cut the fluff* (programs or professional development that do not align) and *keep the stuff* that really achieves your vision—to use an adapted 'Anita Archerism.'

Success and school cohesion leads to authentic student voice and agency

As students learn about their own *learning* and master their subject areas, you will see increases in their ability to articulate their vision for their own education, and to execute agency in their learning. Nothing deprives students of agency more than an ineffectual educational experience.

When the school is functioning as it should academically, student leadership and voice can build pride in learning and school community for each student. Strong school spirit and pride is much more likely when the adults and leaders in the community are all actively working towards supporting teachers to be their best, and taking care of everything else to keep the focus on teaching and learning.

School communication and networking

Network with intent: Join networks of like-minded schools and educational groups to align your work with that of others. Also, maintain and rebuild connections to local community groups and organisations to share your school improvement plans and successes. Build your knowledge of what you need to do next, and make smart decisions when opportunities come your way. *Can we afford the effort and time to do this as a school?*

When you are established as a science of learning leader in your school, consider giving back by opening up as a demonstration school and help spread your successes to other like-minded organisations.

Final thoughts: The leader learns alongside the teachers

Although some have debated whether principals should act more like managers or instructional leaders, we strongly advocate that the leader is actively learning the content of the school's professional development and improvement, alongside their teachers.

It will take significant time and extra resources, but, at least initially, you should *attend any professional development* you expect your staff to complete. The reasons are two-fold:

(1) You need to communicate that you value this new knowledge and expertise and that it really does inform your vision for school change;
(2) You actually need to understand the content of what you are changing to know how best to support your teachers, to make good decisions about purchasing curriculum, or further training and putting the *right staff* in the right positions.

You need to demonstrate your investment and care for your staff to be the best they can be. You should also keep a close connection to teaching: by taking lessons, conducting intervention sessions with your most struggling students, or modelling lessons with teachers.

Recall that the *why*, *what*, and *how* of your school changes must be understood and valued by your staff. To undertake such a science of learning transformation, your school needs sufficient resolve. Remove barriers to professional learning and growth (build the space), and stay true to your vision, celebrate the wins, and avoid distractions (protect and promote the work). This will allow your teachers to focus on the work of managing the cognitive load of students, planning the best possible learning, and enacting the best possible teaching.

Remember . . . *your ultimate role as leader is to* ***protect the attention*** *of your teachers and students*, and to ***manage the cognitive load*** *for teachers of the changes you wish to make.*

Find the flow in the change process, so teachers and students can instil a sense of energy and calm in their work. See the knowledge organiser for this chapter in Table 12.3.

Table 12.3 Chapter 12 knowledge organiser: Our science of learning school improvement framework

(1) Provide time, space, and resources for teachers to . . .	
PLAN THE LEARNING	• Optimise the intrinsic load of what they are teaching • Reach 80% of students the first time with explicit instruction • Stay at least one week ahead of the students • Find the quick planning wins • Start work towards a long-term coherent curriculum
ENACT THE TEACHING	• Minimise the extraneous load for students • Build school-wide values and norms • Support teachers' use of classroom and learning routines to minimise distractions • Embed coaching for effective teaching techniques to increase instructional expertise

(*continued*)

Table 12.3 (Continued)

(2) Simultaneously, reshape school structures that:	
BUILD THE SPACE FOR CHANGE	• Make changes as smooth as possible. • Align vision, professional development, and coaching • Increase and align assessment, and data and support systems (e.g., MTSS) • Facilitate staff/leadership development
PROTECT AND PROMOTE THE WORK	• Celebrate successes of teachers and students • Look for further opportunities to improve • Don't let the 'extras' overtake the 'essentials' • Manage governance and finance • Network within and outside your school and communicate your success

Where to next?

- *Running the room,* by Tom Bennett.
- *Effective classroom setup.* Think Forward Educators presentation by Leah Myers & Jac Dominey. https://thinkforwardeducators.org/meetings-for-members/docklands-mar2022.
- *The pair square: A classroom layout that promotes learning.* https://www.nathanielswain.com/cognitoriumblog/2022/2/pairsquares.
- *Making room for impact: A de-implementation guide for educators* by Hamilton, Hattie & Wiliam.
- *Leverage leadership 2.0: A practical guide to building exceptional schools,* by Paul Bambrick Santoyo.
- *The five dysfunctions of a team,* by Patrick Lencioni.

Check your indicators – Leadership

On-Track Indicators	*Off-Track Indicators*
• Teachers are given time and resources to ensure their teaching materials are clear and effective. • Work is started on developing a long-term coherent curriculum, including shared scopes and sequences and curriculum maps. • Extraneous load for students is minimised through effective teaching practices. • The school's vision, professional development, and coaching efforts are aligned. • There is a strong understanding of what good teaching looks like, and teachers are coached and supported to reach this standard in all their work. • Assessment, data, and support systems are increased and aligned with instructional practices. • Focus remains on essential aspects of teaching and learning and on improving the everyday classroom practice of every teacher.	• Teachers work individually or in small teams for planning, but significant time is spent each week creating new lessons to meet the needs of each individual class. • Planning focuses more on short-term goals, and individual teacher perspectives. • Professional learning is happening but can be on many different topics across the year. • Non-essential tasks and non-academic initiatives take significant focus away from teaching and learning. • Governance and finances make it hard for the school to focus on teaching and learning. • The school is not strongly connected to external networks and is still figuring how best share or learn from other schools.

Discussion questions

1. How well aligned are your school's vision, professional development, and coaching initiatives to support effective teaching practices in your school?
2. What leadership actions can you take to build and reinforce school-wide values and norms?
3. How can you as a leader enhance the use of classroom and learning routines to maximise learning time?
4. How well is the attention of students and teachers protected in your school? Are there unnecessary distractions?
5. How can you, as a school leader, more strategically celebrate the successes of both teachers and students in your school?
6. How can you lead the identification of further improvement opportunities and avoid the 'extras' overtaking the 'essentials'?
7. How could you manage governance and finance, while effectively communicating your successes?

References

Agarwal, P. K., & Bain, P. M. (2019). *Powerful teaching: Unleash the science of learning*. John Wiley & Sons.

Archer, A. L., & Hughes, C. A. (2010). *Explicit instruction: Effective and efficient teaching*. Guilford Publications.

Bennett, T. (2020). *Running the room: The teacher's guide to behaviour*. John Catt.

Dehaene, S. (2021). *How we learn: Why brains learn better than any machine . . . for now*. Penguin.

Drucker, P. F. (2006). *Classic Drucker: Essential wisdom of Peter Drucker from the pages of Harvard Business Review*. Harvard Business Press.

Kirschner, P. A., Sweller, J., & Clark, R. E. (2006). Why minimal guidance during instruction does not work: An analysis of the failure of constructivist, discovery, problem-based, experiential, and inquiry-based teaching. *Educational Psychologist*, *41*(2), 75–86.

Mccrea, P. (2020). *Motivated teaching*. John Catt.

Rosenshine, B. (2012). Principles of instruction: Research-based strategies that all teachers should know. *American Educator*, *36*(1), 12.

Sweller, J., van Merriënboer, J. J., & Paas, F. (2019). Cognitive architecture and instructional design: 20 years later. *Educational Psychology Review*, *31*, 261–292.

Townsend, T., & Bayetto, A. (2021). Supporting school leaders to become more effective in leading reading improvements. *School Effectiveness and School Improvement*, *32*(3), 363–386.

Wiliam, D. (2011). *Embedded formative assessment*. Solution Tree Press.

Willingham, D. T. (2023). *Outsmart your brain: Why learning is hard and how you can make it easy*. Simon and Schuster.

13 A call to action . . . and caution

Nathaniel Swain

I hope you have been uplifted by the stories and insights within these pages. I wrote this book to capture the astounding experiences of teachers and students as they use the science of learning to reshape their schools from the ground up. I leave you now with some calls to action and some cautions.

Not an ideology

The science of learning is not a belief system or ideology (nor is the science of reading). When we use the science to inform our practice, we are making a relentless commitment to implement the best supported practices and techniques available to us to support the greatest number of students. We do this knowing full well that science is an ongoing and dynamic project and that much of what we do now may be proven wrong one day. If you are harnessing the science of learning, you are making it your duty to use the most rigorous and up to date evidence to inform your decisions. As Louisa Moats eloquently stated referring to the science of reading, particularly:

> *The body of work referred to as "the science of reading" is not an ideology, a philosophy, a political agenda, a one-size-fits-all approach, a program of instruction, or a specific component of instruction. It is the emerging consensus from many related disciplines, based on literally thousands of studies, supported by hundreds of millions of research dollars, conducted across the world in many languages.* (Moats, 2019)

My fellow contributors and I may nonetheless be accused of pushing a sort of ideology in this book. Critics of this work may implore us to remember that 'every child learns differently', that there are 'many ways to be a teacher.' This *appeal to nuance* is in my mind a position of profound compromise. When you say that nothing can be more helpful than anything else, you essentially endorse: 'Anything goes!'

I believe that many different perspectives must be accounted for as teachers plan and enact their practice in partnership with their students, but if we neglect the principles and restrictions that underscore how learning happens, we teachers are setting ourselves up for failure.

DOI: 10.4324/9781003404965-16

It's not about 'only one way'; It's about 'best bets'

There are renewed criticisms of attempts to bring scientific findings into the classroom, with some pushing the view that there is no science of learning, or that science cannot be pinned down as 'one thing.'

It is important to remember that the insights contained in this book and the ways in which they have been operationalised in the school examples do not represent a one-size-fits-all approach, nor an attempt to create a universal set of procedures that all schools must follow.

Instead, what we have attempted is a distillation of some of the non-negotiables that fall out of the key insights about how we learn and how best to teach. It's about the best bets right now.

Prepare yourself with critical reading of the research

To continue your journey, you need to become a critical consumer of research (Willingham, 2012). Access the scientific literature, read systematic reviews, and consult with experts that have standing in the research and professional communities.

At a time when the 'science of learning' is at risk of becoming a buzzword, you must always interrogate information or recommendations that come your way in accordance with what we know from the weight of the scientific evidence. Check new programs or initiatives in terms of their alignment with the ideas about:

- cognitive load theory;
- fully guided instruction;
- the Simple View of Reading; and
- the forgetting curve, for example.

It is also important to note that all the recommendations in this book are of course *subject to change* in light of a changing weight of evidence, or the development of better and more accurate theories of learning. As various scientific endeavours come to fruition and offer new ways of understanding, those harnessing this science must accede and adapt their practices. That is the difference between being informed by evidence and being informed by ideology.

Final thoughts

Any teacher or leader looking to kickstart their school improvement must remember that the status quo is strong; it is infinitely easier to stay doing the same old things, or settle for very superficial changes. Leaders need to make the change appealing yet smooth, to help cross the threshold of change resistance. As we have seen, when this occurs and the wins start accumulating, schools can become self-propelling entities that rock the status quo, buck the trend, and perhaps blaze new trails for others to follow.

It is not about choosing one philosophy or agenda over another. It is not about personal preference. It is about a duty to act when there is strong evidence that such changes are "helpful for all children, harmful for none, and crucial for some" (Snow & Juel, 2005).

Morally, how can we ignore this call?

References

Moats, L. M. (2019). Of 'hard words' and straw men: Let's understand what reading science is really about. Voyager Sopris. https://www.voyagersopris.com/blog/edview360/lets-understand-what-reading-science-is-really-about

Snow, C. E., & Juel, C. (2005). Teaching children to read: What do we know about how to do it? In M. J. Snowling & C. Hulme (Eds.), *The science of reading: A handbook* (pp. 501–520). Blackwell Publishing. https://doi.org/10.1002/9780470757642.ch26

Willingham, D. T. (2012). *When can you trust the experts?: How to tell good science from bad in education*. John Wiley & Sons.

Index

Page numbers in **bold** refer to tables, those in *italics* indicate figures.